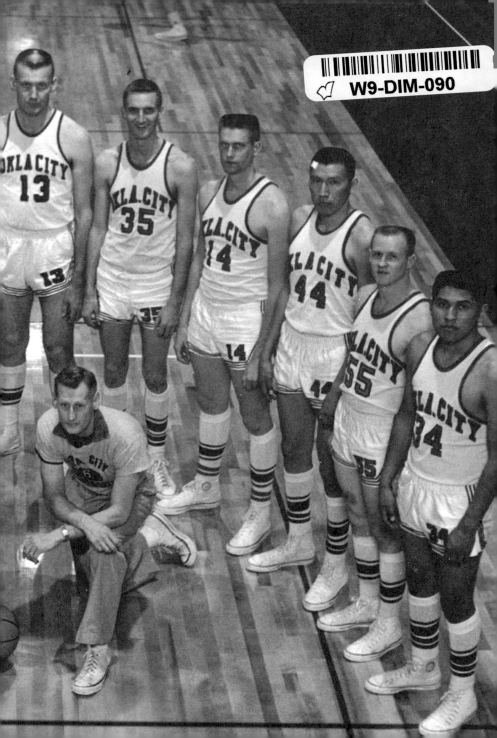

Court Magician

**THIS BOOK MADE POSSIBLE
BY GRANTS FROM:**

The Daily Oklahoman
Dorchester Capital
Kerr-McGee Corporation
Oklahoma City University

ABE LEMONS
Court Magician

BY BOB BURKE AND KENNY FRANKS

FOREWORD BY COACH BOB KNIGHT

Series Editor: GINI MOORE CAMPBELL
Associate Editor: ERIC DABNEY

Printed in the United States of America

ISBN 1-885596-14-6

Library of Congress Catalog Number 99-65514

Designed by 2W Design Group

OKLAHOMA HERITAGE ASSOCIATION
201 NORTHWEST FOURTEENTH STREET
OKLAHOMA CITY, OKLAHOMA 73103

CONTENTS

Jubilant United States basketball players carry their coach, Bob Knight, off the court following their gold medal win over Spain in the 1984 Olympics. Knight, head basketball coach at the University of Indiana, is draped with the net that was cut down following the victory. Courtesy *The Daily Oklahoman*.

FOREWORD

by Bob Knight

When most people think of Abe Lemons, they think of a man with a great wit and sense of humor before anything else. Abe has, throughout his entire career, been far and away the most entertaining person I have ever seen in athletics. I truly believe that his ability to tell stories and his approach to situations in life rival that of any of the great comedians in our lifetime. Yet, simply describing Abe Lemons as a man of tremendous humor, is like saying New York City is big and leaving it at that. There is a depth to Abe that very few people I have met in my lifetime even approach having.

Beneath the wit and the humor is an incredible philosophy of life and how to go about getting things done in the right way and successfully, whether it be basketball or any other endeavor. Just like his fellow Oklahoman, Will Rogers, Abe's wisdom comes through very clearly to those who just listen carefully to him while he talks.

Abe has one of the five best basketball minds I have encountered during my time in coaching. His understanding of the game, and how it should be played, is the equal of any of the great coaches I have known such as Pete Newell, Clair Bee, or Red Auerbach. Yet once again, to describe Abe as one of the great basketball minds, would be like describing the Rockies as pretty high and saying nothing else about them. His wisdom far transcends the game of basketball.

There is an integrity and honesty to Abe that very few people have. These qualities come out very readily in any conversation that you have with him. There is no one whom I have ever enjoyed talking to or listening to more than Abe. His approach to basketball, just like his approach to life, has been very honest, simple, and direct. His coaching methods enabled him to achieve great success at three different universities. In each of those cases, he took schools with very poor basketball programs to national prominence. However, his coaching success is only a part of the story. The real success lies with all those players who were able to develop an understanding of what it was going to take to succeed in life while playing for Abe.

It is interesting to me that Will Rogers and Abe are both from Oklahoma because I can think of no other person except Rogers who can compare even closely to the combination of humor and wisdom that have been so much a part of Abe's personality.

It has been my great good fortune to have known Abe for more than 30 years. During that time, I have been the beneficiary of countless things he has said or discussed in my presence. One of the great privileges I have enjoyed as a coach is having Abe as both a friend and a teacher. I would extend my thoughts in this regard to his wife, Betty Jo. Just as Abe's wisdom is often hidden by his humor, so too is this magnificent lady, always in the background and yet a very integral part of the man that is Abe Lemons.

Like the rarest of books, there is no other in the world like him. The Basketball Hall of Fame will never be complete until Abe has been inducted. As a coach, a teacher, and a man of great integrity, Abe Lemons is truly a man for all seasons.

ACKNOWLEDGMENTS

One of the nicest things about writing this biography was to get to know Abe and Betty Jo Lemons better. What class human beings they are! Their fan club is nationwide. Dozens of former players and associates cooperated with us in a highly unusual fashion to make certain the story of their coach and his bride was told correctly and with enthusiasm.

Herman Meinders, who provided initial funding for the research and writing of the book, and Lee Allan Smith, "Mr. Expediter," provided assistance and encouragement throughout the project. We were blessed with comments about Abe from sports giants like Bob Knight, Dean Smith, Darrell Royal, Don Sanders, and Nolan Ryan.

We are grateful to Frank Boggs, Ed Nall, Kenny Clark, Barry Dowd, Jim McKone, Bill Foster, and Bill Little for helping guide the development of the story line that evolved from boxes of newspaper clippings and notes of interviews of former players.

This book could not have been written without the able assistance of Eric Dabney, research assistant and interviewer extraordinaire, and designer and layout artist Sandi Welch.

We are also indebted to Carol Campbell, Mary Phillips, Melissa Hayer, and Robin Davison at *The Daily Oklahoman* archives, for providing access to their fabulous collection of photographs; to Debbie Neill, Shelley Dabney, and Debi Engles for transcribing interviews; to Kitty Pittman, Adrienne Butler, Melecia Caruthers, Marilyn Miller, and Mary Hardin at the Oklahoma Department of Libraries; to Oklahoma City University Athletic Director Bud Sahmaunt and his staff, including sports information director Tony Sellars and mens basketball coach Win Case, for providing photographs and historical documents; and to Jennifer Poole, Director of Alumni Relations at Oklahoma City University, for being helpful and excited about the project.

We are thankful for the host of Abe's friends and colleagues who reviewed the manuscript and made hundreds of helpful suggestions and corrections. Our reviewers were Frank Boggs, Kenny Clark, Pat Petree, Ed Nall, Lee Allan Smith, Wayne Dabney, Judge Carol Hansen, Judge Jerry Salyer, Judge Norm Russell, Win Case, Tony Sellars, Bill Little, Royse Parr, Herman and LaDonna Meinders, Don Bullard, Steve Hendrickson, Barry Dowd, Bill Foster, Gary Gray, Phil Goss, Berry Tramel, and Manuel Heusman.

Gini Moore Campbell, our esteemed editor, gently massaged our feeble attempt to tell the Abe Lemons story as it should be told, with dignity and humor, woven inextricably together.

Finally, thanks to the Oklahoma Heritage Association, its chairman of the board Lee Allan Smith and president Dr. Paul Lambert, for its noteworthy projects to preserve the history of Oklahoma.

BOB BURKE
KENNY A. FRANKS

1999

— Chapter One —

A Humble Beginning

You've gotta have a sense of humor when
you are small and poor to boot...

Abe Lemons

HOWARD COSELL WAS IN ABE LEMONS' FACE. "COACH, ARE YOU crazy?" spouted the red-faced sportscaster with the wobbly, raspy voice. Cosell pulled no punches in questioning Lemons' sanity in forcing his Oklahoma City University Chiefs players to divide up, shirts against skins, and scrimmage in front of an amused but confounded Madison Square Garden crowd. The Chiefs had performed badly in the first half of a 1968 National Invitation Tournament game against Duke University, so Lemons ordered the team back to the court to practice, rather than to the dressing room for half-time.

The red light on the television camera alerted Lemons that a national television audience awaited his response. There was silence. Cosell's voice quivered as he glared at Lemons, "Coach, won't your boys be too tired to play the second half? Where did you learn this coaching tactic? Did you do this to amuse the crowd?"

Lemons, as determined not to answer the questions as Cosell was at getting an answer, shot back, "Listen mister, you may be big stuff in New York, but you ain't nothin' in Walters, Oklahoma."

Walters is about as far south as you can go in Oklahoma. Named for a prominent local resident, William R. Walter, a post office was established in the community September 27, 1901. The town became the county seat of Cotton County at Oklahoma statehood in 1907. And from Walters, came one of America's greatest basketball minds...Abe Lemons.

The Lemons children scampered around the farm doing their morning chores as the smell of bacon and sausage frying on the old wood stove in the kitchen alerted them that breakfast was ready. Johnnie Lemons had arisen long before daylight to prepare an early-morning feast, including her world-class, flaky biscuits, to give her husband and five children a good start on the new day. Johnnie moved a little slower in the kitchen in early November, 1922, because she was eight months pregnant with her seventh child.

The stock market crash was seven years away, but the Great Depression had begun early on the Lemons' family farm near Ryan on the north bank of the Red River in Jefferson County, Oklahoma. Abraham Eldredge "Abe" Lemons worked hard to keep food on the table for his growing family. With a fifth-grade education, he struggled to earn enough money to keep his family afloat. Because of the hard times, he lost his farm on the other side of the Red River in Jack County, Texas. He made good money pulling drainage ditches and leveling rough ground around oil wells in north Texas and southwest Oklahoma until well-intentioned government officials confiscated his mules during World War I.

The elder Lemons came from a long line of hard-working Texans with large families. His grandfather, George Washington Lemons, the sixth of eight children, settled near Gainesville, in Cooke County, Texas in 1839. His father, John Wesley Lemons, the fourth of 15 children, was a Methodist circuit preacher who moved his family to the New Port community in Jack County just before the turn of the 20th century.

Abraham Lemons was the fourth of eight children. He married Johnnie Thompson June 28, 1903, in Ardmore, Oklahoma, and owned and operated a small cafe there until 1907 when they moved to New Port, Texas. Johnnie's father, Newt Thompson, volunteered in the Civil War at age 17 in Alabama. He was lost from his regiment and hid out in an attic of a rural Alabama farm home until he could rejoin his unit. There he met his future wife, Caroline. After the war Thompson returned to Alabama and married Caroline before heading west to Missouri. [1]

In 1915 the elder Lemons moved his family to a farm near Ryan, Oklahoma. After less than bountiful harvests from the land on the Red River, he took a job as a part-time butcher at Garrison Grocery to supplement his meager earnings. He butchered his own cattle and sold the meat to local grocery stores. He needed extra money to buy Johnnie bolts of cloth that she and oldest daughter Mattie Lee, 18, used to craft shirts and dresses for the Lemons children for the winter. Johnnie earned a few dollars extra by taking in washing from more prosperous neighbors and sewing quilt tops for $1.00 per spool. Her quilts were popular throughout Jefferson County.

The Lemons boys were old enough to be valuable farmhands. Robert Carroll, 16, Samuel Eldridge, 14, and Troy Ovie, 12, worked from sunup to sundown in the fields. At home, Johnnie cared for two younger children, Roy Willis, age six, and Avah Loretta, age two.

In the wee hours of November 21, 1922, Johnnie knew her time was near. A short time later she gave birth to a baby boy. As Johnnie held the baby close to her, she smiled, hoping that this baby would bring as much joy to her as her other children had. However, she could not have anticipated the joy and laughter that her newest son would bring to millions.

The new baby was given an unorthodox name, simply the initials "A. E." The initials officially did not stand for anything, not even Abraham Eldridge, his father's name, even though the family Bible lists the baby as "A. E., Jr." In the fifth grade, A. E. ignored his cousin when she called him "Abe." It was years later, while enlisting in the Merchant Marines, that A. E. was forced to have a real first name. He placed a "B" between his initials and became "Abe" Lemons.

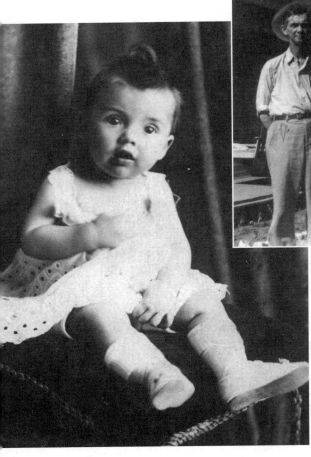

ABOVE: Abraham
Eldridge and Johnnie
Lemons, Abe's parents.

LEFT: Young Abe
Lemons, gazing at the
portrait camera with a
curl on the top of his
head and dressed in
the finest white frock.

When young Abe was two-years-old, a baby sister, Mamie Ruth, was born. A year later his father gave up on the farm near Ryan and moved his family to Walters where he took a job as a full-time butcher. The Lemons moved frequently from one rent house to another in Walters. The elder Lemons worked long hours and took odd jobs to make enough money to provide a decent place for his family to live. He followed the wheat harvest in the summers, cooking for field hands. Young Abe and his brothers went with their father on the harvest and feasted on cooked raisins and apricots, his father's specialty.

Young Abe started school at Walters in the fall of 1928. After a year, the family moved to Grandfield where his father butchered in yet another grocery store. The Grandfield job lasted only a few months and the Lemons moved back to another rent house in Walters, "A house that we were afraid to paint," Young Abe said, "because it might cave the walls in." [2] His father could not scrape up enough money to buy a car so he walked to work or caught a ride with co-workers.

Abe was small for his age. Even as a teenager he weighed

RIGHT: Abe and his sister, Mamie Ruth.

BELOW: Left to right, Abraham Eldridge Lemons, Robert, Samuel "Bud," and Abe.

only 75 pounds. What Abe lacked in size, he made up for in energy, especially in school. He was well liked by his fellow students but was a thorn in the side of many of his instructors. He was constantly in trouble with teachers who paddled him for a variety of sins including climbing in and out of school windows, failing math, and flipping other students on the ear.

The Great Depression was in full swing in Oklahoma in 1936. It began with the stock market crash in 1929 and continued as banks failed, factories closed, and dust storms carried off tons of topsoil from western Oklahoma. Cotton County suffered mightily. The Lemons family barely had enough money for food.

Later in life, young Abe reflected on how lucky he was to grow up in Walters, "They gave you a chance to grow up. The people in Walters were interested in you and disciplined you, but they gave you a certain amount of freedom so you'd mature. I would walk into a paint store and the owner would pick me out a painter's cap my size to wear around, free. We'd have rubber-gun fights in old houses and nobody minded. We never busted things up. We used to have big parades, with a trough of lemonade. Everybody would drink out of the trough, even the horses. Not now. They'd talk about germs. But you know, a kid never died in Walters. We never thought about germs." [3]

Abe began the summer of 1936 with a sore behind. Eighth-grade teacher Walter Holt told Abe on the last day of school, "Bend over. Grab your ankles. You have failed the eighth grade." Holt pounded Abe, Joe Jerrell, and Blackie Beach for what seemed like an hour for not making the necessary grades to be promoted to high school. Abe had flunked math and the failure in one subject forced him to repeat the entire eighth grade.

It was a blessing in disguise for Abe because he dropped back to a younger class with students like Russell Fletcher and Howell Ogletree, boys who became Abe's lifelong friends. Abe said, "Luckiest thing ever happened to me. I grew late, and the only year I played basketball was when I was 19, that extra year. If I hadn't of failed eighth grade, I never would of played on the team, and I'd be back sweepin' the streets in Walters now." [4]

Because Abe was so puny, he found a friend to protect him from bigger kids. James Henry "Red" Kearns was a tall, lanky, red-headed boy who stared hard at other kids who wanted to beat up on Abe. Being small helped Abe develop a sense of humor at an early age. He recalled, "You've gotta have a sense of humor when you are small and poor to boot—and have to ride a girl's bicycle in a little town. You've also gotta be fast, and when a guy comes up to you and says, 'I'm gonna poke you in the nose,' you've gotta be able to look at him and say something clever, like, 'Oh, yeah?'" [5]

In high school, when Abe finally began growing, he quickly outgrew his mother. He might have been a foot taller than Johnnie Lemons, but Abe still respected her every command.

Once the circus came to Walters and set up big tents on the football field about a block from the Lemons house. Red Kearns and Abe convinced the circus master to admit them free if they carried water for the elephants. Abe thought his arm would come off, carrying five-gallon buckets of water half his size. He never knew elephants drank so much water.

Red convinced Abe to go along with another money-making venture at the circus. They would be paid 35 cents to box in front of a crowd. Red, who outweighed Abe by at least 20 pounds, promised to not hit his friend hard. Once in the ring, Red lost his senses. Abe quipped, "He beat the hell out of me. He hit me like a dog. I learned a valuable lesson, you can't believe everybody, even your best friend, when it comes a chance to beat up on you." [6]

Abe saved his earnings from the boxing match and purchased an aviator helmet, equipped with goggles, for a quarter. He used the remaining ten cents to buy a ticket to the Saturday movie in Walters. With his new helmet snapped tightly under the chin, he slipped into the back row of the theater and dreamed of flying while watching the latest episode of "Tailspin Tommy."

Walters car dealer Roy Peck lured bare-footed Abe to go to Lawton with him to fight at the Ritz Theater. Peck was a part-time boxing promoter who saw promise in scrawny Abe who weighed in at a hefty 75 pounds. Abe had plenty of practice fighting in Walters. He and a kid named Kenneth Schrader fought in the middle of the street until one crawled to the bar ditch and gave up. In Lawton, Abe actually fought larger opponents to a draw. When he knocked down Lawrence Woodhouse three times, but was awarded only a draw, he gave up his boxing career.

Johnnie Lemons was the disciplinarian of the household, although Abe reflected later that "her heart wasn't in it." She often dragged the boys down the street, swiftly applying a wiry peach-tree limb to their behinds. Her big threat was to make the boys clean out the chicken coops if they disobeyed. However, when Abe and his friends slipped away for a picnic of possum grapes and wild plums and to go swimming in the nearby Cache Creek, Johnnie pretended she did not notice their wet hair, sun-burned necks, and lips that were puffed to twice their normal size, a result of the boys smoking grapevine. While Johnnie had to resort to whipping Abe, his father only had to look up at him sternly to get his point across.

The elder Lemons opened a grocery store in Walters with his son-in-law, Charlie Todd, in 1937. The Depression cut short the venture and Lemons opened a cafe.

The shortage of money affected young Abe's spiritual future. He attended a Baptist church that required kids to fill out a slip every Sunday that asked questions like "Did you read your lesson? Did you read your Bible this week? Do you have an offering today?" Abe's pockets were bare. He felt so badly about not having an offering, he changed churches and attended a Methodist church that did not ask such revealing questions about his financial condition.

Abe's first dreams of leaving Cotton County to see the world came when he joined the Sea Scouts, a Boy Scout program that taught boys about boats and sailing. Ralph "Buddy" Pearson, a Walters funeral director, was the Sea Scoutmaster. Abe and his fellow scouts built a sailboat and rode the waves of Walters Lake, dreaming of sailing the Seven Seas.

Abe picked up a few extra dollars each month by hustling a variety of jobs. He was paid by the National Youth Administration, part of President Franklin D. Roosevelt's New Deal recipe for escaping the Depression, to sweep out school classrooms. He picked up scrap iron with the help of an old magneto he salvaged from a worn-out car, sold soft drink bottles, and ushered at the Thompson Theater.

Abe learned honesty from his parents and from his part-time job cleaning out the spittoons at the Walters jail. Prisoners whistled at him as he worked. Once out in the sunshine and the fresh air, Abe appreciated his freedom and decided then and there that he never wanted to do anything wrong to end up in jail. [7]

Abe skipped high school football until his senior year. Walters coach John Axton had convinced the local school board to buy new uniforms for the Walters High School Blue Devils. Abe, now a solid 6'3", 145 pounds, saw a uniform in a store window and wanted to be part of the team.

Axton, a native of Idabel and a former All-State football player, and his wife, Mae Boren Axton, came to Walters for their first teaching jobs after college graduation. Mae, the only sister of Oklahoma Congressman Lyle H. Boren, and aunt of Governor, United States Senator, and University of Oklahoma President David L. Boren, later wrote Elvis Presley's first hit song, "Heartbreak Hotel," and played an important role in Abe's life. One day in class, Abe looked out the window and saw a toddler making his way down the street that ran alongside the high school. Abe did a double-take and recognized the child as two-year-old Hoyt Axton, the son of Coach John and Mae. Hoyt made his own name in the entertainment world. He appeared in many national television commercials, penned such rock-and-roll hits as "Joy to the World" and "Bony Fingers," and starred in several movies, including "The Gremlins."

The Blue Devils did not have a banner year in 1940 until they won the big county game against Temple on Thanksgiving Day. Lawton and Duncan both had power-house squads and beat Walters by 30 points. Abe played end and was a pretty good pass catcher for quarterback Raymond "Speck" Snyder. Abe snapped the ball on long punts to Lloyd Graham who once punted the ball so poorly that it bounced back into the endzone for a touchback. In another game, Abe hiked the ball to Graham who promptly planted the pigskin in Abe's behind.

The Walters-Temple game always featured fights among the players. "Chicken" Hays of Temple and Billy Ogletree of Walters did not disappoint the Thanksgiving Day crowd. They staged a fight at one end of the field during the game. Walters beat Temple largely because of the play of Alvin "Fat" Booher. Coach Axton added extra padding on Fat, to allow him more size to stop Temple's famous end-around plays. Abe later recalled, "Every time the Temple runner sprinted around the end, there was padded Fat Booher waiting." [8]

Years later when Abe was honored by the National Football Foundation, sportswriter Frank Boggs commented on Abe's football career, "What a strange award. It's like [William]

"Refrigerator" Perry being given a plaque from the National Jockeys Association." [9]

Axton was also Abe's high school basketball coach in 1940-1941. Abe was part of the Walters track team, running a leg of the mile-relay. Abe's best time in the quarter-mile was 64 seconds. Abe described his performance as "coming around the curve looking like I had an icebox tied to my back. Girls can run faster than that." [10]

Abe was introduced to basketball when his friend William T. "Wimpy" Jones put up a goal in his yard. Roundball soon became Abe's favorite sport, even though his small size prevented him from being an integral part of the team until he blossomed late in high school. In his junior year, Abe tried out for the school play, or really was forced to try out for the play. He spoke softly and was so self-conscious he could not imagine getting up in front of people. When he walked out of the play and refused to participate, he was kicked off the basketball team. He hitch-hiked to Oklahoma City for the state tournament and sat on the bench. Abe started for the Walters basketball team his senior year, at age 19.

Abe graduated from Walters High School in May, 1941. He was earning six dollars a month sweeping out classrooms. He borrowed six dollars from his friend who managed Joe's Drug Store to finance his participation in the senior class trip to New Orleans. In the Big Easy, Abe stuffed himself with nickel hamburgers, one of his favorite culinary delights, and came back from the trip with two dollars in his pocket.

Abe wanted to go to college largely because of the influence of Mae Boren Axton. She insisted he further his education. She took him under her wing and drove him to see her brother, Dr. James Boren, president of Southwestern State Teachers College in Weatherford, Oklahoma. Mae told Abe she thought she could persuade her brother to give him a basketball scholarship and find him a job on the Weatherford campus.

Before he left for college, Abe had to make up one course to officially finish high school. To get the credit, he traveled to Durant to attend a summer course at Southeastern State College.

Abe's high school assistant coach J. D. Norton offered to drive him to Weatherford to begin college. Abe's father had bought him a small trunk in which he packed his few items of clothing. His worldly possessions consisted of a tweed suit his sister had bought him for high school graduation, one pair of shoes, one pair of khaki pants, two homemade shirts, homemade underwear, and three pair of socks. He was 19 and had shaved only once so Abe did not worry about taking a razor with him to college. After Abe finished packing, his father took him aside and opened his worn billfold. The elder Lemons had only two dollars. He kept one dollar for his family and gave the other to Abe.

With a dollar in his pocket and a hunger for adventure, Abe Lemons left Walters in search of his future.

— Chapter Two —

Off To See the World

I was expecting to see Randolph Scott.
Instead I saw Captain Lund whose dog tried to bite me.

Abe Lemons

IN EXCHANGE FOR TUITION, BOOKS, AND ROOM AND BOARD AT Southwestern, Abe cleaned the college president's office, the science room, and three hallways of the administration building each morning. Often President Boren arrived at his office early as Abe was completing his cleaning chores for the day. Boren and Abe became good friends, a friendship that would benefit Abe in later years.

Abe's basketball coach was Rankin Williams whose first love was his job as the Southwestern baseball coach. Williams left much of the teaching of basketball technique to a teacher, Cotton Vickers, who helped Williams coach the basketball team.

From his earliest recollections Abe wanted to be a coach. He loved to teach his teammates a new move or play he had learned from watching any basketball game he could attend. Abe came out of high school basketball with minimal skills, except for shooting the basket. He described himself as a "slow" player with no finesse or know-how to do anything except "barrel toward the basket with the ball." It was Vickers who taught the lanky freshman from Walters how to pivot. Williams thought Abe was too slow, but Abe made the Southwestern team anyway. He was ruled technically ineligible the first semester but played full-time after the Christmas break.

Abe's roommate was Vern McClendon, called the "Golden Boy." Abe enjoyed living in the college dorm with hot showers and cool rooms. His only problem with college life was the lack of quantity of food in the cafeteria. He had never gone without plenty of food in his life, even though his parents were poor. Now he was hungry all the time. He enjoyed feasts of mayonnaise and bread provided occasionally by a fellow student who swiped a gallon of mayonnaise and a loaf of bread from a grocery store near the campus.

Abe's teammates on the Bulldog basketball squad were Red Springer, Pete Jayroe, whose daughter Jayne was Miss America in 1967, Earl Niles, Trapp Rhodes, Roy Dellahoney, Duckey Sullivan, and Abe's best friend, George Stack.

Even before the basketball season began, Japanese planes attacked Pearl Harbor, Hawaii, on December 7, 1941. As America's war effort escalated, the Southwestern dorms were needed to house soldiers and workers being trained for the war-defense industry. Abe and other students were forced to find lodging in private homes in Weatherford. Abe, George Stack, and Pete Landrom rented a room near the campus for one dollar a week.

One of the highlights of Abe's freshman year in basketball was Southwestern's trip to Denver, Colorado, to play in an American Athletic Union (AAU) tournament. The Bulldogs, members of the Oklahoma Collegiate Conference, were beaten in the first round of the tournament even though Abe hit three baskets and his room-mate George Stack scored 12 points. After loading up at their cheap hotel in Denver, the team began the trip back to Oklahoma. They stopped to fill up with gasoline in New Mexico. After paying for the gas, Coach Williams, operating on a lean basketball budget, was left with only 18 cents for each player to eat on. Fortunately, bologna was 15 cents per pound so the players pooled their money and bought a stick of bologna, a loaf of bread, an onion, and a jar of mustard and headed home.

During the school year, Abe, called "Spider" by his basketball teammates, often hitchhiked home to Walters for the weekend. Once he and Doodle Harris went to nearby Temple to check out the girls. Abe was always bashful around members of the opposite sex. He never dated in high school and took his sister or niece to Sea Scout or school dances so he would not be expected to dance with others girls.

On the trip to Temple, he met a pretty young junior, Betty Jo Bills, the drum major of the Temple High School band. Abe thought Betty Jo was something special. However, the feeling was not mutual. Betty Jo had been given wrong information that Abe was a freshman in high school, not college, and would have nothing to do with him. Abe was wearing overalls and looked like a high school freshman. He had not begun shaving until age 19, and then only because his sister-in-law made him.

Betty Jo was born in Temple July 28, 1925, to Ellis and Arah Bills. Her father managed the hardware department at Sears and the B & O Store. [1]

Abe and Doodle asked Betty Jo and two girlfriends to go the movie preview at Walters. After Betty Jo's mother approved, Betty and her friend Patsy Allen wound up in the back seat of Doolittle's car, with Abe in the middle. Betty Jo remembers being afraid that someone might see her and think she was on a date with Abe. [2] That attitude would change later.

For the remainder of the school year Abe feverishly pursued Betty Jo. He sometimes borrowed his sister's car and even once rode a bicycle the 11 miles from Walters to Temple to take Betty Jo to the drugstore for a coke. The relationship was slow to develop. At first Betty Jo did not understand Abe's sense of humor. She thought he was often cruel to his friends with cutting remarks. As weeks turned into months, Betty Jo saw a softer side of Abe. She was convinced he was not as hard as he acted.

As Abe's first year in college ended in May, 1942, the air was filled with frightening talk of war. America was battling fascist forces in Europe and in the Pacific. Abe and his closest friends wanted to serve their country and tried to join the Navy. Even

Seahawks Capture Basketball Title

Coach Lou Zara estimated this week more than 6,000 enrollees participated in SBMSTS' first intramural basketball tourney which the Seahawks won this past month from the Stewards, 23 to 9, in the championship play-off. Gold basketballs were awarded the finalists.

Outstanding player honors went to Abe "Slim" Lemons, Sec. 10C, of the Seahawks, for scoring 105 points in his seven tournament games. In the title game, he took high scoring honors with eight points.

Abe was the star on the championship team of the intramural basketball tournament at the United States Maritime Service training facility at Sheepshead Bay, New York, in 1943. Abe's Seahawks beat the Stewards 29-9 in the championship game. Oklahomans dominated the Seahawks. Left to right, front row, Rusty Fletcher, Walters; Alfred Agler, Walters; Howell Ogletree, Walters; Paul Magness, Geary. Back row, Loyd Murray, Oklahoma City; Ray Loyd, Stigler; Ralph Jacobs from California; Abe; Melvin Niles, El Reno; and Beryl King, Oklahoma City. Abe, nicknamed "Slim" by his fellow Merchant Marines, won outstanding player honors in the tournament, scoring 105 points in seven games.

though thousands of Oklahomans were being inducted into the various military branches, the Navy rejected Abe because of two bad teeth, a spinal defect, and a weak left arm that had been severely fractured when he was 13. Abe tried to join the Army Air Corps but again was rejected because of his medical condition.

Abe had never heard of the United States Merchant Marine until Lester and Bill Thorn of Walters came home on leave from a Merchant Marine assignment. Armed with information about the Merchant Marine, Abe and several friends caught a ride to Oklahoma City with Lloyd Graham and signed up to see the world

Abe, right, joined the Merchant Marine out of a deep love for his country and the desire to help win the war to preserve freedom. In this photo he pauses for refreshment in a bar in Havana, Cuba with fellow Merchant Marine Bill Brewer.

on Merchant Marine ships. Abe had yet to see an ocean but knew he would like sailing on the open sea because of the fun times he had in Sea Scouts.

America's Merchant Marine had a gloried past. Without a Navy, the young United States turned to experienced merchant seaman in privately-owned boats and ships to protect its shores in the war against Britain. One historian wrote, "This story of our nation would have been different were it not for the merchant seaman. He was on the sea with the first throb of independence. The navy, so hastily provided by the infant government, was made up of ordinary merchantmen pierced for guns. With Yankee merchant sailors upon their decks they sailed jauntily to sea to confront the mightiest navy in the world, and just how well they acquitted themselves history amply records." [3]

The Merchant Marine played a significant role in America's victory in World War II. Gliding through submarine-infested waters, ships dodged torpedoes and enemy bombers to deliver cargoes and war munitions necessary for G.I.'s to carry on the battle for freedom.

Abe and Howell "H.C." Ogletree took a train to Sheepshead Bay, New York, to begin Merchant Marine training. Two other Walters boys, Russell "Squirt" Fletcher and Alford "Chickenhawk" Agler, also were at Sheepshead Bay at the same time. Abe convinced his Walters buddies to form a basketball team. They recruited Ray Loyd of Stigler, Oklahoma, and entered an all-Oklahoma team into the Merchant Marine league. Abe was the star of the team. With a full-court press and their novel nicknames, the Oklahoma quintet swept competition on the base against teams made up of the best of the 6,000 recruits. On weekends Abe and Ogletree traveled to New York City. They saw a Frank Sinatra concert and Ogletree ended up dancing one night with baseball star Lou Gehrig's wife. [4]

After five weeks of training, Abe and other Merchant Marine recruits were given an option for advanced instruction. At first Abe wanted to be an engineer and work in the engine room. However, a single excursion into the belly of a ship on a hot day changed his mind forever. Abe signed up for purser school, easily passing the only prerequisite of being able to type at least 21 words per minute. A purser was the member of a ship's crew in charge of the books, payroll, and requisition of supplies.

After three months of purser training, Abe was housed at the Chelsea Hotel in New York City to await assignment. The order sending him to Boston, Massachusetts, soon came. A fellow Merchant Marine received assignment to New Orleans, Louisiana, and asked Abe to trade. Abe had been corresponding by mail with Betty Jo, who had graduated from high school, worked in Dallas, Texas, for awhile and returned to Temple as an audit clerk at Sears. Abe and Betty Jo's relationship grew. Because New Orleans was closer to Oklahoma than Boston, Abe traded assignments and caught a train to New Orleans. Within a few days he was sent to Mobile, Alabama, for his first sea assignment.

Abe had seen his share of gallant ships in the movies. He was excited when he took a taxi to the Mobile dockyards to inspect his first ship, the *Gallant Fox*. He expected to see a sharply-dressed captain who resembled Randolph Scott or John Wayne, with groomed whiskers and a pipe in his mouth, waiting on the bow of a freshly-painted vessel, ready to take on the high seas.

Abe's mouth dropped open in disbelief as he approached the slip where the *Gallant Fox* was anchored. The World War I freighter sat bubbling in the water without a speck of paint in sight. It was the ugliest thing Abe had ever seen. With a lump in his throat, he boarded the ship to meet the captain. It was not Randolph Scott, but Eric Lund, a Norwegian sailor with a dog named Sampson that bit people just for fun.

Abe, as an officer and purser, asked to be shown to his room. He was informed this ship had no separate room for the purser. Instead Abe was shown a room with six bunks next to the kitchen and coal burner. The noise, and stories that the ship was a target for German torpedoes in the Gulf of Mexico, kept Abe from sleeping his first night. He soon learned that the Gulf was called "torpedo junction."

He slept with a lifejacket on so he could jump safely into the water should the *Gallant Fox* be sunk.

Often, when the fear of torpedoes prevented Abe from sleeping, he sat all night under the stars on the ship's deck. Once when an explosion rocked the ship, Sampson ran around barking and biting everyone in sight. Abe scrambled for a life jacket, knowing not what to do or where to go.

Abe's first trip on the *Gallant Fox* was a month-long journey to pick up bauxite at Trinidad in the Caribbean Sea. A typical purser's day on an empty ship was less than stressful. Abe sold clothing and candy to shipmates out of the ship chest, slept anytime he wanted to, and played cards all night.

Merchant Marine duty was not for weaklings. A Merchant Marine history written during the height of World War II praised members of the service, "He knows when he signs on for each

When Abe could convince his Merchant Marine commanders to give him a few days off, he headed for southwest Oklahoma to see Betty Jo Bills. This photo was taken at Pappy's Nightclub in Dallas, Texas, in 1945.

voyage that his chances of returning to port are often doubtful, but, on the other hand, he also knows how often he has cheated death, and he hopes to do it once more." [5]

Purser's pay in the Merchant Marine was $150 per month, plus a bonus when ships traveled into a war zone. Abe spent almost three years in the Merchant Marine as a purser and pharmacist's mate on several different vessels, hauling oil, chemicals, and war machines, including airplanes to exotic destinations such as Australia, India, North Africa, Italy, and islands in the South Pacific.

In the summer of 1946, Abe had a decision to make. Should he sign on for another tour of duty in the Merchant Marine? Or, should he return home to Walters and ask Betty Jo to marry him? Letters between Betty Jo and Abe had grown more frequent and he missed his periodic trips to Walters to date the girl of his dreams. One morning Abe woke up with his mind made up. He went home to Betty Jo.

There was never any question in Betty Jo's mind whether or not she would marry Abe. It was only a question of when.

Abe was 24-years-old and had never owned a car. He knew if he was going to get married he needed two things, a job and dependable transportation. He had saved $700 from his Merchant Marine paychecks and had steady work hauling wheat. He bought a 1937 dark blue Dodge from a neighbor and planned how to approach Betty Jo with his proposal of marriage.

In the middle of a date, Abe summoned the courage to ask Betty Jo the big question. However, Abe did not ask, but simply told Betty Jo they were getting married. She had waited a long time for the moment and said, "Okay."

Abe did not want a large wedding so plans were laid for Abe and Betty Jo to get married secretly in Durant. On August 24, 1946, Abe, accompanied by his best man, Russell "Squirt" Fletcher, and Betty Jo, with her best friend, Janie Dollar, were married by a Baptist preacher. The honeymoon in Durant was very skimpy, as Abe had only $13 to his name.

The newlyweds returned to Walters and went to their separate homes. Betty Jo's parents would not talk to her. Her mother suspected what had happened because nice clothes she had bought for Betty Jo's anticipated wedding were missing during the weekend.

Abe managed to keep his happy secret from his family for two weeks until Abe's father cornered him one night and asked, "Did you get married?" Abe would not lie to his father and confessed. The elder Lemons said, "Bring your wife home." Abe triumphantly went to Betty Jo's house, explained the situation to her parents, and moved his bride and her belongings to his parents' house in Walters. There they stayed until Abe could start college and find a job to support them.

Abe was shocked to learn that his service in the Merchant Marine did not entitle him to benefits under the G.I. Bill. He turned again to Mae Boren Axton who had moved to Ada to teach school while husband John was in the Navy. Dr. James Boren had relocated during the war from Southwestern State College to Hardin College in Wichita Falls, Texas. Mae told Abe to talk to her brother, Dr. Boren, about a scholarship. Abe went to Wichita Falls and showed up on his doorstep.

When Dr. Boren answered the knock on his door, Abe asked, "Do you remember me?" Boren quickly made room on the Hardin basketball squad for Abe and asked basketball coach Paul L. "Red" Rutledge to provide a full scholarship. Because Abe and Betty Jo needed to live off campus, Rutledge agreed to pay for Abe's tuition and books, and provide $35 per month to help with rent. Abe and Betty Jo found a two-bedroom apartment which had once been used as servants' quarters at the home of Bernard Martin, the uncle of Broadway and movie star Mary Martin. Betty Jo worked in the purchasing department at Sears for $25 a week, supplementing the young couple's income enough to at least prevent starvation. The apartment was bare, with only a cookstove and bed. Abe rounded up a card table to serve as a dining table.

There was absolutely no extra money in the Lemons' budget, not for eating out or for movies. Betty Jo rode to work each morning with Martin, an attorney. Abe practiced basketball every afternoon and studied at night. The Hardin basketball team was "a hopeless bunch," losing almost every game. Abe recognized the fundamentals that he and his fellow players should be learning. It was his natural coaching instinct coming to the surface.

The news that Betty Jo was pregnant forced Abe to think about how to earn more money or consider changing schools to make it easier on his growing family. He worked during the summer of 1947 unloading box cars of wheat at the General Mills plant in Wichita Falls. At night he manned the ticket booth at the Spudders baseball park. On July 25, 1947, Betty Jo gave birth to a beautiful baby girl. She was named Dana Lee.

Abe wore number 89 as a member of the Hardin College basketball team.

Abe's future flashed before his eyes. He recognized he must finish college to reach his goal of becoming a basketball coach. Abe was desperate to move to another school because he did not want Betty Jo to work outside the home.

Abe looked for other schools that might pay a larger monthly stipend to supplement his scholarship. The basketball coach at Texas Wesleyan University at Fort Worth offered Abe a full scholarship plus $75 per month. Abe accepted the offer but changed his mind when he read in the newspaper that his old southwest Oklahoma friend Doyle K. Parrack had been named head coach at Oklahoma City University (OCU). Parrack had grown up in the Cookietown community, ten miles west of Abe's hometown of Walters. Parrack had played basketball for the Union Valley High School team and knew of Abe's success at Walters and Southwestern Oklahoma State. [6]

Parrack learned the fundamentals of basketball as a player at Oklahoma A & M in Stillwater, Oklahoma, from 1941 to 1943 and again, after the war, from 1944 to 1945, under legendary coach Henry P. "Hank" Iba. Parrack was a member of the 1945 National

Collegiate Athletic Association (NCAA) championship squad. He coached at Shawnee High School in 1945-1946 and played for the professional Chicago Stags in 1946-1947, a season in which Chicago won the Western Division championship before losing to Philadelphia in the finals. [7]

Parrack was quiet, single, 26, and 6'0", and OCU fans were excited about him bringing the Iba brand of basketball to the Chiefs.

Parrack called Abe and matched the offer from Texas Wesleyan, on the condition that Abe pass rigorous tryouts and make the OCU squad. Abe drove to Oklahoma City, stayed in the YMCA, and gritted his teeth, determined to show Coach Parrack he could still play basketball. After a hard workout, Parrack approached Abe with a smile on his face, and said softly, "You made it kid." As soon as Abe arrived back in Wichita Falls, Betty Jo began packing. The Lemons family headed for Oklahoma City.

—*Chapter Three*—

Becoming a Chief

Basketball is like life, easy to play, but difficult to master.

James Naismith

WHAT APPEARED TO BE A LIFE OF PLENTY FOR ABE AND BETTY JO at Oklahoma City University was anything but that. The young couple was not prepared for the hardships they faced in Abe's last two years of college.

Oklahoma City University was located on 55 acres at the corner of Northwest 23rd Street and Blackwelder Avenue in Oklahoma City. The school began classes in 1904, as Epworth University, largely the dream for a Methodist college in Oklahoma of a young Edmond, Oklahoma, lawyer, Anton H. Classen. Classen made the Oklahoma Land Run of 1889 and used his influence to convince the Oklahoma territorial legislature to establish a teacher's school in Edmond, an institution that later became Central State College and ultimately the University of Central Oklahoma.

However, Classen, a dedicated Methodist, worked diligently to promote a Methodist school of higher learning for Oklahoma City. Known as Methodist University and Oklahoma City College for several years, the school was given its present name in 1923. [1]

Classen became famous for his street-car company and real estate developments in Oklahoma City, but his proudest accomplishment was a Methodist university for Oklahoma.

Oklahoma City University fielded its first basketball team in 1920 and began a series of losing seasons. All of OCU's athletic teams were called the "Goldbugs," at the suggestion of college president Edwin G. Green and *The Daily Oklahoman*. According to legend, ancient Egyptians revered the goldbug beetle as a symbol of resurrection and continuing life. [2] In February, 1944, OCU's symbol was changed to an American Indian and the school's athletic teams were known thereafter as the "Chiefs" until 1999 when the name "Stars" was adopted.

Abe and Betty Jo arrived in Oklahoma City with only a few dollars in their pockets. The only housing they could afford was a tiny, run-down apartment near Will Rogers Field in southwest Oklahoma City in former barracks used by servicemen during World War II. Betty Jo was miserable, spending all day, every day with Dana, alone, cooped up in the apartment, unable to go anywhere because Abe used their only car to travel the 12 miles to school and work.

Betty Jo later described the Will Rogers Field apartment as a concentration camp, "It had a cement floor. Abe's sister gave us furniture or we would not have had anything. We had an icebox that the iceman came by and put a block of ice in. We had no washing machine. I boiled water on top of the range to do diapers and daily laundry." [3]

Betty Jo hung her clothes on a line outside the apartment until winter came and froze the wet clothing before it could dry. Rent was $37.50 per month, half of the $75 cash Abe received from OCU.

Abe and Betty Jo hardly saw each other. He left the apartment early to make a 7:40 a.m. class. Abe worked eight hours a day, for 75 cents an hour, on OCU's paint and maintenance crew. C. A. Redman supervised the crew of athletes required to work on campus to earn their scholarships. Sometimes Redman, known as the meanest man in the world, needed to make work for the boys. He would tell them to move a pile of lumber from one side of the campus to the other. Then, to create another project, he would tell them to move the pile back to where it was in the first place. Redman's practice gave life to the phrase "moving the lumber pile" as a metaphor for doing busy work. [4]

A week after classes began, Coach Parrack called the first basketball practice from 6:00 p.m. to 10:00 p.m. The practices, including double and triple-time sessions on weekends, further limited time that Abe, Betty Jo, and Dana could spend as a family.

Abe grew up in poverty and had never thought much about the luxuries of life he was missing, luxuries such as eating out or going to a movie. However, he was disturbed when he saw Betty Jo's suffering, her unhappiness with the drudgery of spending 24-hours-a-day with the baby in the apartment, with no relief or variation in her daily routine to buoy her spirits.

Abe and Betty Jo literally counted their pennies toward the end of the month to see if there was any money for groceries or milk for Dana. Abe's sister cried during one visit as she heard Abe and Betty Jo trying to figure out how to scrape up enough money to buy a box of crackers. Some months, when the money completely ran out, Betty Jo took Dana and spent a few days with her parents. Abe looked like a skeleton but he was determined to learn basketball and keep his family intact.

Oklahoma City University's campus did not provide an adequate place to play basketball. The Goldbug Gymnasium had been built in the early 1920s but was under-lighted and under-heated, causing OCU officials to rent either the Municipal Auditorium or the gym at Oklahoma City's Capitol Hill High School for home games. Lucky for Abe, the OCU administration approved funds to construct a new gymnasium-cafeteria complex that contained space for bleachers seating 2,000 for basketball games. The Chiefs moved into their new home in November, 1947. [5]

The 1947-1948 OCU season was a good beginning for Abe and Coach Parrack. Using the Henry P. Iba hold-the-ball brand of basketball, Parrack's Chiefs began the season with a moral victory, limiting the sensational amateur team, the Phillips 66 Oilers, to 50 points in a 50-31 loss. Parrack told reporters his team was in good physical condition but lacked experience.

Parrack, who later in his career served eight years as an assistant to Iba, wholeheartedly believed in Iba's slow-motion basketball. Iba was already one of the most respected basketball coaches in the nation. He was hired at Oklahoma A & M in 1934 and won back-to-back national NCAA championships in 1945-1946, the first college to accomplish that feat. Iba also changed the face of college basketball by recruiting Bob Kurland as the first "big man." Kurland, with his 7'0" frame, dominated opponents' backboards in the Cowboys national championship seasons.

With a 5-5 record, and impressive wins over Western Colorado State College and Austin, Texas, College, the Chiefs were invited to the third annual Emporia College Invitation tournament in Emporia, Kansas, just after Christmas. OCU lost a 55-43 decision to Miami University of Ohio but regrouped and outscored Colorado School of Mines and Hastings College of Nebraska to capture the consolation game in the tournament.

Abe started slowly offensively in his rookie season at OCU. Early in the year teammates Farrell Craig, a 5'10" guard, and 6'7" center Delbert Cearley were the Chiefs' leading scorers. In the second half of the season, Abe caught fire, and finished the year with 192 points, 33 more points than his nearest competitor, 6'0" guard Jack Roblyer. Abe enjoyed playing with Roblyer, Craig, Cearley, Don Slocum, Ollie Helderle, Merle Bodkin, Bill Johnson, Bill Stowell, Richard Dozier, Paul Hansen, and Don McClure. Abe, at 6'3" was the tallest player except for the team's two centers, Cearley, and 6'8" Slocum.

After the Christmas break, Abe led the Chiefs to wins over Northwestern Louisiana, Hardin College, Austin College, and East Texas Baptist College. OCU closed out the season by dropping a seven-point decision to Northwestern Oklahoma State College, finishing at 18-13. Abe averaged 6.2 points per game, on a team that averaged only 44 points per outing against their opponents 39.3 points. [6]

At the end of Abe's first year as a student at OCU he was granted permission to work off campus and earn a few extra dollars for his family. He attended classes Monday through Friday until 12:30 p.m. and worked from 1:00 p.m. to 1:00 a.m. at the Wilson Company meat-packing plant where a job opened up after dozens of workers left on strike. Abe later called it the hardest job of his life, "The plant was old and there were no easy jobs. I pulled a buggy full of bacon or meat over bumpy, brick floors. It was cold inside and hot outside. It was slave labor." 7

The new job allowed Abe to save some money and soon the Lemons moved to better housing, a small apartment on Northwest 29th Street near the OCU campus. Family life improved dramatically. He borrowed $75 from OCU president Dr. Cluster Q. Smith to buy a used refrigerator and stove. Smith agreed to allow Abe to pay back the loan over a two-year period, with one percent interest. Smith was president of OCU from 1942 to 1957 and chancellor of the university for three additional years. Born on a ranch in Texas, Smith was a country school teacher and Methodist preacher before being hired as vice president of Southern Methodist University in Dallas, Texas, and serving as superintendent of the Methodist's St. Louis, Missouri, District. 8

There was still not much extra money in the household budget but Abe could walk to school and work, freeing up the car for Betty Jo to escape the house and go grocery shopping or take Dana to play in the park. Abe was proud. Even though his family was hardly making ends meet, he did not want Betty Jo to get a job and leave Dana with baby-sitters.

Abe greatly admired Coach Parrack. He appreciated Parrack for teaching him the basic fundamentals of basketball and expecting him and his fellow players to put out 100 percent even in games in which the Chiefs were trailing badly and there was little hope of winning.

Parrack was very strict with his players. He did not want them to have anything to do with girls. In order to talk to girlfriends, the players arranged clandestine meetings at the OCU library where Parrack required players to go in the evening after practice.

Parrack was also adamant that his players not eat desserts before games, particularly on road trips. However, sharp-thinking players

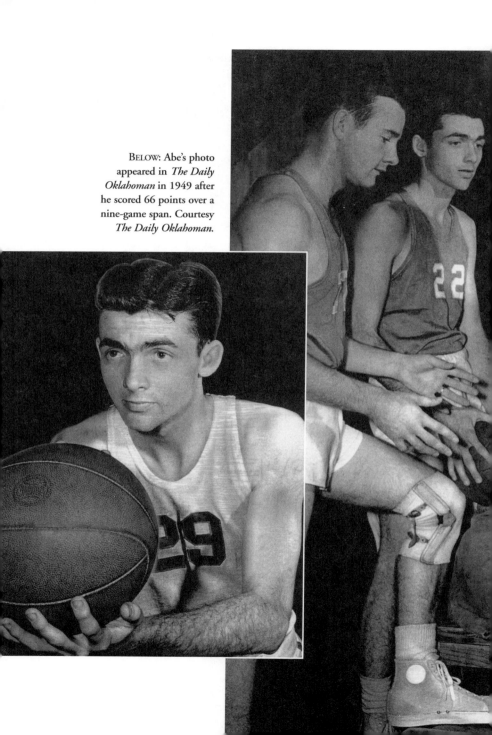

ABOVE: Abe played at Oklahoma City University with Bruce Hodge who became a career agent with the Federal Bureau of Investigation. Hodge had played high school basketball with Paul Hansen at Oklahoma City Central High. In this 1976 photo, Abe, left, and Hodge prepare a sandwich from Abe's favorite food, bologna. Courtesy Bruce Hodge.

LEFT: Abe, center, and Jack Roblyer, left, check out practice balls from Oklahoma City University coach Doyle Parrack. Abe said that the period should be called "Stalag OCU," referring to Parrack's structured, hard-work practices that often ended with "running the stairs" or the "fireman's carry," where players ran sprints carrying another player. When Abe became a coach, he also used the "fireman's carry." Courtesy *The Daily Oklahoman.*

buttered their crackers and loaded them with sugar as a substitute for dessert. [9]

Parrack's hard-work ethic and gentle persuasion of his players paid off in the 1948-1949 season. For the first time in the school's cage history, the 20-win plateau was reached. No one could have predicted the successful season after the Chiefs lost a low-scoring affair to the University of Arkansas Razorbacks 31-29 in their first game in early December. Neither team took a shot at the bucket for the first 90 seconds. When the Razorbacks caught fire and scored 15 points in the first seven minutes, Parrack sent in his wrecking crew of Dick Dozier, Bill O'Neil, and Paul Hansen. A newspaper reporter wrote, "All three of them hawked the ball and stole it several times and at the same time Craig and Hansen were burning the nets with two pointers to get the Chiefs back into the game." [10] The Chiefs got to within two points of Arkansas in the final minute but Arkansas prevailed. Abe was listed as a defensive standout of the game.

However, the Chiefs rebounded and won five consecutive games against worthy opponents, including two wins over the University of Houston. The Chiefs almost lost to the unheralded Trinity College Tigers of San Antonio, Texas, in the fourth game of the season. OCU trailed at half-time but came back to win by eight, 57-49.

Abe was joined in his second season as a Chief by Merle Bodkin; Don Slocum; Bill Stowell; Hansen, an All-City player from Oklahoma City Central High School; Jack Key; Sam Marrs; Ollie Helderle; Don Penwell; Harold "Skeet" Warren from Oklahoma City Central High; LaVerne Laws; Vernon Bowen; Farrell Craig; Dozier; Jack Roblyer; Bruce Hodge; and O'Neil. [11]

Hodge, decades later when he was inducted into the OCU Hall of Fame, said the only reason Coach Parrack kept him around was because he owned a car. Because of the lean OCU athletic department budget, basketball players rode to games in a beat-up aged bus and players' cars. [12]

Abe's quick reaction to crises helped Jack Key out of a tough situation one night on the road at Fayetteville, Arkansas. Coach

Parrack announced the team would be wearing dark jerseys for the game. Key confided in Abe that he had forgotten his dark jersey and only had a white jersey to wear. Abe calmly had an answer to the problem, saying, "Jack, don't even put a shirt on. Just put on your warmups. Chances are you'll never get to play tonight so it won't matter." [13] Key, praying hard that he would not be called upon to substitute, sat throughout the game in his warmups, with no shirt. Key never played and Coach Parrack never knew the difference.

During an unusually tough practice session, Key elbowed Abe after he tripped over Abe's leg. Parrack, to punish the two brawling players, hollered out the order, "Run the stairs!" Abe and Key, neither of whom could afford to rebel against Parrack's command and run the risk of losing their scholarships, ran the stairs from 5:00 p.m. until almost midnight. [14] Key did not mind a physical scrape with Abe now and then, but would not even consider verbal warfare with Abe. Key said, "Abe was smart, cool under pressure, and the witty sayings flowed out of his mouth. You didn't want to ever get in a mouth fight with him cause he'd kill you." [15]

The Chiefs' starting lineup was formidable. Abe and Bodkin, called the most improved player on the club from the previous year, started at forward. The guards were Craig, a 5'10" speedster from Enid, Oklahoma, and Stowell, 6'0" from Tulsa, Oklahoma. At the pivot post was "Slim" Slocum, a 6'8" giant from Addington, Oklahoma. [16]

Abe's wit and humor that would make him a national treasure later in life was discovered by the media early in his career as a player at OCU. As the 1948 season got underway, the student newspaper, *The Campus*, commented, "As with last year, the coolest man under fire was the likable A.E. 'Abe' Lemons, the young dribbler with the dead pan expression. The fans can expect the limit out of this young man." [17]

Parrack's "iron curtain" defense held opponents to only 38.4 points per game in 1948-1949, second best in the nation. After losing road games to the University of New Mexico and Indiana State Teachers College, the Chiefs reeled off nine straight wins against tough squads such as Tulsa, Houston, Centenary, and Wichita State University. On the second night of a tournament at Oklahoma City's Municipal Auditorium, the Chiefs met their old rival Texas Wesleyan, from the cowtown portion of Fort Worth, Texas. OCU won 43-34 in a hard-fought contest in which Wesleyan players threatened to whip the officials for letting the Chiefs win. [18]

The Chiefs became well known in Oklahoma basketball circles in the late 1940s, largely due the efforts of OCU athletic publicity director Jerry Ragsdale, affectionately known as "Fat Rat." As sports editor for *The Campus* and a stringer for *The Daily Oklahoman*, Ragsdale promised Parrack that attendance at home games would double. Ragsdale underestimated his ability as a public relations guru. Attendance was four times greater in 1948-1949 than in the previous season.

Ragsdale and Abe were great friends. In one of his columns in the campus newspaper, Ragsdale quipped, "And that Abe Lemons, what a character he is. When television comes down our way, he will run Bob Hope off the screen." [19] Ragsdale wrote about sports in a light-hearted, super informal style, "Well, 400 of the luckier students here in this institution had the chance to see the round-ballers in action for a buck Saturday night...Doyle Parrack, the genial young coach will be one of the top skippers in the nation in a few years." [20]

With an enviable 18-5 record at the end of the regular season, OCU was invited to participate in the National Amateur Athletic Union Basketball Tournament in mid-March. The tournament, sponsored by the Amateur Athletic Union (AAU), had been held in Denver, Colorado, for years. However, Hal Middlesworth, the sports editor of *The Daily Oklahoman*, convinced AAU officials to move the tournament to Oklahoma City in 1949. So many teams were entered that games were simultaneously held at the OCU gym, Capitol Hill High School, and at the Municipal Auditorium.

With a home-court advantage, the Chiefs moved into the AAU quarter-finals with impressive victories over the Montana Stockmen and Dayton Zimmerman teams. Abe hit the first bucket in the Dayton game and was the lone Chief to foul out of the contest. In a quarter-final matchup against the Peoria, Illinois, Caterpillar-Diesels, OCU ran into a buzz-saw, losing 43-40, ending OCU's best season in history at 20-6.

Abe found an even better apartment a half-block from campus during the middle of his junior year. It had an extra bedroom, a real improvement over the tiny apartments to which Abe and Betty Jo were accustomed. Abe earned extra money by mowing lawns, picking up garbage, and painting houses.

Abe's love for basketball was not adversely affected by his pitiful financial plight. Whenever he could find time, he attended high school and college games, and played pick-up games with any group of basketballers he could find. He drove around town in his aging car. The universal joint had gone out "a thousand times" and a window could be lowered or raised only by pulling a string Abe tied to the mechanism inside the door. [21]

Oklahoma City University began the 1949-1950 season with a veteran team. Only Roblyer and Helderle had been lost to graduation. Slow-down basketball was still Coach Parrack's forte, prompting a newspaper to report, "The Chiefs style of playing will not be changed much this year, with the deliberate type of basketball prevailing. The club is not noted for fast breaks except on occasion." [22]

The Chiefs began their season in the Mayor's Benefit game at the Municipal Auditorium against the Phillips 66 Oilers from Bartlesville, Oklahoma. The Oilers' star player was former Oklahoma A & M All-American Bob Kurland who topped Phillips' scorers with 11 points as the Oilers won 56-39. Abe scored nine points to go with Craig and Bodkins, the leading scorers for the Chiefs with 10 points each.

Abe's senior season was incredibly successful, both for him personally, and for his teammates. He was elected team captain and was second to Slocum in scoring, with 7.7 points per game. OCU was 19-9, with a 13-game winning streak, notching key wins over Emporia State, powerhouse Creighton University, Tulsa, North Texas State, and the University of Houston.

The highlight of Abe's last season as a player for OCU was the Chiefs winning the 1949 All-College Tournament in Oklahoma

City. The tournament was sponsored by *The Daily Oklahoman* and was born in 1936 as a charity event to finance the Milk and Ice Fund for children. Later, in 1957, an All Sports Association was organized with E.L. "Jim" Roederer as its first president. The All Sports Association continues to support the highly-successful All-College, the nation's oldest Christmas holiday basketball tournament. [23]

From its humble beginning in 1936, the All-College Tournament was a hit with colleges in the Southwest which had difficulty scheduling games before Christmas. Teams usually lost money traveling to Oklahoma City, but sought competition to sharpen the skills and reactions of their players. In early years when *The Daily Oklahoman* considered dropping the tournament, college coaches asked the newspaper to keep it going. Some of the great players in American college basketball history have played in the All-College.

With Abe's 14 points, OCU slipped past the Baylor University Bears in the opening game of the All-College 43-32 and entered the dream second-round matchup against Oklahoma A & M. It was student versus mentor, Parrack against Iba. Newspapers called it one of the most important games in state basketball history. OCU upset A & M 37-35, causing one newspaper to write, "The king is dead, long live the king." [24]

The Chiefs continued their winning ways in the All-College final against the Cowboys of the University of Wyoming. However, it took overtime for the Chiefs to capture their first All-College title, 36-35. Farrell Craig was voted the tournament's most valuable player. Craig and Abe were named to the All-College Tournament team.

After their All-College victory, the Chiefs were ranked 23rd in the nation in the weekly Associated Press poll of sportscasters and sportswriters. It was the first season Associated Press gathered and published weekly rankings of college basketball teams.

After the 1950 season, Coach Parrack talked to Abe about staying on as an assistant basketball coach for OCU. Parrack, who had continually encouraged Abe to go into coaching, requested and won approval from university officials to hire Abe as his assistant, and freshman coach, for $3,200 annually. Abe was breathless as he hurried across campus to the apartment to tell Betty Jo the news. They were happy that Abe would actually get paid for doing what he lived and breathed, playing and coaching basketball. The $3,200 salary seemed like all the money in the world. Abe beamed as he predicted he could buy his loyal and beautiful wife anything she wanted.

Parrack was proud of his new assistant coach who he thought was "level-headed, intelligent, a leader, a good recruiter, and strong on academics." [25]

In May, 1950, Abe's mother was present as he became the first member of his family to graduate from college. As Abe walked across the stage to receive his diploma, he remembered the long hours of back-breaking labor and missed opportunities to be with his wife and baby. Surely it was worth it. With a college degree in physical education, Abe had the means to adequately support his family. Abe Lemons was on top of the world.

— *Chapter Four* —

Assistant Coach

**Coaching under Doyle Parrack was like
being in a mock trial.**

Abe Lemons

ABE WAS A NATURAL AS A BASKETBALL COACH. HIS LAID-BACK instruction won the hearts of his players. Sure, there were times when players hated him when the hair bristled on the back of his neck during an "instructional" session so loud that paint chips flicked off the fieldhouse ceiling. But, when the dust cleared, Abe's players had been taught the fundamentals of basketball and understood why they were placed in a particular spot on the floor and were expected to execute in a specific way.

Abe learned much about coaching under Chiefs head coach Parrack. Abe liked offense and Parrack liked defense, a combination made in heaven. Abe was allowed to concentrate on teaching OCU players the intricacies of offensive basketball. Average scores were creeping upward every season as fans demanded more aggressive, wide-open basketball. In learning the technical aspects of offensive basketball, Abe found he was also learning the defense. If a coach knew how to outsmart a defense, that same knowledge could be used to design a defense to take the punch out of any offense.

Abe recognized that any future success he might enjoy as a basketball coach hinged on his ability to coach offense. Rule changes and a better stable of shooters across the nation drove scores up. The glamour was in scoring so high school coaches often put defense at the bottom of their instruction list.

Abe used visits to other schools and coaches' clinics to learn from the masters, veteran coaches like Doc Hayes of Southern Methodist University, Joe Lapchick of St. John's University, Forrest "Phog" Allen of Kansas University, Adolph Rupp of Kentucky University, John Wooden of the University of California at Los Angeles (UCLA), and Henry Iba of Oklahoma A & M.

About Iba, Abe said, "Hank gave the game everything he had. He didn't worry about milking it for all the extras, the radio programs, the television programs, the endorsements. He stayed out of the limelight and gave the game to the kids. Hank always liked it when the writers referred to the team as Oklahoma A & M's team and not the Hank Iba team." [1]

Abe learned both what to do, and what not to do, from the famous coaches. He saw Lapchick as a coach inwardly bleeding to death, taking every loss as a personal affront, losing 15 pounds every season. Lapchick got so worked up during a game, he died a little each week. Lapchick once told a gathering of coaches, "This is a humiliating business. There are no geniuses in coaching. The players make the coach. The coach who thinks his coaching is more important than his talent is an idiot." [2]

From Phog Allen, Abe learned to look at football players as potential basketball players. In years before basketball coaches were not interested in players unless they answered to nicknames like "Slim" or "Bones." Allen saw the parallels of football and basketball, "The two games are first cousins. Both are contact games. Any time you get two or more boys going in the same or opposite direction for a loose ball, you've got contact. Dribbling through a spread defense, for instance, is akin to a halfback running a broken field." [3]

Oklahoma City University basketball was popular in 1950. The school was considered one of Oklahoma's Big Four, along with the University of Tulsa, the University of Oklahoma, and Oklahoma A & M.

As freshman coach Abe was in charge of equipment, typed letters, drafted media guides, and kept the team books on travel

Arnold Short was named the most valuable player of the 1952 All-College tournament. Short and Abe became good friends from the beginning of their relationship, even though Abe was Short's coach. Short enjoyed Abe's humor, his stories about real people and real events. Courtesy *The Daily Oklahoman.*

expenses and meal allowances. After his bookwork was completed, Abe turned his attention to the younger, less experienced players who were assigned to him by Parrack for drilling in the fundamentals of offense. The freshman team, called the "Lemonites" or the "Little Chiefs," was a valuable proving ground for several future Chief varsity stars such as Arnold Short, Claude Kedy, Sonny Hawkins, and Tom Bolin.

Short was an incredible athlete who won almost every long-distance run coaches Parrack and Lemons imposed upon the basketball players. Short, a 6'2" star from Weatherford, Oklahoma, where he played for high school basketball coach Steve Graham, was motivated to try harder because of the example set by his older brother, Eddie. [4]

Abe coached and exerted authority over former teammates who had yet to graduate. Paul Hansen, Bill Stowell, Farrell Craig, Bill O'Neil, Don Penwell, Jack Key, and the smallest man on the squad, Dick Dozier, were now under Abe's tutelage. All were great friends and there seemed no problem in Abe wearing a different hat as the 1950 season began.

Abe developed strong relationships with several new players. Sam Marrs, who had played basketball at the Oklahoma Military Academy, was a good defensive prospect. Corky Jones, a sophomore from Grandfield, Oklahoma, was exceptionally fast for his big, 6'5" frame. Kenneth Rose, an All-State star from New Lima, Oklahoma, planned to be a coach and took great interest in the successful transition from player to coach that Abe had completed. Another new player who wanted to be a coach someday was Doyle Mayfield, the leading scorer for his first two years at Carnegie, Oklahoma, Junior College. [5]

Abe was very close to guard Paul Hansen whose play was hampered by a nagging knee and back injury he had suffered years before at Oklahoma City Central High School. Abe worked with Hansen on shooting and Hansen responded, making his share of OCU points.

Abe came out of retirement in early November to play in the first annual OCU varsity-alumni game in the school gymnasium.

Abe led the losing alumni squad in scoring. He also led the team in stopping by the drugstore on the way home to buy aspirin to help his aching legs and back.

Parrack's and Lemons' 1950-1951 Chiefs posted a 16-14 record. Don Penwell was the leading scorer.

In 1951-1952, OCU fielded a superb basketball team. Forwards Andy Likens and Jack Key, guards Arnold Short, Ken Rose, and Bill O'Neil, and center Don Penwell were backed up by other lettermen Don Dalton, Doyle Mayfield, and Bill Couts. The Chiefs won the All-College Tournament for the second time in three years and received the school's first ever bid to the National Collegiate Athletic Association post-season tournament. Coach Parrack became the first person to appear in the NCAA tournament both as a player and a coach. Penwell was the team's leading scorer with 403 points in 26 games with a career-high 30 points in a single game.

Former player Paul Hansen, earning only $2,600 annually as the basketball coach at Noble High School, Oklahoma, had no money for tickets to the All-College tournament. However, Hansen, who "could charm a bird out of a tree," convinced two ladies running a flower shop at the municipal auditorium to allow his wife, Carol, and him to slip into the arena through the flower shop. [6]

In the NCAA tournament, OCU lost to Wyoming 54-48 but rebounded to beat highly-touted UCLA, coached by John Wooden, 55-53 in the consolation game. Arnold Short led all scorers with 22 points in the OCU-UCLA game. It was in that game that Short's career began to blossom, all because of a heart-to-heart talk about goals, objectives, and life that he and Abe had before the game. [7] The Chiefs finished the season at 19-8.

Fan involvement was at an all-time high at OCU, contrary to a national trend of smaller crowds at college basketball games. OCU was far removed from a horrible national scandal involving 33 players from seven schools, City College of New York, Long Island University, Manhattan University, New York University, the University of Kentucky, Bradley University, and Toledo University. The players were accused of conspiring to fix games in 20 cities in

17 states. Some players and gamblers who conspired with the players went to jail, prompting Seton Hall University coach John "Honey" Russell to proclaim, "The whole business is crazy. Scholarships, big national schedules, win the games or you lose a job—all of it is crazy. If I had it all to do over again, I'd go some place where they didn't give scholarships and they played a simple schedule with schools right around the area. I'd go where all they wanted you to do was take a group of kids and teach them to play as well as possible and then if they lost or they won it wouldn't matter as long as they were getting something out of the sport." [8]

The 1952-1953 Chiefs reached a pinnacle in OCU basketball history to that point. With an 18-4 regular season record, the Chiefs received their second consecutive NCAA tournament bid. Unfortunately, OCU was forced to play the University of Kansas in a regional game in Manhattan, Kansas, in the Jayhawks' backyard. Kansas, the Big Seven Conference champion, beat the Chiefs 73-65. The Jayhawks would eventually lose the national championship by a single point to Indiana University in the NCAA final game. OCU lost a close consolation regional game to Texas Christian University 58-56, to close out a remarkable 18-6 season.

In the All-College Tournament in Oklahoma City the previous December, the Chiefs beat Bowling Green University in the first round, lost to an Oklahoma A & M team that had its hottest shooting night of the year, hitting 80 percent of field goal attempts, and won the third place consolation game against Wyoming. Arnold Short was named the All-College Most Valuable Player.

Short, who played later for the Phillips 66 Oilers amateur basketball team and served six years as athletic director at OCU in the 1980s, was a versatile player who perfectly fit Abe's offensively-minded idea of using agility, accuracy, and speed to get the ball in the hoop quickly and efficiently. Short broke every individual Chief scoring record, averaging more than 22 points per game, and the OCU team broke the team high mark both for a single game and the season total. In the All-College, Short scored 70 points, surpassing the old mark set by Oklahoma A & M star Bob Kurland in 1946. [9] Short was named third-team All-American.

Abe's 1952-1953 freshman team was one of his best, promising a steady flow of talent into the varsity program. The Little Chiefs posted a 14-9 record with 6'3" forward Joe Kile leading the team in scoring. Close behind was 5'10" guard Don Shields and 6' guard Gerald Hoeltzel. Abe worked hard with two big freshmen, Troy Qualls and Don Jones, both 6'8". Qualls and Jones alternated at the post and at center and played all 23 games on the freshmen schedule.

Abe used two Oklahoma small-town basketball stars to lead his 1953-1954 freshman team. Larry Bradshaw, from Cheyenne, was a talented defensive player whom Abe used in his single post attack. Lyndon Lee, a star at Thackerville High School, and Bradshaw were both 6'4". Abe had other promising freshmen to educate about the finer things of basketball. Eddie Kidd, a star at Oklahoma City Southeast High School, Bob Lawson a 6'3" forward from Pryor, Oklahoma, and Don Cunningham, a 6'4" forward from Cox City, Oklahoma, made up a powerful bench for the Little Chiefs. Campus newspaper sports editor Pat Petree wrote, "What makes it even better, this power laden bench is capable of swapping places at any time with the regulars and giving a fine account of themselves." [10]

— Chapter Five —

Ed Nall

**One day of practice is like one day of clean living.
It doesn't do you that much good.**

Abe Lemons

ONE OF THE PRIMARY REASONS OCU BASKETBALL WAS WELL KNOWN across the nation in the 1950s and 1960s was Ed Nall and his creative promotional ideas.

Edwin Powell Nall, a native of Waurika, Oklahoma, began working with OCU's athletic department while still a student in 1950. After he graduated in 1952, head coach Doyle Parrack convinced Nall to stay on as business manager and sports information director.

By 1953, the Chiefs Basketball Network, owned and managed by Nall, was in its third year of operation with sportscaster Bill Bryan serving as the radio voice of the Chiefs. The games were broadcast on KTOK Radio in Oklahoma City. Previously stations KTOW and KOCY had aired Chiefs basketball. [1] At one time the OCU broadcast was fed to 26 commercial radio stations and was heard around the world via the Armed Forces Radio and Television Network (AFRTS). Nall coined the phrase, "Good evening everyone. From coast to coast and around the world, the OCU Chiefs basketball team is on the air," that opened each Chiefs' broadcast.

Finding sponsors to pay for the broadcast of OCU games was often a challenge. Nall used his ingenuity to trade radio time for meal tickets at O'Mealey's Cafeteria so the basketball team could be fed when the school cafeteria was closed. Once when a "no-smoking" sign was needed for the fieldhouse, Nall traded advertising spots for goat feed that he traded to a sign painter who happened to own milk goats. Net cost for the sign to OCU...zero. [2]

When OCU needed a new cafeteria, Nall traded commercials for paint. He often bought cheap cattle at auctions and turned to OCU booster Chick Davies, an official at the Wilson Company meat-packing plant in Oklahoma City, for help in butchering the beef into T-bones and other parcels. Nall traded the good cuts of meat to a meat wholesaler, John Muncy, for bacon, ham, and cheese. The

Ed Nall, left, and Abe at a 1956 banquet for OCU basketball supporters. Nall worked night and day to promote the success of the Chiefs program under the direction of Abe and Paul Hansen. Courtesy *The Daily Oklahoman.*

basketball players were fed from the lesser cuts of meat, prompting one player to exclaim, "All we ever have is roast, roast, roast!" [3]

Nall was always looking for good deals to make his lean athletic department budget work out. When a Humpty Dumpty grocery store announced a close-out sale, Nall bought 1,200 rabbit pot pies that had not sold to the public. The players, eating under the assumption their delicacy was a chicken pot pie, were never told differently. Nall bought almost a ton of butter from a dairy in Tulsa whose truck had turned over, smashing the pounds of butter into odd-shapes. With his savings, Nall fed the OCU athletes for three cents per meal one season.

Nall played hard ball in getting the best prices and best service from vendors on the campus. When the local Coca-Cola bottler refused to provide a new clock for the OCU fieldhouse, Nall had all Coca-Cola machines removed from the campus. The bottling company got the message and bought OCU a new clock.

As the athletic department business manager, Nall was responsible for getting OCU teams to away games. He used cars, buses, trains, and even a World War II C-47 airplane. Pat Patterson, a local automobile dealer, owned the C-47 and accepted commercials on Chiefs' broadcasts in exchange for providing the plane and pilot, Bill Ireland, to ferry the basketball team to distant destinations from St. Louis to Wyoming. [4]

Nall was a master promoter. He hired airplanes to fly over Memorial Stadium in Norman during Oklahoma University football games to promote OCU basketball. On an afternoon before OCU entertained SMU in Oklahoma City, banner trailing the airplane read "OCU vs SMU 8 P.M." Nall published the basketball brochure and media guide, sold advertisements, and season tickets, and assisted in filming the games. He also found time to teach physical education and write, shoot, and edit a color 16mm film promoting OCU.

Nall convinced sportswriters in St. Louis, New York, Houston, Los Angeles, and other major cities to mention OCU basketball. Nall also arranged for the OCU team to be introduced on ABC's Breakfast Club with host Don McNeil. Movie stars Glenn Ford, Edgar Buchanan, and Cathleen Case appeared at OCU to plug the Chiefs.

Nall created the "Chiefs" booster club, the OCU Sports Hall of Fame, and a booster band called the "Band Aids" to play at home games. To interest fans in the "roughness" of a particular game, Nall talked his friend, funeral home owner Bill Merritt, into parking an ambulance in front of the fieldhouse "in case any of the players were injured and had to be taken to the hospital." [5]

The genius of Nall, a pioneer in FM radio broadcasting in Oklahoma, was even recognized by out-of-town sportswriters. A story in *The Wichita Beacon* called Nall "a man of boundless energy and limitless vision who is currently engaged in three important projects, any one of which would be considered a full-time job by the man on the street. Nall is the P.T. Barnum of the campus." [6]

Media experts predicted the 1953-1954 Chiefs would be a one-man team, led by pre-season All-American Arnold Short. But it did not take the Chiefs long to prove they were a team of many players. With an ever-toughening schedule, OCU won 18 of 25 games and locked up a third consecutive NCAA playoff bid, losing in the first round to Bradley 61-55. Earlier in the year, after a strong win in the third place game in the All-College against Wyoming, the Chiefs moved into the Associated Press top ten basketball teams in the country. At the close of the 1954 season, Arnold Short was named a second-team All-American by *Look* Magazine.

Abe's Little Chiefs had their best season ever in 1953-1954. After losing the first two games to the Cameron Aggies from Lawton, Oklahoma, the freshmen reeled off 21 straight victories, including wins over frosh teams from Oklahoma A & M, Wichita, and Tulsa.

The softer side of Abe that wife Betty Jo had spotted in their early dates was evident in the case of Frank Thurber in 1954. Abe had promised Thurber a basketball scholarship to OCU after the 6'7" Thurber averaged 19 points a game playing for Crooked Oak High School in Oklahoma City. Tragically, five days after Thurber graduated from high school in May, 1954, he was stricken with a serious case of both bulbar and spinal polio.

Abe went to an Oklahoma City hospital to visit Thurber who depended upon an iron lung to help him breathe. Abe assured the youngster that the scholarship was still available as soon as Thurber could attend classes. After three months in the iron lung, a month on a rocking table, and painful hours of exercise, Thurber was able to walk, and enrolled at OCU. On Thurber's first day of classes, Abe looked him up and gave him encouragement. When Thurber demonstrated his inability to lift his arms high, Abe quipped, "Sure makes it hard to toss that hook shot." [7]

Oklahoma City University lost its basketball home court June 16, 1954, when fire swept through the OCU fieldhouse. OCU supporters, led by Floyd Van Horn, came to the rescue and asked local civic clubs to help the Chiefs recover from some of the damage not covered by insurance.

The first check OCU received from supporters was from Paul Hansen who was working on his Master's Degree at the University of Minnesota. When he heard about the fire, Hansen sent a check for $50, a lot of money in relation to his $2,600 annual salary at Noble High School. [8]

The West Side Lions Club gave Abe a check for $250 to replace basketball uniforms lost in the fire. With no place to play, the Chiefs moved their home games to Capitol Hill High School.

Without Arnold Short, Parrack's OCU varsity team had its only losing season under his tutelage in 1954-1955, posting a 9-18 record, even though half the losses were by six points or less. With ten sophomores on a 16-man club, the Chiefs lost their season opener to Texas Christian University in overtime. It was a tough season for the Chiefs even though the club upset Houston in the opening round of the All-College tournament in December. The Chiefs, seeded eighth in the tournament, wound up third, behind defending national champion San Francisco University and George Washington University. [9]

While the Chiefs varsity squad suffered, Abe's freshman team flourished. The Little Chiefs won 16 of 20 games, led by tree-topping Hubert "Hub" Reed who would make many headlines as an OCU basketball player. Reed, whom Abe had recruited from Oklahoma City Capitol Hill School, hit 32 points in one February, 1955, game against the Central State College "B" team.

Even though the varsity Chiefs had a disappointing season, officials at the University of Oklahoma touted Chiefs coach Parrack as a possible replacement for retiring OU coach Bruce Drake. When Parrack accepted the job as Sooner head basketball coach, Abe was elevated to the position of head coach of his alma mater. It was just another step toward basketball greatness for the skinny kid from Walters, Oklahoma.

Oklahoma City University president Dr. Cluster Q. Smith introduced Abe to the media at a press conference. Smith said OCU regretted losing Parrack but that the loss was mitigated by the fact "we are not left in the lurch because we have Abe. The squad has expressed utmost confidence in Abe and cheered lustily when he was announced as their head coach." [10]

Abe was optimistic in speaking to the press for the first time as a head coach, saying, "We have a great squad of boys to go with next season. I see no reason why we can't win a lot of games." [11]

Abe announced that all his players were staying at OCU, ending speculation that some of the potential starters, including Hub Reed, might follow Parrack to OU.

Abe picked his good friend and former teammate Paul Hansen as OCU assistant basketball coach. Hansen lettered two years on coach Clarence Breithaupt's Central High School team in Oklahoma City before moving on to Oklahoma A & M. A knee operation prevented Hansen from playing basketball at A & M. However, he was given a scholarship at OCU the following year and played three seasons for the Chiefs.

A back injury in his junior year sidelined Hansen for much of the season. Hansen was married to the former Carol Montgomery. Carol later graduated from law school, was a distinguished lawyer, and served as a judge on the Oklahoma Court of Civil Appeals.

Since graduating from college in 1951, Hansen had coached three years at Noble, Oklahoma, where his boys and girls quintets won 133 games while losing only 25. At the time he was selected by Abe as assistant coach, Hansen was a physical education instructor at Jackson Junior High School in Oklahoma City.

—*Chapter Six*—

Head Coach

You give the ball a shove, and let it fall.
That's what we call basketball.

Abe Lemons

ABE BEGAN THE 1955 SCHOOL YEAR AS THE HEAD COACH and athletic director at OCU. Any inhibitions he had felt coaching under Doyle Parrack were lifted and a new era of wide-open basketball began in Oklahoma. The OCU yearbook described the change, "Oklahoma City had its basketball face-lifted as Lemons removed the stern faced, perfectionist attitude from the blue and white ranks and substituted instead a feeling of 'enjoy the game you play.'" [1]

Shortly after being named head coach in the spring, Abe set out to schedule as many big-name schools as he could. Because his humor had won him friends in coaching circles, Abe was able to line up games against Texas Christian University, Auburn University, Seattle University, the University of Utah, Texas A & M, the University of Houston, and other leading basketball programs. OCU had to play on the big schools' terms, however. Often Abe was forced to play opponents at their home arena. The Chiefs played many road games but OCU was compensated well for the inconvenience. Abe knew the only real drawback of so many road games was playing with "their" officials. He said, "Whether people know it or not, officials have unharnessed bias and prejudices. If it came down to a close call, the official is going to go with the home team so he can move up the ladder in that conference." [2]

Abe molded his 1955-1956 Chiefs around freshmen he had coached in the two previous seasons in which the frosh squad won 37 games and lost only six. The entire 13-man squad was made up of sophomores and juniors. Hub Reed, the 6'10" sophomore, led a solid team that included Lyndon Lee, Leon Griffin, Roger Holloway, Dennis Jeter, Cecil Magana, Bill Juby, Larry Bradshaw, Charles Wheeler, Marvin Pilgrim, Benny Ratzlaff, Fred Dunbar, and Raymond Gilbert. [3]

Griffin was a red-haired, 6'6" sophomore from Pittsburg, Oklahoma. He had led the Chiefs freshman team in scoring the previous year averaging 17 points per game. Jeter, who after graduation served many years as a basketball referee in the Southwest Conference, was 23-years old, having served two years in the Navy before returning to his native Oklahoma to play basketball for the Chiefs. Pilgrim, an All-Stater, was nicknamed "Bones" because of his lean, lankly build. The 6'3" sophomore from Midwest City, Oklahoma, was a starting guard for the Chiefs.

Another example of Abe's small-town recruiting prowess was Gilbert, a 6'4" sophomore from Arnett, Oklahoma. From Piedmont, Oklahoma, came 6'1" guard Fred Dunbar, one of two freshmen who had played in every frosh game the previous season. Ratzlaff was a burr-headed blonde from Corn, Oklahoma, and specialized in a fade-away shot. Magana and Juby came to OCU from Dewey, Oklahoma. Holloway was an All-Stater from Frederick, Bradshaw hailed from Cheyenne, and Jeter graduated from Noble High School. Lyndon Lee was expected to star for OCU after setting a sophomore scoring record the previous season.

Abe stressed ball-handling and fundamentals in the first few weeks of basketball drills. His elevation to the head coaching

position made a positive impact upon OCU supporters. Fan interest was so high at the beginning of the new season that athletic business manager Ed Nall chartered passenger buses for students and fans to attend road games. A five dollar deposit held a spot for a student on the bus. Professors were even urged to be lenient and allow students "meeting grade and attendance requirements" to be excused from classes early to catch the bus. [4]

The largest ticket-selling campaign in OCU history was unveiled by Nall. Over 300 season tickets were sold in the first week. Abe and his players attended a kickoff dinner hosted by Frank Crader, president of the OCU Alumni Association. Several Oklahoma City companies sent representatives to take part in the ticket drive, including Fred Jones Manufacturing, Wilson Company, KTOK Radio, Ralph Horton Insurance, Oklahoma Gas & Electric Company, General Motors, and Frank Murphy Insurance. [5]

Nall, with an eye for publicity for OCU, tried to do his own recruiting of new players. Nall heard about a young giant who lived near Ryan, Oklahoma. Nall found a young man named Lem who was 7'3" in his stocking feet. Nall remembered, "I found Lem in a cotton field. He was a little crippled up where a grain elevator had fallen on his foot, but he sure was tall." [6]

Nall drove back to Oklahoma City thinking how much publicity he could generate for a player nicknamed "Lem the Stem." After a visit to OCU, Nall took Lem back home to Ryan to pack his clothing. However, when Nall showed up at Lem's parents door, Lem's mother said, "Lem decided he don't want to go to no school." Nall had lost his best publicity angle of the year.

Local reporters expected Abe's first season at OCU to be successful. Pat Petree, sports editor of *The Campus*, wrote in his column "Standing PAT on Sports," "This season OCU may see the budding of a championship basketball team planted as a seed some eight years ago in the mind of former Chief coach Doyle Parrack...While Parrack can claim the distinction as the planter, the harvesting of the fertile cage crop rests on the capable shoulders of Abe Lemons. Abe is a qualified coach who has the complete confidence of the club." [7]

An extensive sports publicity campaign was undertaken by OCU to inform the capital city about the new coach and a new brand of basketball. Seventy-five billboards were rented and a half-million pocket-sized schedule cards were printed. Another 20,000 window cards were distributed to area businesses. Short movie strips plugging Chief basketball games were produced for showing at the six leading downtown Oklahoma City theaters. And, a huge blue light was installed on the top of the Gold Star Memorial Building on the OCU campus. If the Chiefs won a game, the blue light was turned on, signaling to the surrounding area the outcome of the game. [8]

The blue light got a good workout in December. Playing home games at the new Capitol Hill High School arena in south Oklahoma City, the Chiefs won their first eight games, blowing out Emporia State University by 19 points, Texas Christian University by 28 points, Auburn University by 18, and racking up solid wins against Wyoming and Western Kentucky.

In the 1955 All-College Tournament in Oklahoma City, OCU beat Pennsylvania University by 12 points in the opening game and slipped by Oklahoma A & M 48-47 in the second round. The Chiefs' eight-game winning streak was ended when they were outscored by the University of Tulsa 65-58 in the All-College championship game. On January 4, OCU traveled to Tulsa for a re-match. This time OCU beat Tulsa 58-50.

In a game at Memphis State, the fieldhouse was sold out and Abe and his team struggled to work their way through the waiting throng to get to their dressing room. Roger Holloway, who after college became a successful high school basketball coach and school superintendent, was shocked when Abe scattered the crowd by throwing an extra 15 or 20 tickets into the air. Holloway remembered, "Abe's trick worked. The fans who had been told the game was sold out scrambled for the tickets and let us through. However, we almost got killed by fans diving for the tickets on the floor." [9] The Chiefs traveled all over the nation by train and bus to play basketball. In January, 1956, Abe took his team on a murderous six-game road trip into the western part of the United States. In a week and a half, the Chiefs beat Drake University in Des Moines, Iowa; split two games with the University of Seattle, in Washington; lost by two points to highly-rated Utah University in Salt Lake City, Utah; beat Brigham Young University at Provo, Utah; and narrowly escaped with a one-point win against Wichita State University in Kansas.

KOCY sportscaster Pat Petree and *Oklahoma City Times* sportswriter Jay Simon accompanied the Chiefs on the swing west. Petree was the radio voice of the Chiefs. Simon called the matchup of OCU and Seattle as a tilt between two of the nation's top independent basketball powers.

After two games with Seattle, Simon agreed with Abe about the poor officiating. Abe said the Chiefs "got a hose job." *The Daily Oklahoman* headline read, "Sad Officiating Hits Touring Chiefs Twice." [10] Simon wrote, "Basketball teams expect slightly different interpretations of the rules when they leave home for intersectional games and often you hear of teams getting the business when they go to this place or that. But it is highly unlikely worse basketball officiating exists any place on this planet than that which plagues the western division of the Skyline conference." [11]

Abe kept his cool during the bad officiating. However, he glared at officials and sent his players out with cryptic messages. Co-captain Lyndon Lee told a ref, "Isn't it a foul anymore when they hang on your arm?" [12] Abe found a referee from Oklahoma and forced Seattle officials to accept him to call the game the second night. OCU won by four points.

Abe's good humor and love for the lighter side of life rubbed off on his players. After the win over Brigham Young University, one of the Chiefs placed a bright yellow Chiefs schedule card squarely in the middle of the glass backboard in the Brigham Young University gym. One player commented that the yellow card would give the Cougar players something to think about the next day at practice.

Hub Reed, bruised and scratched from the battering he took under the boards, told Abe after the game at Brigham Young University, "Coach, I'm sure glad I don't have a temper or I might've really hurt someone out there tonight." [13]

Sportscaster Petree, who doubled as correspondent for *The Campus*, wrote, "If you were to give coach Abe Lemons and his cast of basketballers a TV audience that appreciated the lighter side of sports, the OCU gang would probably rank as the greatest video attraction since Milton Berle or western movies." [14]

Abe was fast becoming recognized as the prize wit among the nation's basketball coaches. After reviewing press clippings from Utah newspapers that said OCU's win was due to Brigham Young University playing their worst game of the season, Abe, with a sly wink, added, "Durn considerate of them, isn't it?" At the hotel after the Brigham Young University win, Abe remarked, "We usually try to make basketball fans happy. Tonight we disappointed 10,000 of them, and enjoyed every minute of it." [15]

Abe wanted his players to enjoy road trips. A reporter, after observing Abe's tactics on a trip to New Orleans, wrote, "Abe keeps the whip-cracking at a minimum on out-of-town treks and the lack of regimentation seems to have paid off. The OCU performers have had fun, which Lemons thinks is the No. 1 factor in winning—if you have the horses of course...the sharp-witted Lemons also came up with another good quip as he was explaining how much some of the players eat on the road. Said Abe: Leon Griffin and Hub Reed are just like chickens in a brooder house. Every time you turn the light on, they get hungry." [16]

The national press closely followed the Chiefs' progress in 1955-1956. OCU was ranked in the top 20 teams by the Associated Press nine of the 11 weeks the poll was conducted. The Chiefs reached as high as number ten following their first eight wins of the season but plummeted out of the top 20 after their upset loss to Tulsa in the finals of the All-College. Sportswriters placed the Chiefs back into the top 20 after a five-game winning streak against Brigham Young University, Texas A & M, Loyola of New Orleans, and Wichita twice.

Abe won the hearts and loyalty of Oklahoma sportswriters by always telling them the truth and giving them stories for their columns. Volney Meece, a writer for *The Daily Oklahoman*, said he wrote his columns by just repeating Abe's stories from press conferences. An early 1956 Meece column provides a good example:

Then the Lemons sense of humor comes to the fore as he describes the final seconds of a two point road win, 'We lost the ball, they lost the ball, we lost the ball, they lost the ball and we finally ended up winning. I don't remember much about it; guess I musta' blacked out for awhile.'

'We try to keep a good mental attitude,' Lemons continues. 'We want to at least play reputable ball so we can look people in the eye the next day.'

Lemons can talk for hours, without scratching the surface about occurrences on the long rail trek to the West, things like center Hub Reed and guard Larry Bradshaw just sitting at the window for hours looking at nothing in the barren wastes of Montana. Or Reed taking a drink out of the Great Salt Lake and spitting cotton the rest of the day. Or the flash pictures he took of his elongated players trying to sleep in the train berths, or the cackling of his two gigglers, Roger Holloway and Ray Gilbert.

Commenting on Reed's battering under the basket, the handsome, dark-haired coach, drawled, 'Reed was hung up like a pig in a poke. I hated to call time out 'cause when Reed lay down near the bench he sure hated to get up. He looked like a camel getting to his feet. Bradshaw told me after the game they were giving Hub such a bad time inside, he was ashamed to throw the ball into him.'

That's the kind of coach-player camaraderie that exists in the OCU camp. The Chiefs get their kicks out of playing but that's not all the story. A small sign that hangs on the wall of Lemons' office adds, 'We Play to Win.' 17

Abe started 22 of the 24 regular-season games with the same lineup of four juniors and one sophomore, Hub Reed, at center. The juniors were Holloway and Lee at forward and Magana and Bradshaw at guard.

The Chiefs ended their regular season with an impressive 76-67 win over Houston and became the first team in NCAA history to draw five consecutive playoff bids. Reed led Chiefs scorers with a 20.1 average per game. Lee was second in scoring with a 14 point average. Holloway was the club's top rebounder and Bradshaw and Magana were recognized as the team's top defensive aces.

The Chiefs set out to change school history in the NCAA playoffs. OCU had never made it past the first round of the national tournament in its first four appearances. The Chiefs were matched up against high-scoring Memphis State in the first round at Wichita, Kansas. Memphis State was averaging 89 points per game, fourth best in the nation and had won 20 of 26 regular-season games.

Trailing by as many as 12 points on two occasions, the Chiefs were down 70-69 when they poured in four straight baskets to take command of the game with 6:30 left. Jeter ignited the late-game spree with a driving layup to put the Chiefs on top for the first time. Reed led the Chiefs with 27 points even though he spent 10 minutes on the bench after drawing a fourth foul in the first minute of the second half. When Reed fouled out, the Chiefs had outscored Memphis State 22-7. The Chiefs won 97-81, the most points ever scored by an OCU team to that point. [18]

Abe and his players were elated. They had made it to the Sweet Sixteen of the NCAA and moved on to the regional finals at Lawrence, Kansas, to take on Big Seven champion Kansas State University. The team received telegrams from OCU president Dr. Cluster Q. Smith and Oklahoma City Chamber of Commerce president Ray J. Spradling who said, "Oklahoma City is very proud of the fine showing you and your boys have made this year. Best of luck tonight." [19]

The Chiefs took the floor at Phog Allen Fieldhouse, the nation's second largest basketball arena, to face the Wildcats. Most of the 17,000 fans were from Kansas and booed the Chiefs ferociously as they took the court. However, Abe and his crew were not rattled by the home-state advantage enjoyed by coach Tex Winter's Kansas State club. The Chiefs won 97-93 in a hectic affair that went down to the wire.

Abe had a 24-hour rebuilding job to do. The win over Kansas State had taken an emotional and physical toll on his young club. OCU faced Southern Methodist University in the regional finals. The winner would earn a trip to the Final Four in Evanston, Illinois, and a shot at the national championship.

Oklahoma City University's dream of playing for the national crown faded as Southern Methodist University dominated the Chiefs 84-63. Abe blamed fatigue for his Chiefs' inability to match their output of 97 points in the two previous tournament games. Southern Methodist University, the nation's leading free-throw team, continued its proficiency, hitting 34 of 44 free shots, six of the misses coming after the game was decided. The

Mustangs hit 16 of 33 first-half shots from the field to build a ten-point half-time lead. The Chiefs were never in the game in which Southern Methodist University breezed to its 19th consecutive victory.

Reed was named to the NCAA All-Tournament team, prompting one sportswriter to laud him as exemplifying a top-flight attitude, "Reed has a burning desire to play winning basketball no matter what the personal sacrifice. As a result you're liable to see Hub practicing to correct weak points 12 months a year and at all hours of the day or evening." [20]

The Chiefs were met at the train station in Oklahoma City by cheering fans. Making it to the final eight of the nation's basketball world was recognized as an incredible feat by OCU officials, supporters, and state sportswriters. In *The Campus*, the new style of OCU roundball was applauded, "This was the season of a complete changeover from a strict defensive pattern of play to the wide open, razzle-dazzle type of ball where you speed like the Super Chief, shoot like Davy Crockett and gamble like a tourist in Las Vegas. The installation of the fast break as a primary offense inserted a new thrill for Chief followers. You put up more shots, hope to hit more, and at the same time take a chance that your opponents can't catch up to you." [21]

Looking back on the year, a local reporter recalled, "Pleasant memories of college life are built on the things you did and things that happened to you. Herewith, then, a neat pile of stardust from a glittering basketball season that you may want to scatter among the grandchildren in years to come." [22]

The OCU campus newspaper used the successful basketball season to applaud Abe's efforts and to call for the construction of a new fieldhouse. In *The Campus*, Pat Petree editorialized:

> The new regime of athletics at Oklahoma City University is off to a tremendous start...and the man primarily responsible for it is the new athletic director Abe Lemons. The lanky native of Walters, Oklahoma made it quite clear, quite early, that OCU was going to move ahead (and fast) in the field of national

sports. He has made his vow good so far and from all indications this is only the beginning...The pressing need right now is for a new fieldhouse that the Chiefs can call their own. While most people dream, wish and think, Lemons is working full time to make the hope come true.

As a first year man, OCU's new sports boss hasn't had a chance to make too many influential contacts. But his bargaining line is something even stronger. He has a quality product to exhibit and a sincere, straight-forward approach that shows without a doubt that he means to get what he needs.

Whether the ultra-modern arena pictured in the Chiefs' press book will be the eventual home of OCU basketball or whether it will be a smaller but still adequate fieldhouse, it's pretty safe to assume that 1956 is the last year OCU's big time basketball show will be staged constantly on the road. [23]

Abe publicly called for a new fieldhouse, "We've got to find someplace of our own, at least for practice. We've been practicing in parks department gymnasiums...In a lot of places we are considered bush league because we don't have our own gym. Name teams say, 'What's the use of playing OCU? They don't even have a gym.'" [24]

Abe begged school officials to act, "If we can just get something, even dig a ditch to show a fieldhouse is on the way, it will help in both scheduling and recruiting." [25]

Abe had his first season as a head coach under his belt. He was extremely pleased with the performance of his players. The Chiefs ended the year at 20-7, ranked 11th in the nation in the final Associated Press poll.

A Tribute by Dean Smith

of Abe:

I have known Abe Lemons for a long time, beginning back when he was an assistant coach to Doyle Parrack at Oklahoma City University. Our Kansas team was playing them in NCAA tournament and, even then, Coach Lemons could make remarks in the paper that were extremely funny. Then, when he was head coach at Oklahoma City, our paths would cross from time to time. He was especially good to me, having been a former Kansas player.

I remember the 1967 Final Four in Louisville, when our North Carolina team was defeated by Dayton University, losing an opportunity to play number one-ranked UCLA with Lew Alcindor in the finals. As a relatively young head coach, I was extremely disappointed and ran into Abe twenty-five minutes after the end of the game. After telling Abe that perhaps I should quit coaching, he gave me a pep talk and told me to hold my head high. After a ten-minute serious talk with Abe (and I have seldom seem him serious for that long), I surely felt better and looked forward to coaching

ABOVE: Legendary University of North Carolina basketball coach Dean Smith makes a point during an Oklahoma Coaches Association clinic in Oklahoma City in 1990. Smith knew Abe from their early years in coaching. Courtesy *The Daily Oklahoman.*

again the following season. Incidentally, we met UCLA in the finals the next year and were handily defeated.

I have heard many jokes from Abe, and I have heard his speak on many occasions, and not once have I failed to have uncontrollable laughter. He is so naturally funny that it can happen on the spur of the moment. An example of this occurred in Lexington, Kentucky, during the Final Four in 1985. Our convention was at the Marriott Hotel. They had one elevator serving the far reaches of the hotel, while most of them were at the front end near the lobby. My wife and I decided to take the one isolated elevator up to our room one evening and, as the door opened, there was Abe, all alone. Very quickly, without saying hello, he indicated that he was "taking an elevator ride with all of his friends." Of course, Linnea and I have known Abe and Betty through many meetings of the National Association of Basketball Coaches Board of Directors. We always looked to sit near Abe, knowing full well that there would never be a dull moment.

I am sure you folks have his reasoning behind the players scrimmaging at half time of an NIT team. You probably have his idea for the reason he did not have a curfew was to say, "You have to stay out until such and such a time."

What is lost through all this humor is that basically Abe Lemons was a tremendous college basketball coach. In my opinion he would have been an excellent NBA coach, because his players always played hard and knew what he wanted. They also had a looseness about them that enabled them to play up to their potential.

—Chapter Seven—

We Play To Win

**Lemons and right-hand-man Hansen featured a fast break
that popularized OCU basketball coast to coast.**

Volney Meece, sportswriter

ABE KNEW THAT A WINNING BASKETBALL SEASON WAS BORN years before on the recruiting trail. The OCU mentor had his own rules about recruiting. He scanned the newspapers reporting on high school games. He talked to other coaches and OCU supporters who were on the lookout for good talent. However, there was no substitute for driving hundreds of miles around the state to tiny towns and steamy gymnasiums to watch high school players perform.

Recruiting was a battle primarily against the other three schools of the Oklahoma Big Four. Henry Iba at Oklahoma A & M and Doyle Parrack at Oklahoma University often had their pick of the best players. Clarence Iba at Tulsa was also a formidable recruiting foe. But Abe held his own. His wit and straight-forward style won points with parents and school officials concerned that their kids might get lost in a large school like OU or A & M. When the Chiefs were not playing, you could always find Abe in some small town "buying a kid a hamburger and a coke and convincing his parents why he ought to play for me at OCU." [1]

Abe looked for a certain attitude in a player. He wanted kids who would accept instruction and be willing to be both a good student in the classroom and a hard-working player on the basketball court. Abe had a sixth sense about players. He talked with kids one-on-one, trying to get down to their level. He asked them what was important in their life? Abe recalled recruiting Hub Reed, "He was not a good student to start with, but he made more improvement than any kid I've seen. By the time he got out of college until he came back, seven years in the pros, he became a different student and person. He was tough as a boot, the best human being I ever knew. He never knew how good he was. He always wanted to play with the underclassmen because he was embarrassed to play with the older guys. I knew those things from the first time I met him." [2]

Abe went out on a limb before the 1956-1957 season. He had lost five seniors, four of them starters, from the previous year's squad. However, Abe, said, "I think we'll have one of the finest teams in this part of the country this year."

Reed was Abe's big gun in his second season as OCU head coach. Magana, Bradshaw, Lee, and Holloway were seniors. Returning juniors were Reed, Dunbar, Jeter, and Griffin. New faces on the Chiefs varsity were Bill Hanson, Oklahoma A & M transfer Jerry Wallace, Troy Hill, Mike Kelley, Ed McCraw, and Gary Gardner.

Wallace had transferred from A & M because he wanted to play his final two years with his old Capitol Hill teammate Reed. A newspaper story about the transfer said "a real plum fell into the hands of OCU head basketball coach Abe Lemons when Wallace decided to transfer from Iba's Aggies."

For the first time in the Lemons years, out-of-staters joined the Chiefs squad. Mike Kelley was a bandy-legged speedster from Borger, Texas, who led Paul Hansen's OCU freshman team the previous season. Joe Gavlik, a sophomore teammate, graduated from high school in faraway New Jersey.

Abe became a second father to most of his players. In the summer, before the fall school term began, Abe helped his players find jobs and checked up on them periodically. In the summer of 1956, Reed, Juby, Griffin, Wallace, Hanson, and Hill all worked at the

Wilson Company plant in Oklahoma City. Holloway and Dunbar worked for Oklahoma Gas and Electric Company constructing a new power plant at Harrah, Oklahoma. Magana worked in a foundry at Dewey, Oklahoma. Bradshaw, Lee, and Gilbert were busy working on farms and ranches.

With success comes notoriety. OCU players such as Hub Reed were even discussed in the off-season on the hunting and fishing pages of *The Daily Oklahoman*. Columnist Vernon Snell wrote, "Hubert has not been able to do much fishing this year. He's only been on one trip and didn't catch many then. The entire OCU basketball squad went on an outing at Lake Texoma during the last week of school last spring...Reed has been squirrel hunting several times this year. He hunts near Binger over in Caddo County. He has had some pretty good kills on those outings...Asked about what new basketball techniques he's picked up, the big OCU basketball player, tabbed as a certain All-American before he finishes his career, said, 'I didn't know anything until last year. I've got the right guy as a teacher. Coach Lemons has taught me everything I know.'" 3

Abe opened fall practice in mid-October at the Taft Junior High School gym in northwest Oklahoma City. Assistant coach Hansen took his freshmen players to the city recreation center at Northwest Seventh Street and Shartel Avenue for scrimmages. Abe and Hansen ran their Chiefs through daily workouts, doubling the workout schedule on Saturdays. Because the Chiefs were a veteran team, Abe was able to immediately begin

Paul and Carol Hansen in 1996. Courtesy Carol Hansen.

working on play patterns, mixed in with a fair sprinkling of fundamentals. Without a home to play in, the Chiefs were still nomads.

Hansen was a busy man. He coached the OCU baseball team and, as the assistant basketball coach, had equipment manager responsibilities, which included laundering the players' uniforms. Once when the school dryer was broken, Hansen's wife, Carol, had 18 jock straps drying on her clothes line in the Hansen back yard on Northwest 27th Street, surely a world's record. [4]

Two weeks into practice, Ray Gilbert, a 6'4" junior from Arnett, Oklahoma, tore cartilage in his right knee and underwent surgery. As the season opener neared, Abe told reporters that his starting lineup of Reed, Holloway, Lee, Bradshaw, and Griffin would be the tallest starting five in the nation.

Abe was blessed with a talented group of players. *The Campus* ran down the prospects, "The depth, and here's the dessert, running through the squad position by position, Lemons has talent to favorably compare with that of OU's football powerhouse. The center position...'Tis in good hands...the hands of a probable All-American, Capitol Hill's Hub Reed. His 27 point clip over last season's final ten games definitely marks him as one of the nation's best." [5]

If Reed was unavailable, Holloway could adequately fill in at center. Lee or Griffin also could play valuable minutes at center. Surveying the forwards for the new season, *The Campus* commented, "Usually a coach grits his teeth when unable to pick from a covey of players...But Abe, when it comes to his forwards, just beams, shuts his eyes and points. That's how good his front line talent is. Lee and Holloway, top two a year ago are hardpressed to hold their starting spots, mainly from the rugged Griffin, who went on a 35-point spree in his first start last year, and Jerry Wallace. Others rating just behind these four are three strong sophomores, Ada's Bill Hanson, Ed McCraw from Putnam City, Joe Gavlik from New Jersey, Rod Campbell from Blackwell, and Gary Gardner from Lemons' hometown of Walters." [6]

At guard, Abe was blessed with Magana and Bradshaw, both two-year starters. Backing them up were Juby, Jeter, and Dunbar. Mike Kelley was only 5'9" but his quickness provided an edge over

other players. Freshmen coach Hansen told Abe that Troy Hill, a 5'10" speedster from Chickasha, would be a key player on the varsity. Hansen said Hill was the player a coach wanted in a tight game, "He'll make the breaks for you." 7

Sports scribes predicted another great year for OCU. *Street and Smith's* annual basketball preview pegged the Chiefs as the best independent team in the Missouri Valley region and predicted the club would have no difficulty in reaching the NCAA tournament.

Athletic business manager Ed Nall began his sixth year on the job and increased the number of radio stations broadcasting Chiefs games on the OCU Basketball Network to 25.

The 1956-1957 Chiefs shuttled in and out of the Associated Press top 20 all season. They were 3-1 when the All-College Tournament rolled around the week after Christmas. The Chiefs had beaten San Jose State, Mississippi Southern, and Wyoming while dropping a game to Southern Methodist University. More than 2,000 fans jammed into the Capitol Hill High School arena to see the Chiefs beat Wyoming.

The 21st annual All-College Tournament began in Oklahoma City's Municipal Auditorium two days after Christmas. It was a feast for basketball fans who liked high scoring. Nine players on the tournament teams were averaging more than 18 points per game. Seattle's Elgin Baylor was scoring above 26 points per game, followed by teammate Dick Stricklin, OCU's Reed and Griffin, Jim McCoy of Marquette University, Bobby Kimmel of Georgia Tech, Win Wilfong of Memphis State, and Cal Grosscup of Tulane.

In the first game of the All-College, OCU weathered a furious closing bid by Idaho State's previously unbeaten Bengals and won 70-66. Reed led the 11th-ranked Chiefs with 31 points, including 19 in the first half.

In playing what Abe called the best game of the young season, the Chiefs won their second round game against Marquette, 63-58. Reed scored 20 points in the lowest-scoring game of the tournament. For the fourth time in eight years, the Chiefs reached the All-College finals.

In the championship game, OCU led Seattle by 14 points with 10 minutes remaining. But Seattle, with three of its stars including the great Elgin Baylor on the bench, clawed back and forced the Chiefs into overtime. With four seconds left in the extra period, Bob Miller, a Seattle substitute, stepped to the foul line and sank the second of two free throws, giving Seattle a 70-69 victory, even though the Chiefs held Baylor to eight points. The All-American was only one-for-eight from the floor. The Chiefs were crippled in the closing minutes when their three top rebounders, Bradshaw, Holloway, and Griffin fouled out.

Several All-College scoring records fell during the tournament. Memphis State hit 40 field goals in one game. Marquette and Georgia Tech combined for 180 points in a game. Tulane's Grosscup had 35 points in a losing effort against Seattle, Wilfong of Memphis State hit 33, Baylor of Seattle had 32, and Reed of OCU scored 31 points in individual games. However, no one approached the 50-point explosion of Furman's Frank Selvy in 1953.

OCU's Reed was named to the All-College tournament team, the first Chief to bag that honor since Arnold Short.

In early January it was rumored that Abe was being considered for the head basketball coach job at Florida State University. A reporter asked Abe if he would use the interest shown by Florida State to get a raise at OCU. Abe responded, "I'm getting more than I'm worth now." Actually, Abe was earning only $7,500 per year at OCU. He kidded the reporter, "I'm not going anyplace. I'm too happy here. Of course, every coach says that. Now I might change my mind if someone came along and offered me a Cadillac, pot of gold, 90-year contract, beach house and yacht. I think I'd have to accept that offer." [8]

Lyndon Lee caught fire for the Chiefs after the Christmas break. He scored not less than 22 points per game in wins over Oregon, Arizona, and Memphis State. Abe observed, "Lyndon has suddenly become the player everyone had him pegged to be when a sophomore. He's looser and with him, the whole club has loosened up." [9] Rumor had it that Lee blossomed as a player when he threw away his high-topped basketball sneakers and switched to the new low-cut fashion. Business manager Ed Nall, always looking for ways to cut the athletic department budget, said if the low-cut shoes improved Lee's play so much, why not put the whole squad on the court barefooted and save a lot of money. [10]

Abe took his Chiefs in January to Bowling Green, Kentucky, where the Western Kentucky Hilltoppers had lost only three times in the previous 117 games. In front of 5,000 screaming fans, Lee led OCU with 23 points as the Chiefs upset Western Kentucky 85-78, despite a 35-point performance by Hilltopper center Ralph Crosthwaite. Reed allowed Crosthwaite three goals in the first four minutes before Abe decided to sacrifice players to try to stop the big center. Before the end of the game both Holloway and Bradshaw fouled out.

Oklahoma City University lost three of its next four games. Losses to Seattle, TCU, and Idaho State overshadowed a 69-68 road win at Utah. Abe told his players that they needed to get down to business or there would be some lineup changes. Griffin was almost thrown out of the Idaho State game when he complained about the officiating. Griffin yelled to a teammate, "You guard that guy, I'm gonna guard this guy in a striped shirt."

On a road trip west to New Mexico in late January, the Chiefs shattered the old single-game scoring mark of 97 by beating New Mexico in Albuquerque 107-86. The Lobos were helpless as the Chiefs attacked a zone defense and poured in baskets at will. Lee had 31 points for OCU, with Griffin and Reed chiming in with 25 and 24, respectively.

After wins over Texas A & M, Wayne State, and Western Kentucky, the Chiefs were gliding toward the NCAA post-season tournament. Reed scored 39 points in the romp over Western Kentucky with Griffin hitting a season-high 27 points. Reed left the game with two minutes to go with a sprained ankle. Volney Meece wrote in the following morning's *The Daily Oklahoman,* "Abe Lemons is still up in the air about the near-perfect performance of his Chieftains in the scuttling of Western Kentucky Monday, and crack center Hub Reed is just up in the air period. Reed, a deep-voiced pencil-shaped junior who most of the time is a scoring sensation but at other times acts like he's dead set against making All-American, shrugs off questions about the sprained ankle. 'It was just a slight turn, it's OK,' said the Capitol Hill sky-scraper as he strides off, sans limp, to eat lunch, eating being another league in which he stands out." [11]

After the Western Kentucky game, Abe wanted to talk about his star player. He said, "He could do it more if he'd just shoot. On defense when Western tried to screen him off near the circle, Hub was sliding through a knothole of space that a mouse couldn't get through." [12]

The Chiefs' scoring machine faltered in a game against Kansas State. OCU gave up 100 points in the 100-82 loss, the first time a Chiefs team had ever allowed an opponent to reach the century mark.

In February, 1957, OCU attempted to abandon its role as an independent basketball power and joined five other schools to form a cage conference for a one year trial-run. The Chiefs were matched with Regis College of Denver, Colorado, and Creighton University of Omaha, Nebraska, in the western division of the new hoop loop. The University of Detroit; DePaul University of Chicago, Illinois; and Marquette University made up the eastern division. The idea for the new conference was a result of the participating schools having problems scheduling games.

However, because most of the schools in the new unnamed conference were Catholic, church officials objected to the alliance. The new conference never was officially sanctioned and failed to get off the ground.

Oklahoma City University was 17-8 after a regular-season-ending victory over Creighton, 97-70. The Chiefs enthusiastically accepted a sixth straight invitation to the NCAA tournament. The team was also invited to play in the National Invitation Tournament (NIT) in New York City but players voted to go to the NCAA tournament.

In a coin toss OCU won the right to host the first round of the NCAA against the other at-large entry in the region, Loyola University of New Orleans. Going into the post-season, Reed led the Chiefs in scoring with 24 points per game, followed by Lee with 14.4 and Griffin with 13.4 points per game. The Chiefs were ranked tenth in the national Associated Press poll at the close of the regular season, the highest end-of-season ranking ever for an OCU team.

Abe gave his players a few days off. He told them to completely get basketball off their minds. Abe thought he needed a change of pace for his team that had lost to Loyola earlier in the year, 67-61.

Athletic business manager Ed Nall asked Abe to hold a news conference to promote the NCAA game with Loyola. Knowing he needed to stir up fans to attend the game, Abe pledged that if OCU lost, he will kill himself right after the game. He told the press, "I haven't decided on the method I'll use yet, but I promise you I'll make it as gory as possible." [13] The next day in the mail came a razor, a tongue-in-cheek suggestion from former University of Oklahoma assistant coach John Grayson.

In front of a home crowd at the Capitol Hill sports arena, seniors Lee, Bradshaw, Magana, and Holloway played their last home games. After a shaky start in the opening minutes, OCU bombed Loyola 76-55. Reed scored 24 and Holloway turned in his best performance of the season with 18 points. The rebounding of Holloway and Reed was the difference in the game. After the contest, Abe demanded, "How many of you guys came here for my funeral?" No one raised their hand.

The win over Loyola vaulted the Chiefs to the Southwest NCAA regional in Dallas, played at Moody Coliseum on the SMU campus. OCU surprised tenth-ranked St. Louis University and won 75-66.

The Chiefs faced second-ranked Kansas in the regional final in Dallas. The Jayhawks were led by 7'0"center Wilt Chamberlain. "Wilt the Stilt" had been embarrassed the night before when the Moody Coliseum crowd sang "Bye-Bye Blackbird" as the black superstar left the court. Hub Reed approached Chamberlain before the OCU-Kansas game the next night and said, "I want you to understand that all of us down here don't feel that way." [14]

Kansas had beaten Southern Methodist University on its home court the night before and when the Chiefs took the floor, Dallas fans were still irate at the number of fouls called on whomever was guarding Chamberlain. The OCU-Kansas game had to be stopped in the first half when fans showered the court with coins and seat cushions as Chamberlain ran over a smaller OCU player and no foul was called. [15]

Southern Methodist University athletic director Matty Bell pleaded with the crowd to show sportsmanship. Abe was extremely upset at what he thought was obvious favoritism shown

Chamberlain by the officials. Abe's temper boiled. When he hollered repeatedly at a referee, Kansas coach Dick Harp told Abe to shut up. Abe replied, "You make me!" The fierce competition of the game kept Abe from heading to the Kansas bench to make his point. [16]

Chamberlain was too much for the Chiefs as Kansas bombed OCU 81-61 and ended the Chiefs season at 19-9. For the first 20

Abe displays a bright yellow basketball of the type proposed in 1957 for use in televised games. The basketball was the gift of appreciative chamber of commerce members in Oklahoma City. The yellow basketball idea never caught on. Courtesy *The Daily Oklahoman.*

minutes the Chiefs played well, trailing only 27-24 at halftime. Reed matched his more-publicized foe, Chamberlain, basket for basket before Chamberlain finally moved ahead late in the game to outscore Reed 30-26.

After the game Abe expressed his anger at the officiating by accusing the two referees of playing on the Kansas squad, "It was the toughest seven-man zone defense we faced this year." Abe blasted the protection of Chamberlain, "I can't understand it. If you touch him, it's a foul. But if he touches you, it isn't a foul. He can go up in the air, dunk a shot and fall over a little man and it's no foul. But if anybody brushes against him—foul." [17]

A Kansas fan accused the Chiefs of roughing Chamberlain up because he was black. Abe, who thought one rhubarb during the game started when a Kansas fan hollered at a red-headed Chief player, "Get that red-headed SOB," shot back, "That proves the Jayhawks were the ones who were discriminating. And it burns me up. Just because the redheads are a minority group, I don't see why they should be discriminated against." [18]

Abe appreciated the superb Chamberlain, but said, "They don't need to give him all that protection." [19] Kansas went on to play for the national championship, losing to North Carolina in triple overtime in the national championship game in Kansas City. Abe, knowing that Kansas fans were probably still upset at him for criticizing the way officials coddled Chamberlain, told a reporter, "Those folks up there feel so strongly that I didn't even come through Kansas on my way back from Kansas City. I went over to the border and walked around the state." [20]

After the basketball season, Abe spent more time with Betty Jo who was pregnant with their second child. On May 4, 1957, another baby girl, Jan Denise Lemons, was born in Oklahoma City. The Lemons still did not have a lot of extra money and looked forward to weekends alone when they could take the girls down Northwest 23rd Street and stop at a watermelon stand or drink orange slushes at the dairy queen.

On rearing children, Abe made a deal with Betty Jo, "You take care of the girls, I'll take care of the boys."

—*Chapter Eight*—

The Kentucky Connection

*I'm not interested in playing teams close. I want to beat a team.
Beat a team 30 points if I can. I'll settle for less in hard times.*

Abe Lemons

CHIEFS' STAR HUB REED WAS KNOWN AROUND THE COUNTRY
for his love of food. Abe said, "He always starts every meal with a
piece of pie and glass of milk. I think he could eat a whole pie. Ask
him what kind of pie he likes and he says, 'Just pie.' I know they
say pie isn't good for you when you've got to play, but I give him all
he wants. He thinks he ought to have pie, and if he can make 30
points a game, I think he ought to have pie, too." [1]

Fortunately for Abe and the Chiefs, there was plenty of pie in
Oklahoma in 1957. Reed had a career season, finishing out his
three-year stint at OCU with 1,885 points, breaking the Oklahoma
collegiate career record of 1,669 points scored by Oklahoma State
University's Bob Kurland in four years of play. Reed also owned the
single game record of 43 points when he graduated in the spring of
1958. He averaged over 20 points per game for his entire career and
was ranked eighth in scoring nationally his senior year. He was
named honorable mention All-American and played in the East-
West game in Kansas City and the All-Star game in New York City.

He was captain of both all-star squads and was high-point man in each of the all-star tilts. Sportswriters speculated that if the Chiefs had had a better season, Reed may have been voted by the Associated Press and United Press International to their first or second All-American teams. Future National Basketball Association stars dominated the All-American list in 1958, including Elgin Baylor, Oscar Robertson, Wilt Chamberlain, Guy Rodgers, and Bailey Howell. [2]

The 1957-1958 season was an up and down year for the Chiefs. Abe had bluntly told reporters in a pre-season news conference that the outlook was "cloudy" for the year. Even though Reed and fellow senior Leon Griffin were the mainstays of the team, OCU finished the year 14-12, winning bigtime at home and losing disastrously on the road. Except for Reed and Griffin, no player on the squad had more than one year's experience.

Abe and his Chiefs. Left to right, back row, Abe, Lyndon Lee, Larry Bradshaw, Leon Griffin, Hub Reed, Roger Holloway, Bill Hanson. Middle row, Jerry Wallace, Rod Campbell, Gary Gardner, Dennis Jeter. Bottom row, Cecil Magana, Troy Hill, Mike Kelly, Ed McCraw. Courtesy Oklahoma City University.

In early December the Chiefs opened the season with an 85-76 victory over a good University of Houston team. In the next few weeks the Chiefs lost to Texas Christian University twice and to Oklahoma State 57-50.

In November, 1957, the OCU Board of Trustees approved plans to construct a new $100,000 gymnasium and physical education building on the campus. The facility would become Frederickson Fieldhouse, a home for OCU basketball that Abe had campaigned for since he first arrived on the campus. The fieldhouse was named for George Frederickson, a prominent Oklahoma City business leader and vice president of Oklahoma Natural Gas Company, who had served on the OCU Board of Trustees for 30 years.

Frederickson, the first president of the Oklahoma City Golf and Country Club, was a solid supporter of OCU athletics and endorsed the idea of Abe and business manager Ed Nall that the Chiefs must have a permanent home.

Frederickson Fieldhouse was designed to be the world's largest hyperbolic paraboloid structure. Oklahoma Natural Gas Company contributed the first $10,000 toward the construction price of $100,000 for the new arena.

With a 3-4 record, OCU entered the 22nd All-College tournament in Oklahoma City. Slipping by Tulane and Tulsa, the Chiefs made it to the tournament final for the third consecutive year, but lost to two-time national champion San Francisco University. The Dons whipped the Chiefs 60-45. Reed was named to the All-College tournament team for the second straight year, scoring 63 points in OCU's three games in the tournament.

The Chiefs began 1958 in the winning column, beating New Mexico at home 89-60, paced by Reed's 39 points. OCU lost three of its next four road games, dropping contests to Memphis State, Western Kentucky, and Dayton University of Ohio. After picking up wins against Creighton, Wyoming, and Western Kentucky, the

Chiefs hit a three-game losing skid, the worst losing streak in three years. During the streak, OCU lost to Loyola of New Orleans, Miami of Florida, and Florida State University.

In January, the Chiefs traveled to Buffalo, New York, to play Canisius College. The New York team used a strange offense. Abe called it the "Crapshooter's Weave." The players handed the ball to each other rather than pass and ran in opposite directions at the top of the key, like crapshooters handing the dice to each other. Abe described his defense to the crapshooter's offense, "It's a terrible looking thing. We don't know what to do against it. So we used a part zone and part man-for-man on defense. It had them worried. Of course, it had us worried, too, because we didn't know what we were doing. We just sort of stood around in their way." [3]

During the game at Canisius, 5'9" guard Mike Kelley repeatedly dribbled into the middle of the Canisius players and lost the ball. Abe brought Kelley to the sideline and said, "Kelley, one of these nights, I'm gonna take a blunt knife, run out there and stab you right on the floor." [4] Somehow, the Chiefs won the game 76-66.

With a 10-12 record, the season looked dismal. However, the Chiefs won their final four games against Memphis State, Loyola of New Orleans, Creighton, and Regis University of Denver. Reed scored 37 points in the final game of his brilliant career. [5]

The Chiefs had no mascot in 1957-1958. The traditional OCU mascot for years had been a dignified faculty member wrapped in an Indian blanket and wearing a headdress. However, Dr. James J. Hayes retired, prompting the school newspaper to launch a search for a willing faculty member to assume the mascot role.

Even in the midst of a less than spectacular season, Abe was a fierce competitor. He was never happy with second best, telling an interviewer, "You either win a chase or you lose. I would hate to be in a job where you can't see whether you've won or lost. More competitors came out of the depression than any other period. It's hard to be a competitor when you have everything." [6]

Asked what made him a competitor, Abe responded, "I don't know. It's like asking what makes bird dogs point. They just do. I know I find it awfully hard to say the better team won—if we lose.

It is hard for me to give the other team credit, tough to concede that maybe we were overmatched." [7]

Betty Jo was interviewed by Mary Jo Nelson of *The Daily Oklahoman* in 1958. Betty Jo admitted that the only time Abe lost his sense of humor was when his team lost, "I've learned one of the duties of a basketball wife is to keep everyone quiet for a few days after a loss until Abe brightens again." [8] Betty Jo said when the Chiefs win again, the whole family joins in the

6'10 O.C.U. CENTER HUB' REED CITY ALL-AMERICA '58

Hub Reed, a 6'10" product of Oklahoma City Capitol Hill High School, was Abe's first All-American. Courtesy Oklahoma City University.

celebration. Betty Jo and daughters Dana Lee and Jan sat with Paul Hansen's wife, Carol, on the sidelines each home game.

Betty Jo and Carol were almost widows during the basketball season. Abe taught two classes at OCU in addition to directing Chief practices and running the business end of being head coach and athletic director. Betty Jo told the newspaper reporter that most people think a basketball coach's wife's life is glamorous. She said her life was not glamorous, "but is certainly exciting." Betty Jo had a full-time job taking care of the two girls and was active in church and did occasional modeling for a local dress shop.

After the basketball season, Abe spent much of his time visiting prospective players. Abe had made many trips with his Chiefs to

Kentucky to play the Wildcats of Western Kentucky University in Bowling Green. While in Kentucky, Abe built a friendship with Denval Barriger, the Bowling Green High School basketball coach, later the personnel director for the Bowling Green school system. Barriger had coached basketball in Kentucky for years and had a knack for spotting talent. He was intrigued with the OCU offense and asked Abe for details. After Abe returned home from the road trip he jotted down a few secrets of his offense and sent them to Barriger. Abe's sharing of his success bonded his friendship with Barriger.

During a trip to western Kentucky in the spring of 1958, Abe learned from Barriger about an honor student who averaged 20 points per game in his senior year at Bowling Green High School. The Kentucky All-Stater was 5'11" Larry Jones, the son of a Bowling Green couple that cut hair for a living. Barriger suggested that Jones could easily fit into the OCU offensive scheme.

Abe met Jones and his family and convinced them that he would not be lost at a small school like OCU. Jones, nicknamed "Preacher" because he planned to become an evangelist, accepted Abe's scholarship offer and began classes at OCU in the fall of 1958. Before Jones accepted the scholarship offer, Abe had all the Baptist preachers he knew to call Jones' parents. However, Jones said, "Why you have all the Baptists calling me, I'm Methodist?" Abe changed his line of attack and had all the Methodist preachers call and emphasized that OCU was a Methodist University. [9] To make Jones feel more at home in Oklahoma, Abe offered a scholarship to Jones' teammate Lowell Hammars. Abe got more than a star basketball player out of recruiting Jones. Abe got a free haircut from Jones' father and a world-class meal at Ferrell's Chicken every time he went back to Kentucky.

Jones, as an OCU ministerial student, was held to a high standard by Abe. At the end of one season, Jones and other players decided it would fashionable to shave their heads. They forced their wishes on fellow players. Jones explained, "We had one guy who was an actual barber, Gary Duncan. So we connived to get players in our room. I was sitting up high on the back of a chair and locked my legs around their necks while Gary shaved them. Unfortunately, one of our victims was the team manager who was scheduled to be in a wedding that weekend. Abe was mad. He took us off meals for a week. He held a team meeting and asked who was involved. I stood up, along with three others. Abe looked at me and said, 'You're a preacher, you're the ringleader.' I really felt bad." [10]

Jones was a star at OCU in the following years and became world-renowned as founder and president of Feed the Children, one of the nation's most respected and successful charitable organizations. Jones wrote a book entitled *Practice to Win*, largely based upon Abe's admonition that "You'll never play better in a game than you play in practice." [11]

Jones was the first of many basketball stars Abe recruited from the hills of Kentucky. Sportswriter Frank Boggs accompanied Abe on a recruiting trip to Kentucky and wrote, "The back roads are narrow and winding and rarely permit passing. You see signs tacked onto trees in front yards that say 'Antiques' and you know the place is legit if the stuff inside is as ancient as the house that holds it. There are stands with rocks for sale and pink swans made out of plaster. Wildly colorful chenille bedspreads flap in the breeze and the sunshine fades their attractiveness now because the tourist season is idling...Abe is here searching for talent. This state is full of scenery, friendly people, tobacco farms and lanky basketball players." [12]

Boggs and Abe finally found the backwoods house where a prospect lived. The 6'6" youngster was not at home, but Boggs observed, "There are two old hunting dogs stretched out on the front porch near the swing, which weaves ever so slowly as if an invisible old lady is sitting there knitting. A bucket of coal is by the front door." [13]

After waiting 20 minutes, the young man returned home from hauling a load of feed to the next town. Abe introduced himself and told the boy about OCU, how the team played all over the United States, and how he could never get lost in a small school like OCU. The boy announced he was just 17, made good grades, and would graduate near the top of his class of 24 in the small, rural school. The boy did not know anything about scholarships and was puzzled when Abe offered him a four-year free ride on books, tuition, and room and board. With a handshake, the boy promised to visit OCU after graduation. [14]

Abe enjoyed his recruiting trips to Kentucky. He was a talker and impressed prospects' fathers, discussing the latest tobacco crop, and their mothers, with his sincere concern for her son. Abe emphasized the extensive travels his basketball team made each season. He told parents how important it was for a small town kid to see the world, much like Abe had done in the Merchant Marine. Abe, himself raised in a small town, identified with the Kentucky youngsters and their parents. More often than not, hot prospects signed on the dotted line with OCU and became Chiefs stars of the future.

Abe and assistant coach Hansen were the perfect recruiting duo. Longtime Oklahoma City sportscaster Jerry Parks called Abe and Hansen "Batman and Robin." Parks once told a crowd attending a roast for Hansen, "What a team they were. Paul had trouble hearing and Abe needed glasses to see good. So when they're out recruiting around Gotebo or Slapout and come to a railroad track, Abe would listen and Paul would watch for the train." [15]

In the fall of 1958, Abe was not optimistic about fielding a championship team for OCU. He secretly figured to win no more than half his games because of the loss of Reed, his scoring leader for the past three seasons. OCU also lost Griffin, who with Reed, had accounted for half of the Chiefs' scoring the previous year.

However, Abe spent long hours changing his style of play. He knew his 1958-1959 team would be much shorter so he emphasized a free-shooting attack and stepped up plans to increase the relentless pressure defense he taught his players. Dale Ransford, sportswriter for the OCU campus newspaper and radio voice of the Chiefs, was unusually optimistic, despite not having a potential star on the team, "Teams possessing such stars in past years were not necessarily assured of winning seasons...This season could be the most interesting in quite some time. The team seems to be well balanced." [16]

Abe returned three starters from the previous year, 6'4" forward Fred Yeahquo and guards, 6'1" Ed McCraw and 5'10" Troy Hill.

Abe expected a good performance from junior college transfer Joseph "Bud" Sahmaunt and sophomores Harry Vines, David Hale, and Fred Moses. The three sophomores had averaged in double figures for Hansen's freshman team in 1956-1957.

Vines met Abe at an All-Star game in Hutchinson, Kansas. He liked Abe's big car and believed he could trust what Abe said about OCU. Vines later became nationally known as volunteer coach of the "Rollin' Razorbacks," a wheelchair basketball team that has won four national championships and, in 1999, made a tenth consecutive appearance in the Final Four of wheelchair basketball. [17]

Sahmaunt, known for his hustle as a player, had begun the school year at Kansas State University after agreeing to play for the Wildcats under coach Tex Winter. Sahmaunt had starred at Cameron Junior College in Lawton, Oklahoma, where Winter's brother was a dentist. The Cameron team, coached by Ted Owen, later coach for the University of Kansas, had made it to the semi-finals of the national junior college tournament the previous year and attracted attention from four-year college coaches across the country.

One of Sahmaunt's best friends was Fred Yeahquo who tried to convince Sahmaunt to play with him at OCU even after Sahmaunt had committed to Kansas State. Both were full-blood Kiowa Indians. [18] Abe jokingly talked about recruiting Yeahquo and Sahmaunt on the Kiowa Indian reservation, "They did a dance for me. They danced so hard and it rained so much, I couldn't get out for days." [19]

After only a few days in Manhattan, Kansas, Sahmaunt wanted to return to Oklahoma. He called Abe, who told him, "Talk to Coach Winter first." After Winter gave Sahmaunt his blessing to attend OCU, Sahmaunt called Abe back and offered his services. Luckily, for both Sahmaunt and OCU, a scholarship had opened up. Sahmaunt packed his bags and rushed back to the Sooner State to join Yeahquo and the Chiefs. In 1987, years after starring on the hardcourt for OCU, Sahmaunt became the school's athletic director. [20]

The Chiefs averaged only 6'1" among the starting five but substituted fight for height. After surprising Southern Methodist University 74-51 in the opening game, on a 20-point effort by Fred

Moses and another 15 points added by Sahmaunt, OCU hit the Associated Press top 20 and remained there all season. The Chiefs lost their second game to Texas Christian University but then improved dramatically and won nine straight games, including three games in the All-College.

In the game against Drake, OCU trailed by seven with eight minutes to go. During a time-out, Abe brought his team to the sideline and laid it on the line, "Get out there and win the game. You figure out how. You'll get big steaks if you win and hamburgers if you lose." [21] The Chiefs came back and won and Abe bought the players big steaks, explaining, "I want my boys to know the difference between winning and losing, and that's a good way to drive home the point." [22]

The Lemons family gathers around the latest collection of newspaper clippings just before Christmas, 1958. Left to right, Betty Jo, Jan, Dana, and Abe. Courtesy *The Daily Oklahoman.*

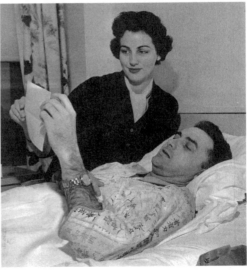

ABOVE: Abe and OCU cheerleaders, Patsy Wheeler, left, of Oklahoma City, and Clara Sevier, of Muskogee, helped rally students before a December, 1958, game against Southern Methodist University. Courtesy *The Daily Oklahoman.*

RIGHT: Betty Jo consoles Abe after having his tonsils removed in December, 1958. Courtesy *The Daily Oklahoman.*

Abe used food as a teaching tool. He said, "When we lose, we don't eat. When we win, we eat real good. I don't eat after we lose, and I don't expect them to, either. When we get beat, we never discuss it as a group. Nobody likes to look at film of a defeat when they're at fault. It'll gnaw at you. Like the golfers say, you can't play good golf if you can't forget your last shot."

The Chiefs went into the All-College with a 5-1 mark. They beat San Francisco 72-64 in the first game and then played one of their best tournament games ever, blasting Xavier University of Ohio 81-54 in the second game. Sahmaunt and Moses each hit 21. In the tournament finals, OCU romped to a 75-59 win over Duquesne University, scoring 53 points in the second half. The win ended a seven-year frustration of being the bridesmaid rather than the bride in the All-College. McCraw led Chief scorers in the win over Duquesne with 15 points. [23] Sahmaunt was named the All-College Most Valuable Player. He was the ringleader of the pint-sized Chiefs who gave up an average of six inches per man to their foes in the tournament. In the Xavier game, Sahmaunt held Hank Stein, the most valuable player of the previous season's National Invitation Tournament, to eight points. After bagging the All-College crown, OCU rose to 13th in the Associated Press poll.

In the second half of the season, OCU continued its winning ways, with victories over Idaho State, Florida State, twice, Memphis State, and Loyola of New Orleans. The Chiefs dropped games to Houston, Centenary of Shreveport, Louisiana, and Georgia Tech. The six-point, triple-overtime loss to Georgia Tech came after the Chiefs had a monumental struggle getting to Atlanta, Georgia, to play the game. Fog canceled the flight from Oklahoma City so Abe resorted to packing his team on a train, headed for Dallas. The train was late and the Chiefs missed their connections at Dallas Love Field. Finally, the team caught a late afternoon flight to Atlanta. But bad weather forced the plane to land in Montgomery, Alabama. By car, the Chiefs headed for Atlanta, arriving just three hours before game time. [24]

A morale booster for OCU was the completion of the new Frederickson Fieldhouse. Fans loved the new facility. They were closer to the action than at the Municipal Auditorium where the crowd was seated a long way from the court. Athletic business manager Ed Nall resigned and was replaced by Steve Sanger.

Reporters kidded Abe about the new clock in the Frederickson Fieldhouse. The space on the clock that displayed the score had three digits, instead of the two spaces most basketball clocks still contained. "How could the Chiefs ever score 100 points?" one reporter asked. Abe pumped up his players for the first game in the new fieldhouse against Florida State University. Sure enough, the Chiefs scored 103 points, proving the necessity for the extra space on the scoreboard. [25]

Oklahoma City University finished the regular season at 20-5 and accepted a bid to play at Madison Square Garden in New York City in the National Invitation Tournament. It was the Chiefs first trip to the NIT and their first time to play in the Garden. OCU could have gone to the NCAA tournament for a seventh straight year but the players voted to go to New York.

Abe and his players enjoyed the sights of the Big Apple. Paul Hansen, his wife, Carol, and Betty Jo took a ride on the Staten Island ferry one night. Abe refused to go along, saying it was "too dangerous." [26]

When the fourth-seeded Chiefs took the floor, they got "gardenitis." Unable to get their offense in gear, OCU lost in the first-round game to the Violets of New York University.

Even though the Chiefs lost in the NIT, the 1958-1959 team was successful. The final record was 20-7 and the Chiefs were third in the nation in shooting, hitting 45.8 percent of their shots from the field, behind Auburn and Cincinnati. McCraw and Moses were eighth and ninth, respectively, in national individual scoring. McCraw hit 54.1 percent of his shots while Moses sank 53.9 percent of his attempts. Sahmaunt was named honorable mention on the United Press International All-American team. Moses led the Chiefs in individual scoring, averaging almost 15.4 points per game. The Chiefs ended the season at number 17 in the Associated Press poll.

Immediately after the season, Abe was offered the job as head coach at Rice University.

Retiring coach Don Suman recommended Abe for the position. True to form, when asked by a reporter if he had been contacted by Rice officials, Abe said, "I refuse to answer on grounds that it might incriminate me." [27]

One advantage Abe saw about the Rice job was that the university was part of the Southwest Conference. Being part of a conference would eliminate much of Abe's work in scheduling games for the Chiefs. However, Abe was comfortable and successful at OCU. In his first four years as head coach, his teams had compiled a 73-35 record, enviable in any coaching circle.

After discussing the job offer with Betty Jo and OCU president Dr. Jack Wilkes, Abe was given a raise by OCU and decided to remain as the Chiefs' head coach.

—Chapter Nine—

Just Dropping In

You have to get the boys. You've got to be a salesman. I'm getting ready to go on a trip to Kentucky and Indiana to see a couple of prospects. That's about a 900-mile trip, and then I have to act like I just happened to drop in.

Abe Lemons

ABE WAS A MASTER RECRUITER. HE COULD TALK INTO THE wee-morning hours with prospects and their parents about almost any subject. He perfected his spiel about how the small-school atmosphere at OCU was far superior to big campuses. He once told the parents of a boy who was considering attending a major state university, "Have you ever been there? Well, I have. And they've got some buildings that must be 20 stories tall. There is no way you can possibly learn all they've got stored up in those buildings. But at OCU, we've got a lot of little ol' buildings. You can just tell by lookin' that in four years a boy wouldn't have any trouble learning everything in there." [1]

Abe spent a lot of his time on the recruiting trail. His technique was simple, "I don't give the kids a bunch of malarkey. When they come to the campus, I turn 'em over to the boys. I take 'em out for hot dogs instead of steaks, because they'd rather have hot dogs. I

For added publicity for the OCU basketball program, KNBQ Radio owner Ed Nall talked Abe into doing a weekly football prediction show during the pigskin season. Here Abe is interviewed by Harry McFarland, center, announcer and chief engineer for KNBQ, as Nall, with headset, monitors the broadcast, Courtesy *The Daily Oklahoman.*

don't treat 'em any different that they'll be treated here later on, and that's why we've never lost a kid." [2]

When a prospect arrived on the OCU campus, Abe put him up in the dorm so he could eat, sleep, and live with the players. He was convinced that young men learned more from the potential future teammates than ever could be learned in discussions with coaches. Abe refused to sign a prospect while he was still on campus. If a prospect told Abe he wanted to come to OCU, Abe would say, "No, you go back home and think about it a couple of days, and I'll get in touch with you later. Then, when you do make up your mind, I'm going to count on you." [3]

In a *Sports Illustrated* feature on Abe several years later, Abe talked about recruiting, especially his enticement of Hub Reed, his first All-American, "I got him with just fishin' and orange slush. I still think you cain't do no better'n a grape sody and a hamburger. Hub dropped by the gym one day after he graduated from high

In a staged public relations stunt, Abe pretended to recruit a 7'6" giant at the circus in Oklahoma City in 1959. Courtesy *The Daily Oklahoman.*

school. 'Shore I'll go fishin', Hub,' I said, though I ain't much for fishin' because I can't stand myself that long." [4]

Abe believed the old adage that a handshake was a man's bond, "Before the NCAA made me sign all these contracts," he lectured, "the only agreement I had with a boy was a handshake. Some of them thought they was smart to get it written out, and shore, I give it to 'em. Course, they didn't know they was better off with just a handshake. To me, a handshake was a four-year obligation. A contract was written just for one year." [5]

Abe opened practice for the 1959-1960 season at OCU with only 12 players. That number dropped to 11 a week later when 6'6" senior Don McGee was forced to the sideline with a heart condition.

Abe had outdone himself in scheduling some of the top basketball powers for the new campaign. On the heels of the highly successful Chiefs season the previous year, many coaches wanted to add OCU to their schedule. It was the toughest schedule in years for OCU with games slated against San Francisco, Southern Methodist University, Clemson, Bowling Green, Houston, Alabama, Miami of Florida, St. Louis University, Bradley, and Memphis State.

L.H. Bengtson, Jr., took over the job as the play-by-play announcer for Chiefs games broadcast on KYFM, owned by former OCU athletic business manager Ed Nall.

Fred Moses, at 6'3", one of the shortest post men in major college basketball, highlighted the list of returning starters for the Chiefs. Moses led the team in scoring and rebounding the previous season. From Arnold, Pennsylvania, a suburb of Pittsburgh, Moses had nine years of basketball experience. After high school, and All-State recognition, he played basketball for the Air Force. [6]

Harry Vines, a mobile 6'6" center and former All-Stater from Little Rock, Arkansas, figured to be the top rebounder for the Chiefs. Abe counted on juniors David Hale, 6'5" from Guymon, Oklahoma, and 6'10" Henry Oeltjendiers from LaGrange, Texas, and five sophomores, Bill Johnston, Ponca City; Rex Norton, Cushing; Eugene Tsoodle, a full-blooded Kiowa Indian, Fort

Cobb; Chester Kyle, Oklahoma City, Northeast High School; and Larry Jones, Bowling Green, Kentucky.

Abe knew he could count on his American Indian players, Tsoodle, Sahmaunt, and Fred Yeahquo, a 6'4" forward who averaged almost seven points a game the previous year.

Abe, proud of his own American Indian ancestry, always had something funny to say about his reputation as making the Chiefs program more interesting by recruiting Indian players. Once Abe said, "You got to obey the White Man's law out here—never steal anything larger than a state." [7] To a visiting coach bringing his team to OCU, Abe retorted, "Custer should have learned you guys—never play the Indians on the road." [8]

Oklahoma City University won six of its first eight games in 1959, including two games over San Francisco and Montana State to give the Chiefs the Treasurer State Classic tournament title in Bozeman, Montana. After Christmas, OCU entered the All-College tournament as the first seed, a new honor for the team. In the opening game, Sahmaunt and Yeahquo starred for the Chiefs in opening up leads of 8-1 and 22-8. Clemson coach Press Maravich asked for a time-out and asked an official, "What can we do?" The referee suggested circling the wagons. When OCU continued the pounding, by outscoring Clemson 48-24 by half-time, Maravich sent a note to Abe, pleading, "Pull 'em off." Abe hastily scribbled a reply, "White man must pay for sins." [9] OCU won the game 84-57.

Maravich, whose son "Pistol Pete" later became one of America's best known college basketball players, explained to a reporter how Abe used easy courses for his players. Maravich said, "These Indians fouled up the program. He had this course in basket-weavin' that he enrolled his players in, but these two [Sahmaunt and Yeahquo] got the curve up so high the others were flunkin' out." [10]

The Chiefs won the second round game of the All-College, slipping past Bowling Green University 84-82. But unbeaten Utah State outscored OCU 75-59 to win the All-College title.

Yeahquo graduated at mid-term, completing his career with a 12-point per game scoring average. The Chiefs collapsed, winning only two of their last 11 games without Yeahquo in the lineup. *The*

LEFT: Guy Quoetone, center, the uncle of Bud Sahmaunt, presents Abe with a Kiowa war bonnet. Abe was given the Kiowa name of "Chief Tone-Yope-Keye, which means "leader who will always lead others to victory." At left is OCU president Dr. Cluster Q. Smith. Courtesy *The Daily Oklahoman.*

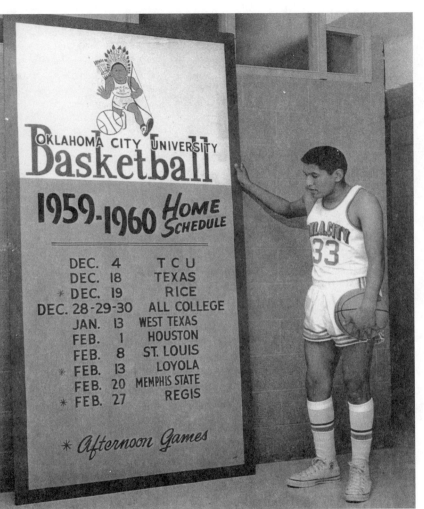

OKLAHOMA CITY UNIVERSITY

Basketball

1959-1960 HOME SCHEDULE

DEC.	4	T C U
DEC.	18	TEXAS
* DEC.	19	RICE
DEC. 28-29-30		ALL COLLEGE
JAN.	13	WEST TEXAS
FEB.	1	HOUSTON
FEB.	8	ST. LOUIS
* FEB.	13	LOYOLA
FEB.	20	MEMPHIS STATE
* FEB.	27	REGIS

* Afternoon Games

ABOVE: Returning starter Bud Sahmaunt, later athletic director at OCU, looks over the schedule for the new season. Courtesy *The Daily Oklahoman.*

LEFT: Abe shows reporters a map of the out-of-state games slated for the 1959-1960 Chiefs. Courtesy *The Daily Oklahoman.*

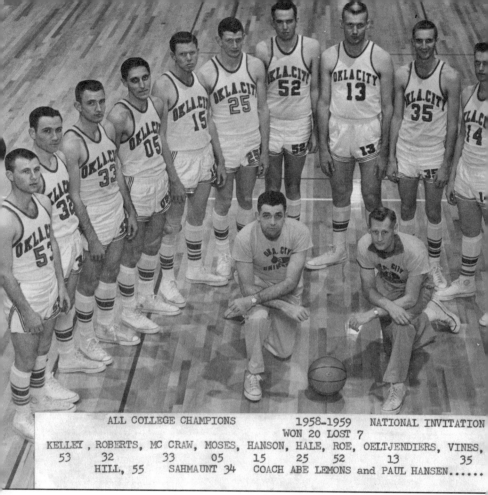

ALL COLLEGE CHAMPIONS   1958-1959   NATIONAL INVITATION
                           WON 20 LOST 7
KELLEY , ROBERTS, MC CRAW, MOSES, HANSON, HALE, ROE, OELTJENDIERS, VINES,
   53   32   33   05   15   25   52   13   35
         HILL, 55   SAHMAUNT 34   COACH ABE LEMONS and PAUL HANSEN......

Campus sports editor Ron Nance reasoned, "The tall senior left a vacancy that could not be filled. At the time of his departure, OCU was riding high with a fancy 10-4 mark...Yeahquo's steady rebounding and scoring along with the confidence his fellow teammates held of him dealt a severe blow to the makings of a fine team." [11]

Abe had more problems. Sophomore Rex Norton, unhappy with the amount of playing time he was getting, dropped out of school at OCU and enrolled at Central State College in Edmond, Oklahoma. [12]

The 1958-1959 Chiefs were All-College champions and played in the National Invitation Tournament. Abe and Paul Hansen kneel in front of the players. Courtesy Oklahoma City University.

A disastrous road trip, seven straight games on opponents' courts, spelled disaster in the second half of the season. OCU lost at Houston; Centenary; Alabama; Miami of Florida; Houston, again; St. Louis; and Regis University in Denver. The Chiefs, after mid-term, managed to end up in the victory column in home games against Loyola of New Orleans and Regis. The final record of 12-13 was Abe's first losing season at OCU.

Oklahoma City University officials called the final game of the year against Regis "Bud Sahmaunt night" to honor the senior in his last game. Sahmaunt scored six points in the win over Regis after scoring 20 or more points in four of the last six Chiefs games.

Even though the Chiefs did not perform well as a team in 1959-1960, individual players did well statistically. Moses, with a 15.5 per game average, led the Big Four schools in Oklahoma in scoring. Sahmaunt was fourth among Oklahoma college teams with a 12.1 per game mark. Larry Jones was the third-leading scorer on the Chiefs squad with a 11.2 per game average, followed by Vines with 10.6.

The season was not a good one for Oklahoma major college squads. Only Oklahoma University finished above .500 at 14-11. OSU was 10-15 and University of Tulsa was 9-17.

The 1960-1961 OCU season got off to a fast start. An overflow crowd of more than the capacity of 3,500 screaming fans greeted the Chiefs as they opened the season at home against the Southern Methodist University Mustangs. OCU started three returning veterans, 6'3" center Fred Moses, lanky 6'6" forward Harry Vines, and speedy playmaker 5'11" Larry Jones. Gary Karr, a 5'7" junior college All-American transfer from Coffeyville, Kansas, Junior College, started at guard and David Hale, a 6'5" senior from Guymon, Oklahoma, was the other forward.

The Chiefs toppled Southern Methodist University 84-78 with Vines pacing OCU with 21 points. The Chiefs next beat Texas Christian University with Moses firing home a 55-foot baseball-type fieldgoal in the final seconds of the game. Jones was the top scorer in a win over the University of Texas at Austin. The Chiefs beat Hardin-Simmons at Abilene and then won their fifth straight game against Baylor, winding up one of the most successful road trips through Texas in OCU history.

Local fans were given an opportunity to see their Chiefs on television in the 1960-1961 season. OCU public information director Hugh Scott hosted a weekly 30-minute program featuring film highlights of Chiefs games on KOCO-TV in Oklahoma City.

Oklahoma City University entered the 25th All-College tournament with a 5-2 record. For the first time in 10 years, the Chiefs were bounced into the consolation bracket with a first-round 73-65 loss to winless Baylor, the tournament's Cinderella team. OCU followed its loss to Baylor with a victory over in-state rival Tulsa University 83-62, sparked by a career-high 31 points from Moses.

Moses scored 30 points to keep OCU in the third-place All-College game against Houston which eventually prevailed 86-82. He broke his own single-game scoring mark with 36 points against Loyola the following week

After mid-term OCU was an up and down club, winning against North Texas twice, and Loyola of New Orleans, but losing key games against Southern Methodist University, St. Louis, Tulsa, and Wichita State

The Chiefs finished the campaign at 14-12.

Abe was so mad at his team after the loss in St. Louis, he told them, "I'm embarassed. Find your own way home. I'll see you in Oklahoma City." Abe carried a half-dozen players in his car and Fred Moses hauled the rest of the road team in his vehicle. Abe whizzed through an amber light and left Moses to make a decision, stop and be lost in downtown St. Louis, or run a red light. Moses ran the red light. Moments later he heard a siren and saw the lights of a police car in his rear-view mirror. [13]

Frantically, Moses told the police officer, "We got beat last night and that guy up there took off and we'll never catch him. We'll be left here and I don't have any gas in my car." [14] The understanding officer turned his siren on again and headed after Abe. However, Abe had disappeared on the road toward Oklahoma City. Moses and the players in his car scraped up a total of $5.13 among them, enough for bologna, bread, and cokes purchased at a Tulsa Safeway grocery store, and enough gasoline to make it back home. Larry Jones rode in the back seat of Moses' car and remembered, "Fred's heater went out. It was sleeting and snowing and we almost froze to death." Abe told the players later that the experience would make them play better. [15]

During the season, Moses came up to Abe one night before a game and said, "Coach, I only need 10 more points to catch you," referring to Abe's scoring total while a player at OCU. Abe grinned and said, "You ain't playing any more, Moses. You'll never catch me." Moses said, "Hell, I got 15 more games to go." Abe said, "Don't be too sure, Moses." [16]

Moses did get to play and became the fourth man in OCU history to score 1,000 points in his career. He averaged 19.4 points per game his senior year and closed out his service in a Chiefs uniform with 1,299 points. Trailing Moses in scoring were Jones with 13.9, Vines at 12.9, and Gary Hill at 11.9 points per game.

Hill was Abe's first recruit from the tiny Washita County, Oklahoma, town of Rocky. Abe had watched with interest the excellent high school teams produced at Rocky by coach Raymond "Red" Miller. Abe saw potential in Hill even as a sophomore in high school. Abe enjoyed the small town atmosphere of Rocky, with its ice cream socials and friendly people. Hill's father, Floyd Hill, liked Abe and, with the help of coach Miller, steered Hill toward OCU basketball. After college Hill became a coach, school teacher, and drug and alcohol abuse counselor.[17]

Hill's recruitment at OCU suffered a setback when Abe allowed Bill "Bird" Johnston to use his 1951 Ford to drive Hill and his father to the Frontier City amusement park in Oklahoma City during a recruiting visit. Johnston's floor-boarding scared Floyd Hill so much he told Abe, "My boy can go to school here, but he can't ride in a car with Johnston." [18]

Johnston starred in another capacity for OCU in 1961. Teammates persuaded him to run for *Keshena* Queen, a beauty and popularity contest sponsored by the OCU yearbook. The pageant was previously open only to girls. However, Johnston, wearing a long dress borrowed from Carol Hansen, the wife of assistant coach Paul Hansen, won the queen contest, but was forbidden by the OCU administration from accepting the title. [19]

A bright spot in the season was the Chiefs performance against Hardin-Simmons, setting a new scoring record of 106 points, including 43 field goals, shattering the old record of 37.

Another encouraging sign of things to come in Chiefs basketball was the play of Bud Koper, a 6'5" scoring ace from Rocky, Oklahoma. Koper averaged 25.7 points per game on the OCU freshman squad, making him the highest scoring freshman in Chiefs history, even better than Arnold Short or Hub Reed. [20]

An OCU player who developed rapidly for Abe was Manuel Heusman. Abe had taken Larry Jones and Bill Johnston to Heusman's home in El Reno while he was still in high school. At El Reno High School, Heusman played for coach Jenks Simmons. Heusman spent many nights as a youngster with his ear glued to his transistor radio, listening to the Chiefs play on KOMA Radio. He knew he wanted to play basketball at OCU. [21]

Abe started practice in earnest in October for the 1961-1962 season. As usual, Abe ran his troops through the Figure 8 drill, where players ran at top speed up and down the court while passing the ball. Abe had a rule. If anyone of a threesome missed a basket or pass, or loafed, all three players repeated the exercise. To help with ball-handling, Abe had his guards wear work gloves during practice. He believed the gloves made the players more aware of their hands. [22]

The new edition of the Chiefs was a scoring machine. Even though the 1961-1962 Chiefs posted a mediocre 14-12 record, the same as the previous season, OCU was the highest scoring team in Oklahoma college history to that time. The Chiefs averaged 82.1 points per game, led by senior star Larry Jones, who clipped off 19.7 points per contest, and junior Gary Hill, with 17.4 points per game. Sophomore Bud Koper added 15.9 and senior Eugene Tsoodle contributed 14 points per game. It was the first time in OCU history that four players ended the season averaging in double figures. [23]

The success of the outstanding offense of the Chiefs was dimmed by the lack of defense. OCU gave up 81.5 points per game, mostly on second shots, a result of a serious rebounding deficiency.

Frankly, Abe thought the new season would be a good one. The Chiefs beat coach Buster Brannon's Texas Christian University Hornfrogs 97-91 in the season opener and followed with a 79-64 thumping of Baylor. With his big guns of Jones, Hill, Koper, and Tsoodle, Abe started 6'3" junior Manuel Heusman at forward. Midwest City's Gary White also played a lot of minutes for the Chiefs. Abe counted on a strong bench made up of Ray Siner, Bill Stephens, Pat Hawkins, Dale Tracy, Bill Hill, Tim Horan, Larry Faulkner, John Kent, and John Axton, the son of Mae Boren Axton, who had played such an integral part in Abe's early life.

The Chiefs squad continued to reflect Abe's prowess at recruiting in small-town schools. The team included John Kent from Borger, Texas; Dale Tracy from Cheyenne, Oklahoma; Tsoodle and Hawkins from Fort Cobb, Oklahoma; Koper and Hill from Rocky, Oklahoma; Ray Snider from Nowata, Oklahoma; Gary Duncan from Cayuga, Texas; Larry Faulkner from Rush Springs, Oklahoma; Bill Johnston from Ponca City, Oklahoma; and Heusman from El Reno, Oklahoma.

After the first two wins of the season the Chiefs hit a three-game losing streak, dropping contests to Wyoming, Baylor, and Southern Methodist University. KTOK Radio in Oklahoma City carried the Chiefs games live with OCU junior James Clark handling the play-

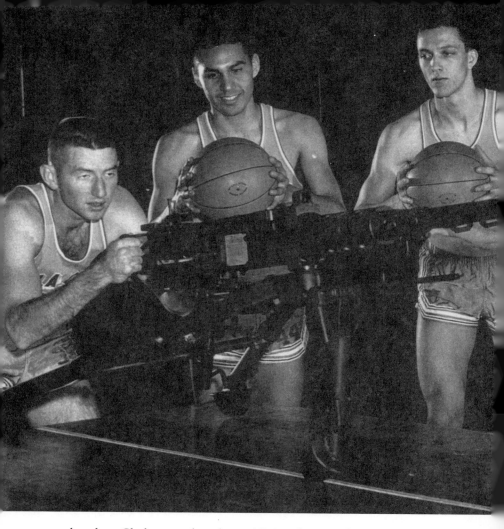

by-play. Clark was also the publicity director for the athletic department.

The Chiefs ran into a buzz-saw in the 1961 All-College tournament. OCU fell to Utah State in the first round, regrouped and beat Texas Christian University the next day, and lost in the consolation final to Texas A & M 71-69 in double overtime. The only positive in tournament play for the Chiefs was the one-two punch of Jones and Hill who hit 64 and 51 points, respectively, in the

The Chiefs in 1961-1962 were among the nation's leading teams on offense, hitting 46.4 percent from the field and 75 percent of free throws. The machine-gun offense gave a photographer the idea for this posed shot. Left to right, Larry Jones, Eugene Tsoodle, Gary Hill, Bud Koper, and Bill Johnston. Courtesy Oklahoma City University.

three games. The All-College was won by Bowling Green of Ohio, led by superstar Nate Thurmond. It was one of the strongest eight-team fields of the All-College in years. Coming into the tournament, Seattle was unbeaten and Wichita was ranked fifth in the country. [24]

After the holiday break, OCU resumed battle on a long southern road trip. They beat Christian Brothers College, got ambushed by Florida State 99-74, and then broke an OCU scoring record by piling up 118 points in a 118-113 win over Miami of Florida. It was not a good game for defense-lovers.

While in Miami, Abe showed his "father-figure" side by nursing Manuel Heusman back to health. Heusman was running temperature of 104 degrees but Abe kept him walking along the beach, stopping occasionally for a glass of orange juice. Abe was concerned about Heusman's wife who was stuck back in Oklahoma City in the middle of an ice storm. Huesman later recalled, "He [Abe] gave me confidence and said I could play sick a lot better than other guys could play well. I believed everything he told me." [25]

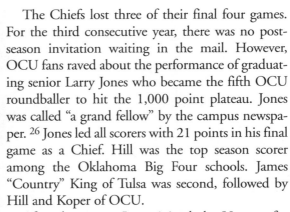

The Chiefs lost three of their final four games. For the third consecutive year, there was no post-season invitation waiting in the mail. However, OCU fans raved about the performance of graduating senior Larry Jones who became the fifth OCU roundballer to hit the 1,000 point plateau. Jones was called "a grand fellow" by the campus newspaper. [26] Jones led all scorers with 21 points in his final game as a Chief. Hill was the top season scorer among the Oklahoma Big Four schools. James "Country" King of Tulsa was second, followed by Hill and Koper of OCU.

After the season Jones joined the Venture for Victory team, a group of Christian athletes led by coach Don Odle. He spent the summer playing basketball in Hawaii, the Philippines, Japan, and Korea. Jones, already a veteran minister, preached to thousands of people during the half-time of the 75-100 games the team played on foreign soil. [27]

LEFT: Abe talks to his team during a time-out after a nine-point Chiefs lead had been slashed to one point in a January, 1962 game. Courtesy *The Daily Oklahoman.*

Views

A Tribute by Frank Boggs

of Abe:

His players never knew exactly what the man was thinking, or what he might do for punishment, and no more effective discipline ever existed. Funny thing was, though, coach Abe Lemons did not know, either, what punishment, if any, might be meted out.

Late in his second decade as a coach, another excellent Oklahoma City University team was on a two-game Texas swing, playing first at Baylor, then at Southern Methodist. The Chiefs should win them both and, late in the game at Waco, that appeared a certainty. But Baylor rallied and Baylor won and Abe Lemons was furious.

We loaded into a long station wagon and I, for a reason never explained to me, always had the opportunity of riding in the front seat. The beaten players, none daring to speak, were wedged into the back rows.

Ahead, somewhere between Waco and Dallas, was a sleazy looking joint that sold beer and hamburgers. The station wagon swerved into the gravel parking lot, rocks flying. Abe got out,

ABOVE: Frank Boggs, sportswriter for *The Daily Oklahoman* made a living by showing up on slow news days and watching Abe's Chiefs practice, gleaning funny stories and one-liners. Players remember a smooth-talking Abe turning into a mad coach shouting instructions at the top of his voice as soon as Boggs entered Frederickson Fieldhouse. Courtesy *The Daily Oklahoman*.

slammed the door and went inside. The rest of us sat in silence. All we were sure is that he had not stopped to buy a beer for his boys.

He returned with two paper sacks full of hamburgers. Even today, all these years later, I am positive those hamburgers hold the NCAA record for smelling delicious. He threw the two sacks into the darkened back seats.

The gravel flew again and they were back on the highway.

Finally he told me, "We'll eat at a nice place when we get to Dallas." Oh, but those vanishing hamburgers in the back seats smelled wonderful.

At Dallas he checked his "team" into the hotel and announced we now would go eat. It was about 1:00 a.m. and everything was closed. Well, he found one seedy joint that had not locked up yet. He instructed me to go in because I suspect, looking back, he did not know if I would get out of there alive. All they had were hamburgers — about 12 for a dollar as I recall.

They were severely over-priced.

There was the time the Chiefs flew into Laramie, Wyoming, where the north winds were invented. Marvin Rich, a wonderful young player, wore a thin wind-breaker, no challenge for a Wyoming winter.

Abe had words for him. "Why didn't you wear a coat? Don't you know it gets cold in Wyoming?"

Rich knew, of course. But he never had owned an overcoat, nor had he ever had money to purchase such luxury.

The next morning Abe took him into a store and bought him his first winter coat.

"That's against NCAA rules," Abe said. "Maybe they can put us on probation."

Such transgressions were pretty much the limit of Abe's cheating.

The range from buying hamburgers for the "dogs" to purchasing the coat for Rich Travis is a good example of how Abe treated his players. About 99 percent of the time, they received the Rich Travis form of treatment.

Abe did not make rules. No curfews. The result was that if you did something wrong, no telling how severe the punishment might be. So the safe road of conduct was to go to class, practice hard, play hard, and behave yourself.

Coaches forever had been judged primarily on the number of victories. This is wrong. Great coaches are those whose players, whatever their background may have hinted, develop into strong and useful citizens. Our country is full of Abe's examples.

Among his peers, Abe was — and remains even all these years after his retirement — one of the nation's most respected coaches.

I saw this magnetism in only a few. In football, Paul "Bear" Bryant of Alabama comes to mind. When he entered a room, he quickly disappeared behind other coaches who swarmed around him like bees, each hopeful of hearing that southern drawl say something.

The same was true with Abe Lemons at NCAA Final Fours.

When a man attracts such respect, his reputation has achieved the ultimate.

At one long-ago NCAA convention Abe was on the coaching panel, entertaining and teaching hundreds of fellow coaches. In the audience was Bruce Drake, who had retired several years earlier and whose name was vanishing as younger generations took command of the game.

Abe told his fellow coaches that those who coached before should be listened to, that knowledge gained from the past never should be forgotten. "We have here today a man who knows more about coaching basketball than any of us ever will. He coached at the University of Oklahoma and his name is Bruce Drake and I want him to stand."

I will not forget the look on Bruce Drake's face. I think I saw tears forming.

The next year, and for many thereafter, a coach from the past was placed on the lecture staff at the Final Four. Bruce Drake was the first. Abe Lemons was responsible.

Abe Lemons is a complicated man. He is tough. He is honest. He never forgot his hometown of Walters. He never forgot his upbringing. He learned to work hard almost before he learned to walk.

He never worked at saying funny things. He simply speaks a different language than the rest of us. He looks at the passing world from a different locale than the rest of us. He does not always begin his sentences at the start, and expects the listener to understand. I am not sure Casey Stengel could have caught everything Abe says.

Never was there a better coaching team than Abe Lemons and Paul Hansen. Together they turned out teams with marvelous won-lost records. But, far more importantly, they turned out men.

Abe Lemons cannot be adequately described. There are too many facets to his personality; too many thoughts and ideas that spring forth without warning.

So, it must suffice to say, he's a remarkable and beautiful man. One who never can be copied.

Thank God we got to observe him.

—*Chapter Ten*—

War with the Striped-shirts

If something flagrant happens, you can't keep from
jumpin up. A guy can't sit around and watch his house burn.
If he's insured, he might lay back and watch it go.
But a coach's job is not insurable.

Abe Lemons

ABE DID NOT LIKE LOSING. HE ALWAYS FIGURED IT WAS SOMEBODY'S
fault and he usually blamed the referees. He had been picked on so
much as a kid, he vowed to not let striped-shirt officials ruin his life. [1]

Abe did not hesitate to question an official's call. Even if his
protest resulted in a technical foul, and it often did, Abe attacked
the official with a venom. The NCAA did not spend a lot of time
training its officials and local schools often picked up a high school
referee to call a home game. Abe can recall many times when an
official cost him a game.

On one occasion, the Chiefs were ahead and stalling in a game
at Salt Lake City, Utah, against the University of Utah. The officials

You can tell by the expression on Abe's face that he did not like the last call. The gentle touch on the referee's arm was Abe's way of disarming the official so that he could get the call right next time. Courtesy Oklahoma City University.

stopped the clock for no reason at all, sending Abe through the roof. Utah coach Jack Gardner bragged about his home-grown officials, "Abe, after the clock shows no time, we still have eight seconds, if we're behind." [2]

Memphis was a town in which Abe thought the Chiefs got the short-end of officiating fairness down through the years. In the late 1950s, it got so bad that Abe refused to play Memphis State University anymore. When he resumed the series, hoping that the one-sided referees had retired, he was disap-pointed again. After a game in Memphis where three of his players fouled out, and he drew three technical fouls, two on one play, Abe said, "That was the worst officiating I've seen in a long time. We've been averaging 13 fouls a game and had only one man foul out in our other 12 games. We're a finesse club, and every move we made they had their hands on us. We don't play this snatch-and-grab type basketball. I've never had this trouble anywhere but Memphis." [3]

Abe was convinced that officials thought they had to call fouls or they would not be paid. When a Miami sportscaster rushed up to Abe and asked what the Chiefs would have to overcome to beat the the University of Miami Hurricanes, Abe said, "Fields and Caldwell." The reporter said, "Fields and Caldwell, they're not play-ing." Abe responded, "That's right. They're officiating." [4]

Abe openly told the press that officials tended to favor the home team in the fun cities like Miami, New Orleans, and Las Vegas because they stood a better chance of being invited back, to make it a pleasure trip with their wives. After a game in New Orleans, Abe ran into one of the referees with his wife on his arm. Abe had yelled at the official during the entire game so the referee expected to get an earful at dinner. All Abe said was, "Have a nice time, Charlie." The referee, looking like he was taking his coat off for a fight, said, "I don't have to take that from you." Abe laughed and said, "Okay, you're going to get mad, so don't have a nice time." [5]

Abe drew three technical fouls in a game once in Moody Coliseum in Dallas against Southern Methodist University. A near riot developed and Abe said, "I'm having a little trouble with the guy with the whistle. I honestly believe if they sent this guy to Vietnam, he'd stop the war in two weeks—or else start another one of his own." [6]

Abe frequently complained about the officiating of Dave Mahukona and Mel Chan, "Dave's a pretty good official, but that Chan never calls anything. He just stands around and smiles." [7]

When Abe was kicked out of a game against the University of California at Berkley for misconduct, he intended to challenge the official outside the dressing room. Turned out the referee was an off-duty cop and was packing a pistol. So Abe just said, "Hi!," and left it at that. [8]

Once an OCU player got his tooth knocked out in a game against Nevada-Las Vegas and Abe said, "Hey, some places this would be a foul." When a dentist jumped from the stands to say he could save the young man's tooth, Abe quipped, "No, don't take him away, we need him." [9]

Abe enjoyed rattling officials who missed calls on the road. In the locker room after a loss at Denver, Abe sat reporters down and spun the story, "This official was always telling me to shut up...So he puts two technicals on me, and I know he's gonna run me in the second half. [automatic ejection after three technicals] I just beat him to it. I stayed in the dressing room and sent a runner out every five minutes. There's no rule says I got to stay out there. When the other team walks by your bench and says, 'You got another bad call,' you begin to wonder. I asked the other coach why he didn't leave, 'cause they weren't doing him any favors, either. He said he would, if he hadn't been at home." [10]

After three less-than-brilliant seasons, Abe brought his Chiefs back to winning basketball in 1962-1963. He added strength and height under the boards to improve rebounding, a weakness of the two previous squads. Rebounding was a lot easier with players like 6'9" Bill Johnston and 6'6" Jim Miller.

Oklahoma City University fielded the tallest team in the nation, especially after 7'0" Edward Wayne "Eddie" Jackson became eligible for the second semester. The starting five of Jackson, Gary Hill, Bud Koper, Miller, and Johnston averaged 6'7". [11]

Chiefs games were broadcast locally on KOMA Radio. The season opener against Southern Methodist University was selected for broadcast around the world on the Armed Forces Radio Network. [12]

For the first time ever, the Chiefs entered the All-College in December with a losing record, at 2-4. However, OCU re-bounded and beat Baylor 76-60 in the opening game. Then the Chiefs lost a one-point game to Wyoming and a three-point affair to Memphis State in the next two games in the tournament.

The entry of Jackson into the lineup after Christmas break was big news. He was OCU's first seven-footer and the first

This cartoon appeared on the sports page of *The Daily Oklahoman*, announcing to the world the impact of 7'0" Eddie Jackson on the Chiefs. Courtesy *The Daily Oklahoman*

black player to put on a Chiefs uniform. When Jackson visited the home of assistant coach Hansen, Hansen's three-year-old daughter, Judy, asked, "Daddy, there is something different about Eddie Jackson isn't there?" Somewhat startled, Hansen said, "What do you mean?" assuming Judy was talking about Jackson's color. The innocent child said, "What makes him so tall?" [13]

A pre-law major, Jackson had led his Moore High School team in Waco, Texas, to a state championship and transferred to OCU from OU. He became eligible after serving the NCAA-ordered one-year layout assessed for changing schools. Jackson had been pursued by 50 colleges and universities after making headlines as a Texas high school star.

Jackson, who after college turned down professional basketball and Harlem Globetrotter offers to eventually become a prominent bank president and lawyer in Oklahoma City, made a difference in the Chiefs lineup, averaging 11 points and 14 rebounds in his first two games. Abe said Jackson gave the team a new image, "They have to keep him closely covered because of his size. The other teams have to put their centers on Bill Johnston so that gives another advantage." [14] Sportswriter John Cronley wrote in *The Daily Oklahoman*, "Jackson can be quite an asset to the team...There's nothing goonish about him, despite his height, for his 220 pounds are smoothly distributed and he moves gracefully." [15]

Oklahoma City University caught fire and won 13 games in a row over worthy opponents such as Baylor, Southern Methodist University, Brigham Young University, and Loyola of New Orleans. After a regular-season ending loss to Houston, the Chiefs won a bid to the NCAA tournament.

Gary Hill provided the clutch basket as OCU knocked off Colorado State University in a March 9 district match at Lubbock, Texas. Hill scored nine of the Chiefs final 11 points.

The Chiefs traveled to Lawrence, Kansas, to compete in the Midwest regional against ninth-ranked Colorado. With their worst offensive performance of the year, the Chiefs fell to the Buffaloes 78-72. It was another game in which Abe thought the officials affected the outcome. Three Chiefs were tossed from the game for arguing. In the middle of the night after the game, there was a knock on Abe's hotel door. It was Eddie Jackson who said some guy approached him in a restaurant and tried to bribe him if he would not hit 20 points the next day. Abe, knowing that Jackson could not score 20 points "with a gun to his head," figured that the fan attempting the bribe thought he was talking to Pan American University star Lucious Jackson. Both Jacksons were from Texas and both were black. [16]

The Chiefs were demoralized after the loss to Colorado. Abe could not get his players up for the next contest. In the consolation game, OCU lost to Texas 90-83, completing the season at 19-10. Abe was extremely disappointed because he sincerely believed the team had the skills to go to the Final Four.

The 1962-1963 Chiefs were led by two stars from Rocky, Oklahoma, Hill and Koper. Hill, a 6'4" senior, averaged 21.1 points per game, second only to Koper's 22.8 average. Koper, a junior, and Hill graduated a year apart at tiny Rocky.

Hill was an outstanding ball handler, a great defensive player, and a high percentage shooter. His efforts were rewarded at the end of the season when the Helms Foundation named him to its All-America team. Koper also was honored by being selected honorable mention All-American by United Press International. In February, 1963, Koper set a new school record by posting 45 points in a game against Centenary.

With the loss of Hill, Abe turned to Koper and Jackson to carry his team forward in 1963-1964. *Sports Illustrated* ranked the Chiefs 13th nationally in a pre-season poll. Abe counted heavily on several spunky sophomores who had burned up the courts on the freshman team the year before. James Ware, a 6'7" jumper from Natchez, Mississippi, showed promise, along with three Kentucky recruits. Dick Bagby was a 5'11" guard from Russellville, Kentucky. Abe spotted two would-be great players during a pick-up game in Glasgow, Kentucky. Jerry Lee Wells was 6'2" and jumped like he had "a coil spring injection." [17] Charles H.T. Hunter was 6'4" and had been the top scorer in All-Star high school games in Kentucky.

Both Hunter and Wells would create a lot of OCU history in the next three years.

Hunter, whom local sportswriter Doug Todd nicknamed "Big Game," led his region in Kentucky in scoring his last two years in high school under Frank Terrell, the long-time basketball coach at Ralph Bunche High School in Glasgow, Kentucky. Hunter had been recruited heavily by the University of Louisville who tabbed him as its first black player. However, when Louisville would not offer a scholarship to Hunter's good friend, Jerry Lee Wells, both players decided to stick together and go west to Oklahoma City.

After the 1962-1963 season Gary Hill was named All-American and was selected to play in the East-West game in Lexington, Kentucky, where he took high scoring honors with 18 points. He was chosen as an alternate on the Pan-American team and was selected in the second round of the NBA draft by the San Francisco Warriors. Courtesy Oklahoma City University.

Later, Western Kentucky head coach Ed Diddle told Abe that, in recruiting Hunter, OCU had picked up the best player in Kentucky that year.

Abe became a father figure for Hunter who had grown up in his Kentucky home without a father. Hunter says Abe was a role model, "He taught me how to be a man, how to live and prepare for the future, how to eat in a restaurant with good manners and how to travel." [18]

Koper scored 37 points in the season opener as OCU beat Texas Christian University before a full house of 3,437 at Frederickson Fieldhouse. After losing to Wyoming in a high-scoring contest, 96-90, the Chiefs beat Denver and Southern Methodist University and upset top-ranked San Francisco University 97-84. Jackson and Ware held San Francisco's All-American Ollie Johnson to eight points.

In the Southern Methodist University game, Koper broke the Moody Coliseum record with 21 field goals and 44 total points. After the game Abe said Koper was the best shooter he had ever

Stumbling, Paul Silas of Creighton loses the ball in a January, 1964 game, while OCU's Eddie Jackson, left, and James Ware watch. Courtesy *The Daily Oklahoman.*

seen in college basketball. Southern Methodist University coach Doc Hayes went over to Koper after the final buzzer and shook his hand. Hayes told reporters, "It was the greatest shooting performance I ever saw." [19]

Abe's unorthodox coaching methods took an unusual turn during a practice session when Ware and Jackson got into a fierce physical and verbal battle. Abe sent for a set of boxing gloves and ordered the two players to "duke it out." After a few moments of sparring by the 7'0" Jackson and the shorter Ware, Abe called it off and the Chiefs got back to business. [20] Gary Gray says some OCU players may have been offended by Abe's actions at the time they occurred but realized later in life that Abe never intentionally hurt anyone's feelings and always had the best interest of the player in mind when he took disciplinary action or spoke harshly during practice or a game. [21]

Abe took his team to the Bluebonnet Classic, a tournament in Houston, Texas, in mid-December. OCU won its first matchup against Texas A & M but lost in the finals of the tournament to Houston University. Koper hit 27 points in each of the games and was chosen the Most Valuable Player of the Bluebonnet Classic. [22]

In the 1963 All-College, the Chiefs went to the finals with wins over Idaho State and Wyoming before losing to tournament champion Wichita State. Koper was named first team on the all-tournament team. Jackson and Ware were selected for the second team. The Chiefs' 104 points against Idaho State set a new tournament scoring record. [23]

Koper moved into the number two slot behind Hub Reed in career scoring at OCU in a game against St. Louis in early February. Abe punished Wells and Hunter for missing a practice by not allowing the two players to make the road trip to St. Louis. Wells and Hunter had driven all night back from a quick trip to Kentucky and missed a scheduled practice. The punishment was a near mortal blow to the players because they had invited friends and family in Kentucky to drive to St. Louis to see them play. Both were so upset with Abe that they thought about leaving OCU. However, cooler heads prevailed and both continued their excellent careers. [24]

The Chiefs were up and down in the second half of the season, losing four in a row, including defeats at the hands of Nebraska and Southern Methodist University.

OCU was 15-10 when the Chiefs lost their final game of the season to Creighton, after beating the Bluejays earlier in the year. Abe was frankly surprised when the Chiefs were awarded the final at-large bid for the NCAA tournament. However, he was disappointed that OCU was matched up for the first round game in Dallas against Creighton, again. The Bluejays beat the Chiefs by 11, ending OCU's season at 15-11. Future NBA star Paul Silas paced Creighton.

Koper ended his career at OCU second to Hub Reed in scoring. His 50-point explosion against North Texas State was a single-game record for the Chiefs. After the season, Koper was named to *Look Magazine's* first team as an All-American, was designated All-American by the Helms Foundation, and was selected for the 1964 United States Olympic basketball team tryouts.

Ed Nall helped Koper win All-American honors by flooding the nation's sportswriters and broadcasters with photos and information about Koper.

Abe almost ran out of adjectives to describe Koper's play. Describing a long shot in a victory

Bud Koper was an All-American for Abe's Chiefs. In his senior year, Koper was 11th nationally in big college scoring and won the scoring championship among Oklahoma Big Four schools for the second straight year. Courtesy Oklahoma City University.

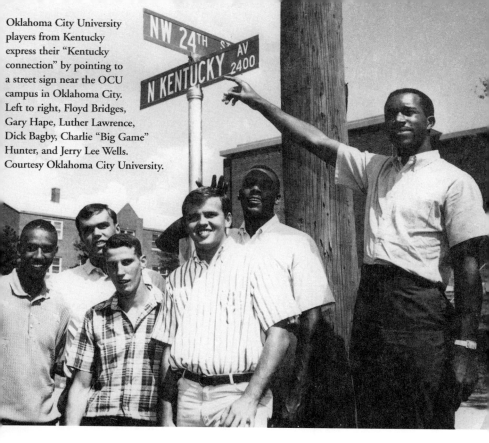

Oklahoma City University players from Kentucky express their "Kentucky connection" by pointing to a street sign near the OCU campus in Oklahoma City. Left to right, Floyd Bridges, Gary Hape, Luther Lawrence, Dick Bagby, Charlie "Big Game" Hunter, and Jerry Lee Wells. Courtesy Oklahoma City University.

over San Francisco, Abe said, "It searched out the bucket like a Nike missile." Abe described his game plan, "We don't have any picks or plays for Koper. We don't set him up. The only instruction Bud has is, 'When we throw you the ball, do what you want with it.'" [25]

Eddie Jackson, Charlie "Big Game" Hunter, Jerry Lee Wells, and sophomore Gary Gray paced the Chiefs in 1964-1965. Wells was the leading scorer and Ware, who was killed years later in a logging accident, became the Chiefs' best rebounder in history, picking up 27 rebounds in one game against Houston. Abe sometimes used the tallest lineup in the country with Jackson, Ware, John Hopkins, Joe Gibbon, and transfer student Gary Hape.

Gray, from Fort Cobb, Oklahoma, was a promising sophomore for Abe. He had set a freshman scoring record the previous season with just under 28 points per game. He scored 50 points in a freshman game against Central State College of Edmond. Abe leaned on Dick Bagby as a playmaker. Ware, who gained 20 pounds in the off-season, weighed in at 212 pounds and was strong on the boards for the Chiefs.

The Chiefs went 21-10 with big wins over Southern Methodist University, Creighton, Rice, and Houston. The first home game at Frederickson Fieldhouse was exciting as Gray hit a 30-foot jump shot with four seconds remaining to clinch a 78-76 victory over Centenary. OCU scoring was spread around. Hunter scored 31 points, with 11 rebounds, in a win over Wyoming while Wells was top scorer with 25 points in a gigantic victory over Southern Methodist University. [26]

Abe was big on Jerry Lee Wells, who had finished high school at 17 and laid out a year before going to college. Abe described Wells as "for his size, as good a player as I've had in 10 years at OCU." Abe called the Wells the complete player, "with a fine sense of balance, hits inside or out and can play 40 minutes without relief." [27]

Abe was comical with his players both on and off the court. Once guard Dick Bagby approached Abe in the school cafeteria and complained of having a bad cold. Abe shot back, "That's probably from the draft from all them ol' boys rushin' past you with the ball." [28]

Oklahoma City University finished second, for the umpteenth time, in the All-College, losing to DePaul University in the finals. Wells had a career-high 34 points in an early second-half victory against Hardin-Simmons.

After losing to Denver University in mid-January, Abe took his team on the road trip of a lifetime, to Hawaii, where they beat the University of Hawaii twice in a row. When Gary Gray asked about when the Chiefs could practice, Abe quipped, "Practice? These guys are just five feet tall in Hawaii." [29]

Abe thrived on showing his players new and exciting parts of the world. On the trip to Hawaii, Abe introduced many of his players to Chinese food for the first time. When the team began ordering from the Chinese menu, Ware ordered a steak. Abe laughed until he cried. [30]

While in Hawaii, the Chiefs scrimmaged against an armed forces all-star team. It was good practice for Abe's players to stay sharp while enjoying the beaches and the vacation atmosphere of paradise.

The tired Chiefs returned to Colorado Springs, Colorado, and lost to Air Force 86-74. At home, Jackson completed his eligibility by scoring 22 points in a win over West Texas State.

At 19-9, OCU won another trip to the NCAA post-season tournament as a leading independent. In the first round, the Chiefs beat Colorado State 70-68, lost in the second round to San Francisco 91-67, and then won a consolation game against Brigham Young University 112-102. In the Colorado State game, Abe almost had a heart attack when the game wound down to a final shot. He did not want the ball to go to Ware. Abe thought Ware's thick glasses prevented him from getting a good look at the basket. Abe picks up the story, "We had a rule, you don't throw the ball at Ware. If he gets it any other way, shoot it. So he's got the ball and he's getting his glasses adjusted at half court. Gary Gray sees what's going on, comes over and slaps the ball out of Ware's hands, and goes down the sideline. He gets flogged and throws the ball to 'Big Game' who has circled to the other side. They reverse Charlie who shoots the ball as he falls out of bounds. He hit the bottom of the net and we win the game." [31]

The funniest thing about the spring of 1965 that jogs the memory of "Big Game" Hunter concerned eating chicken. Hunter and Wells could not go home to Kentucky during Easter break. The OCU cafeteria was closed so Abe gave the players a handful of Kentucky Fried Chicken coupons. After eating three meals a day at Kentucky Fried Chicken for several days, Hunter and Wells decided they could not stand the sight of more chicken. They showed up on Abe's doorstep with their complaint. Understanding the overdose of chicken, Abe gave the young men a few dollars to eat on until the cafeteria reopened. Needless to say, Hunter and Wells shied away from chicken for weeks. [32]

ABOVE: Abe was presented a new Chevrolet Caprice by OCU boosters in March, 1966. Courtesy The Daily Oklahoman.

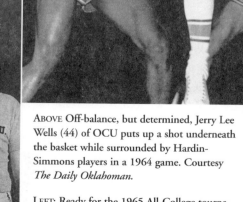

ABOVE Off-balance, but determined, Jerry Lee Wells (44) of OCU puts up a shot underneath the basket while surrounded by Hardin-Simmons players in a 1964 game. Courtesy *The Daily Oklahoman.*

LEFT: Ready for the 1965 All-College tournament are OCU's Charley "Big Game" Hunter, left, and Abe. Courtesy *The Daily Oklahoman.*

BELOW: Abe's Big Four, James Ware, Gary Gray, Jerry Lee Wells, and Big Game Hunter, were immortalized in this 1965 cartoon. Courtesy Abe Lemons.

Abe's team in 1965-1966 was the winningest Chiefs team to that point in basketball history. With Ware as one of the nation's top college rebounders, and with the scoring of Wells, the Chiefs finished at 24-5.

On December 1, the Chiefs kicked off the season in a special doubleheader game played at the State Fairgrounds Arena in Oklahoma City. OCU was pitted against Oklahoma University before 6,800 fans. Hunter and Gray were the stars as the Chiefs beat the Sooners 74-71. Hunter sank two free throws with two minutes left and Gray drilled two charity tosses at the 52-second mark to put the game out of reach for OU.

Abe had two Kopers, from Rocky, Oklahoma, both sopho- mores, on his 1965-1966 squad. 6'4" Henry Koper was a brother of former star Bud and a cousin to 6'5" Ron who led the OCU freshmen team in scoring the previous year with a 20-point aver- age. Rocky only had a population of 250 and Abe seemed to cream the basketball crop from that rural Oklahoma school year after year.

The Abe Lemons-Rocky, Oklahoma connection is a legend. From 1959 to 1964, Abe gave basketball scholarships to seven play- ers from Rocky, a school that had only 55 students from the ninth to twelfth grades. Gary Hill and Bud Koper became major college All-Americans. All seven players, Hill, Bud Koper, Ron Koper, Henry Koper, Jay Harris, Dennis Harris, and Steve Fite completed college and are successful.

Abe took his players from Buffalo, New York, to Hawaii in 1965-1966. In between, the Chiefs won the 30th All-College with impressive victories over Virginia Tech University, Bowling Green, and Rhode Island. Ware was voted the tourney's Most Valuable Player.

Abe liked his players' attitude. Some of his stars disliked being substituted for even in practice. The Chiefs lost only their third game of the season on January 8, 1966, at Memphis, bounced on by the Blue and White of Memphis State 97-87. Coming home, OCU began a ten-game winning streak, knocking out good teams such as Air Force, Creighton, Nebraska, West Texas, and Loyola of New Orleans along the way.

A home win against Memphis State, a game broadcast around the world on the Armed Forces Radio and Television Service, was especially sweet revenge for Gary Gray and other Chief players who had been infuriated in an earlier game that season in Memphis in which the crowd yelled racial slurs at OCU's black players. [33]

Even with a 19-3 record and scoring an average of 96 points a game, OCU was still not ranked in the top ten in the wire service polls in mid-February. Abe was not unhappy about that, "I'd just as soon stay out of there [the top 10]. The only time I want to be rated is at the end of the season. Those ratings are nice for your scrapbook. You can say, 'Look, I was no. 10—for two whole days. And I was fired two days later.'" [34] The Chiefs beat Portland University 124-96, the most points an Abe Lemons' team had ever scored.

In Chicago, the Chiefs prepared to play Loyola University. The pre-game warm up for OCU was less than artistic-looking. Chiefs players were falling all over each other, tripping on their feet, and missing everything thrown toward the bucket. Abe bowed his head and thought to himself, "This is gonna be a long night. We're gonna get killed." The warm up was so bad that Loyola players stood at half court and laughed.

However, when the opening horn sounded, OCU hit the floor and "shot the lights out." Wells scored 36 points and Gray added another 35 as the Chiefs pounded Loyola 105-88. After the game Abe heard his players laughing and shaking hands a little more exuberantly than usual. Upon immediate inquiry, Abe discovered that his players had purposely looked awful in the pre-game warmup. There was added incentive when the Loyola player assigned to guard Wells told him during the warm up that he was going to hold the OCU star to four points that night.

Nearing the end of the season, Abe flew his Chiefs back to the paradise of Hawaii, throttling the University of Hawaii 104-77 and 104-76 in back-to-back wins. The Chiefs were ranked number three in the country as they beat Centenary in the final regular season game and headed to the NCAA tourney for the fourth straight year. Only Kentucky matched the Chiefs' accomplishment in that department.

After the season ended in March, 1966, Jerry Lee Wells became another in the long line of All-American basketball players produced by Abe Lemons and Paul Hansen at Oklahoma City University. Courtesy Oklahoma City University.

Oklahoma City University players were tired from their long trip to Hawaii. After being in the islands for eight days, the Chiefs had to wait ten hours in the Honolulu airport for the flight to Los Angeles. The time difference finally caught up with the Chiefs in their first-round matchup with unbeaten Texas Western University, coached by Don Haskins, a former basketball star at Oklahoma State University. Texas Western's name was later changed to the University of Texas at El Paso (UTEP).

The Chiefs could never get their offense going and lost to the Miners, the eventual national champion, 89-74, even though Hunter scored 31 points.

The loss to Texas Western in the NCAA was the last game for the Big Three for the Chiefs; Wells, Ware, and Hunter. Abe called Wells "an All-American if there ever was one." Wells led the Chiefs in scoring in final two years on the varsity. When he scored 41 points on a road trip even though he was sick, Abe said, "I think I'll stand him out in the cold and see if he can't catch pneumonia." Wells scored the winning basket in a mid-season game over Nebraska, saying later in the dressing room, "I was scared to death. I had to hit it." [35]

Phil Van Ostrand, sports editor of the OCU campus newspaper, called Ware "a mild-mannered senior from the south." Ware was nicknamed "Weasel" and Abe told reporters he could not win without "Weasel" in the lineup. [36]

Hunter's talents were summed up by Abe, "He's a sweet ball player." Hunter led the chiefs in field goal percentage his senior season. Hunter stayed around the OCU campus after the spring semester to take a couple of summer courses he needed to complete graduation requirements.

When Hunter was ready to return home to his native Kentucky, he approached Abe with a problem. He had no money to get

One of the drawing cards Abe used to entice outstanding high school players to enroll at OCU was the exciting road schedule. Here the Chiefs pose for a team photo after arriving in Hawaii to play games against military teams and the University of Hawaii. Left to right, back row, Floyd Bridges, Charlie "Big Game" Hunter, Henry Koper, Ron Koper, Gary Gray, Jerry Lee Wells, James "Weasel" Ware, Abe, and one of several OCU students who paid their own way to make the trip to Hawaii. Bottom row, left to right, Frank O'Brien , Gene Morrison, a walk on who   actually played in a game for Abe, and other students who accompanied the Chiefs. Courtesy Oklahoma City University.

home. Abe loaned Hunter $30. A few years later, when Abe was recruiting in Kentucky and saw Hunter, Hunter could not talk about anything else but the outstanding $30 loan. Two months passed and Abe received a $30 check from Hunter, who had landed a job as a school teacher. Hunter wrote, "Sorry I am just now writing. I made a debt and said I would pay it back. Here it is." Sportswriter Frank Boggs, who was in Abe's office when the letter arrived, saw the seasoned coach get a little misty-eyed.

Before Christmas that year, Abe wrote a letter to Hunter's three-year-old daughter Annetta Lynn. He told the girl, "I know little girls have a hard time getting money around Christmas. I have little girls of my own and know how much extra expense there is at Christmas. So here's $30 for you to buy your mommy and daddy something for Christmas." [37]

Hunter was drafted by the Boston Celtics but a torn ligament in his ankle kept him from performing well in camp. He went home to Kentucky and began a distinguished career as an educator and human resources specialist for major corporations such as Cummins Diesel, Olin, and Mobil Chemical. In 1999 Hunter was teaching "world of work" classes at a Kentucky Job Corps center, using the same information about how to live in the real world he had learned from Abe 35 years before. [38]

—*Chapter Eleven*—

Creating a Myth

**I ain't much for them little-bitty places
you got to swap planes to get to.**

Abe Lemons

BECAUSE OKLAHOMA CITY UNIVERSITY WAS AN INDEPENDENT,
Abe had to start all over each season to find teams to play his Chiefs
to fill out the schedule. He walked a tightrope with opposing coaches
who did not want to play OCU if they thought the Chiefs were
either really good or really bad. Abe was forced to create a myth.

When Abe knew in his heart that his team would be a winner
the next season, he told other coaches, "I've got some good kids but
I just don't think they'll do anything." More often than not, opposing coaches bit on Abe's offer, relishing an easy win over the Chiefs
the next year.

When the game was finally played, and OCU won, Abe's job
was to make the other coach feel like the Chiefs were just lucky that
night. It often seemed that Abe was not bragging on his team
enough, but the pessimistic view of the future was absolutely necessary to line up willing future victims.

The Chiefs' extensive travels were necessary for two reasons.
Abe had to hustle games at each end of the continent because

most colleges and universities were tied up in conference schedules after the Christmas break. Also, Abe used exotic trips to Hawaii and New York City as a recruiting tool. He asked prospects, "Where can you go to school, except OCU, and get to lay on the beach in Hawaii and attend a Broadway play in New York City?"

Because Abe always struggled to play within his meager basketball budget, he often agreed to play games at the opponent's home court, for a certain price. He once told Miami of Florida head coach Bruce Hale, "Let's play a home-and-home series, but let's play 'em both at your place." Abe suspected there was more for his players to do in Miami than in Oklahoma City. [1]

Abe knew his scheduling tactics created a tough schedule. The long hours of travel wore his players down. "We have a lot of intersectional games," Abe told reporters, "When you move out of your area, you're asking for trouble. Very few people move out of their bailiwick as much as we do." [2]

There was one good thing about OCU being an independent. If Abe disliked playing a team, or thought he was cheated by officials in a certain city, he could simply quit scheduling that team. After Houston beat OCU for the tenth straight time in Houston in 1965, Abe vowed to never return. The Houston crowd had thrown wadded-up cups on the floor after Chief James Ware had gotten into a fight with Houston's Jim Jones. Abe said after the game, "I've already got 'em scheduled for next year, but I'm not coming down. I'll let 'em sue me. We'll never play 'em again as long as I'm coach." [3] Abe had forgotten about a rematch with Houston in a few weeks, which OCU won. However, Abe refused to go to Houston the next year and never played the Cougars until he was forced to at Texas, as a member of the Southwest Conference.

It was tough on Abe to take his team into hostile territory. When he played Loyola of Chicago, it was quite an experience. Abe recalled, "You take 10 guys, yourself, and a radio announcer and go into a hostile crowd of 13,000. Every time you score, there's dead silence. They score, and a band plays and everyone of the 13,000 cut loose." [4]

Abe recognized another benefit to a schedule of games scattered across the continent, "A lot of our games are so far away that by the time the news travels back home I can beat it there and tell the local newspapers anything I want." 5

Abe leaned heavily on Gary Gray in the 1966-1967 season. Gray, a 6'1" Delaware from Fort Cobb, Oklahoma, had been spotted by Abe when Gray attended an OCU practice session to see his idol, Eugene Tsoodle. Gray sank a few practice shots himself, prompting Abe to give him an OCU tee-shirt and say, "We want you." 6

Gray was an Oklahoma All-Stater in high school and was a human scoring machine. He set a Frederickson Fieldhouse record with 50 points in a game as a freshman, hit a season-high 36 as a junior, maintained an excellent grade-point average, and had plenty of time to play with his young son.

In 1966-1967, OCU was the highest scoring team in the country and Gray was the sixth leading scorer in major college ranks. Gray later reflected on how precise Abe's methods were in sizing up opponents, "He had an incredible ability to look at film of another team and develop a way to exploit the other players' weaknesses. We had no set offense or set defense. Abe could change the way we played every game. But it worked. When Abe figured out what we were going to do for a particular game, he then left the details to our world-class assistant coach, Paul Hansen." 7

Before the first game, *Dell Sport* picked OCU to finish seventh in the nation. But the season began dismally, with three straight losses to New Mexico State, Southern Methodist University, and North Texas. The Chiefs were 2-4 going into the All-College tournament in December.

Oklahoma City University was not even seeded in the All-College but surprised everyone, including Abe, by beating Massachusetts and Stanford in the first two games. No one gave the Chiefs even a slim chance to win the title game against Montana State. However, OCU rose to the occasion and forced the Bobcats into overtime before losing 82-81.

Abe's 1967 Chiefs. Courtesy *The Daily Oklahoman.*

Abe stopped going to the dressing room after games, explaining, "You don't know what to say if you lose, and there's nothin' to say if you win. It's just like going to a funeral. What can you say? You just walk by to let them know you're there." [8]

Gray was the high-point man in almost every game of the 1966-1967 season. His supporting cast included top rebounders 6'9" Gary Williams and junior college transfer Houston Thomas, Ron and Henry Koper, Melvin Workman, Floyd Bridges, Frank O'Brien, a 6'0" transfer from Kilgore, Texas Junior College, and Rich Travis, who Abe thought might be the Chiefs' leader of the future.

After the All-College, OCU beat Texas Christian University and Centenary. In a swing through the South, the Chiefs lost to Miami of Florida and Loyola of New Orleans but upended Jacksonville. Heading west, Gray set two new scoring records against West Texas State. He scored 55 points on 23 field goals, long before the introduction of the three-point shot, in a game which the Chiefs won

128-103. Gray's record-setting performance was helped by teammates who began feeding him the ball when they saw him hitting buckets from about any spot on the court. OCU's other guard, Rich Travis, scored 31 points. The 86 points scored by the Chiefs two guards in the game may be an all-time basketball record. [9] In the West Texas State game, Gray broke Bud Koper's 50-point and 21 field-goal record and was the fifth leading scorer in the nation going into February.

On a road trip way out west, to Hawaii again, the Chiefs set a team record by beating Hawaii

GARY GRAY
GUARD
1967 ALL-AMERICA

ABOVE: All-American Gary Gray led the Chiefs to a 16-10 record in 1966-1967. Courtesy Oklahoma City University.

LEFT: Gary Gray drives past a Centenary player on his way to another basket in a January, 1964 game at Frederickson Fieldhouse. After the super successful season, the Chiefs' Club, headed up by former Chief basketball player Roger Holloway, presented Abe with a brand new Chevrolet and assistant coach Hansen with a color television.

by 48 points, 133-85. That record fell the following night as OCU romped over Hawaii 116-63, a 53-point margin.

Returning to North America, OCU finished the season by winning eight of its last nine games. Wins over Creighton, Temple, Jacksonville, Loyola of New Orleans, and four other teams overshadowed a loss to LaSalle. [10]

In the final game of the season, Gray became the third highest scorer in OCU history and went out in a blaze of glory, hitting 41 points. He was selected All-American and almost won the national scoring championship with 715 points, a 27.5 per game average. Gray was drafted by the Cincinnati Royals of the National Basketball Association. After a short time in the NBA, he became a successful banker before he changed careers and graduated from the Harvard University law school at age 45. He now heads a major international investment capital company in Houston, Texas. [11]

Ron Koper was one of the best foul shooters in the country in the 1966-1967 season, hitting over 90 percent of his attempts. Travis set an OCU sophomore scoring record. Roger Zelnick in *The Campus* praised two senior Chiefs, Gray and O'Brien, who "never backed away from a tussle for the ball because they knew that possession means victory." [12]

With a record of 16-10, the Chiefs were passed over by the tournament selection committees of both the NCAA and the NIT.

In September, 1967, Abe led a group of college coaches on a United States State Department-sponsored tour of military installations in Spain, England, and Germany. Abe and other coaches, including Vic Bubas of Duke and Hugh Durham of Florida State, put on basketball clinics for American servicemen. Abe balked at getting his passport photo made, explaining that they never made him do anything like that in Walters. At the news conference announcing the European trip, Abe looked at reporters seriously and said, "You realize in the future I won't have as much time for you. As a representative of the United States government I'll probably have to give you a lot of 'yes' and 'no' answers." [13]

The Chiefs were much improved in 1967-1968. At the urging of the Oklahoma City All Sports Association, the Chiefs moved

The Chiefs surprised most everyone by winning the 1966 All-College tournament in Oklahoma City. Left to right, Gene Tsoodle, Rich Travis, and Abe admire the All-College trophy. Courtesy *The Daily Oklahoman.*

their home games from Frederickson Fieldhouse on the OCU campus to the State Fair Arena, in hopes of attracting larger crowds. Season tickets in the amount of $8,000 were sold, assuring the rent would be paid on the State Fair facility. OCU students did not like the arrangement and Abe felt like a man without a home, saying, "It feels like we're on the road all time." Columnist Frank Boggs urged OCU to bring in a brass band and liven up the State Fair Arena. Boggs wrote, "Up until now it has been like watching television with the sound turned off." [14]

Abe predicted a banner season. The Chiefs were led by Rich Travis, Joe Hayes, Willie Watson, Ron Koper, and Houston Thomas, a Chicago, Illinois, native who corralled 20 or more rebounds in three different games. Abe was blessed with a strong bench that included Charlie Wallace, Mike Wachob, 6'8" Ardell England, Melvin Workman, and senior Henry Koper, from OCU's "farm club," Rocky, Oklahoma. Koper wore number 25, the same as his famous cousin, Bud. Another senior, 6'5" Floyd Bridges from Glasgow, Kentucky, had one of the softest and most accurate shots on the squad. John "Java" Vas, a 6'5" senior from Chicago Heights, Illinois, was a transfer from Cameron Junior College in Lawton, Oklahoma.

Junior guard Rich Travis broke Bud Koper's Frederickson Fieldhouse record by scoring 52 points in an opening game victory over North Texas State University. Travis dropped in OCU's first five field goals and had 29 of the Chiefs' 53 points at half-time. "T," as Travis was known, had been recruited by Abe out of Bowling Green High Street High School in Kentucky. Abe first noticed Travis when the youngster was in the eighth grade and hung around basketball games Abe attended. It was easy to spot Travis who was 6'1" by the time he was 14 years old and was heavily recruited by the University of Michigan, Western Kentucky University, and Davidson College. While Travis was still in high school, Abe sent him postcards from exotic destinations on OCU road trips. [15]

In 1967-1968, Travis broke the OCU scoring record with 808 points, an average of 29.9 points per game, despite being double-teamed much of the season. When Travis was initially overlooked in the 1968 Olympic basketball trials, Abe was furious and said no way were there 48 better players in the country than Travis. A few days later Travis was added to the tryout squad.

Travis was often triple-teamed when he headed for the basket. He went into the air to put up a shot with such force that his momentum carried him off the court. When the Chiefs played at Frederickson Fieldhouse, young fans such as Patrick McGuigan, now the chief editorial writer for *The Daily Oklahoman*, banded together and cushioned Travis' fall out of bounds. [16]

The Chiefs won their first eight games in the fall of 1967, including victories over Texas Christian University, Southern Methodist University, Baylor, Fordham University, Auburn, and

Brigham Young University. The last three wins came over powerful opponents in the All-College tournament in Oklahoma City. Travis was named the tourney's Most Valuable Player. After the All-College, OCU went cold, losing to Nevada Southern and Portland University, beating San Francisco, and then losing to Creighton and West Texas State.

After semester break the Chiefs began another long winning streak, beating Southern Methodist University, Arkansas, Denver, Loyola of New Orleans, Centenary, and Creighton. Travis, 6'8 1/2" Watson, and Wallace were the scoring leaders during the January blitz of opponents. The victory over Arkansas was a 92-90 overtime win, the first time an OCU team had ever beaten the Razorbacks. Travis led OCU with 35 points. Sophomore Joe Hayes came into the game late and inspired the team with good passes, fast breaking, and good shooting. [17]

A fight broke out during the game against Loyola in the old fieldhouse on the Loyola campus in New Orleans. OCU players fended off irate fans with folding chairs until police entered the fray and restored order. Abe, dressed to the gills in a new dark green suit and alligator shoes, told a reporter, "They tore my suit and that's OK. But if they had stepped on my 'gators, we'd still be out there fightin'." [18]

Travis, who later attended law school at California State University and now heads up a labor relations law consulting firm in a suburb of Detroit, Michigan, was the fourth highest scorer in the nation's college ranks as the regular season wound down. The Chiefs finished the season with an incredible 20-6 record and received a bid to the NIT in New York City.

New York sportswriters called Abe the "Jonathan Winters of coaching," as Abe's reputation preceded him to the Big Apple. Abe walked into Madison Square Garden and whispered, "Whoo-ee, look at this place. 19,000 people. More than they got in some counties in Oklahoma."

Oklahoma City University played Duke University in the first game of the NIT at the Garden. The first half was a disaster for the Chiefs who could not shoot, hang on to the ball, or pass accurately.

The Blue Devils led 49-28 at intermission. Immediately after the half-time buzzer sounded, Abe had half his players don white jerseys, while the other half remained in the OCU blue road jerseys. Abe threw a ball on the court and told the players to scrimmage.

Fans listening by radio and the players themselves were shocked. Abe later said he was not trying to embarrass the players but they were tight and he was trying to loosen them up. Abe was frustrated, telling his players, "Fellas, all I want you to do is hustle a little, so they don't boo us right out of town. Make up your mind to do something and do it. I don't care what it is, do it. If you want to throw the ball into the third row, do it. Do something." [19]

The Chiefs could never overcome the half-time deficit and lost to Duke 97-81. [20] Abe said, " I felt like that rat in the trap. I don't want the cheese. I just wanted to get out of the trap." [21] There was even a fight during the game that did not end until the scorers' table at courtside was knocked over.

After the season, on May 9, 1969, Abe was presented a list of grievances by several of his black players. Senior Floyd Bridges was the spokesman for the upset players that included England, Art Yancy, Hayes, Watson, and Wallace. All-American Rich Travis did not take part in a meeting with Abe in which the grievances were presented.

Abe was irritated by the 14 grievances presented him. Some were serious, some were funny, and, Abe thought, "Most were stupid." [22] The grievances were:

1. We feel that there is unnecessary "bitching" toward the players during regular practice sessions and in the games.

2. We feel that there aren't enough black freshmen being recruited.

3. We feel that we have been definitely overlooked after the home basketball games concerning meals.

4. We feel that we should have some type of transportation to drive, since none of the black athletes have cars.

5. We were left on our own this past season to get a way out to the arena for the home games and we feel that this is an injustice.

6. We feel that you should provide meal tickets for the black athletes for meals on Sunday evenings, during the season and off-season as you have done on certain Sundays in the past.

7. We are tired of former alumni coming up to the black athletes after home games congratulating them and then not speaking to the black athletes on the streets and in the public.

8. We feel there should be a better communication between the coaching staff and the parents of black athletes, especially the parents of out-of-state black athletes.

9. We feel we are being discriminated against when former alumni go on away trips and take our fellow white teammates out and spend money on them, while the alumni leave the black athletes in their hotel rooms and don't give them a penny.

10. We feel that you should start or at least play five black athletes at once, if they have the ability and out play their fellow white teammates in practice and in games.

11. We feel that you hold personal grudges toward athletes and usually don't play them in games and in practices because of personal reasons.

12. We feel that at least 12 athletes should be given a chance to travel and that those athletes should be chosen on ability and not on your personal feelings toward them.

13. We feel that you have shown favoritism toward certain black athletes while others are overlooked and treated unequal.

14. We feel that we are adults and should be treated with the respect and dignity of young men, not as slaves working for a slave driver. This "bitching" is very sensitive to black athletes because of the way our fathers and forefathers were treated in the past.

The list of grievances closed with a strong statement, "These grievances...can not and will not be tolerated in the future." [23]

Abe's problems with some of his black players developed into the biggest storm of his coaching career. He refused to meet with only the black players, pointing out that most of the complaints concerned the whole team. Abe answered the grievances one by one.

He sarcastically said he would no longer bitch at the black players but would do his best to speak "in a low voice."

Abe told the black players that many of the requests, such as for transportation, were contrary to NCAA policies and would result in sanctions for OCU if he complied with their wishes. Abe did admit that he might have held grudges against some players for personal reasons, saying, "I don't like lazy guys. I don't like guys who don't hustle. I don't like guys who don't work." [24]

In sarcastic terms only Abe could get by with, he responded to the allegations about him bitching at players, "I am a bitching kind of coach for all who play me. But I will make an exception in your place. I promise not to holler at you or bitch at you. Do you mind if I bitch and holler at the white players? As for working for a slave driver, you won't have to run wind sprints or do any of the conditioning drills. Do you mind if the white players run these drills? When you mess up on plays over and over again, that will be OK. But do you mind if I get after the white players and maybe even give them a penalty when they continue to make the same dumb mistake over and over when they know better?" [25]

A well known Oklahoma City civil rights leader, State Senator E. Melvin Porter, involved himself in the fray when black players told the press they were suspended for not following rules. Porter sent a scathing telegram to OCU President Dr. John F. Olson, including tart comments such as "Negroes are not slaves anymore even in modern America. When the day comes we can't express ourselves to the self-indoctrinated white master, then perhaps we need to re-examine our methods of communication. Your actions indicate the bigots you are." [26]

Abe was pressured by Dr. Olson to create a plan so the black players could be reinstated to the basketball team. Olson and the OCU Board of Trustees fully supported Abe's position but wanted a quick resolution. Abe began cleaning out his desk and told Dr. Olson that maybe he should just "go on down the road." Olson again expressed his support for Abe and talked the coach out of leaving.

Abe typed his responses and asked the players to sign the agreement. Five of the six players said they wished the incident had never occurred. Those five were reinstated and Abe promised to continue to play his best players and create a winning, family-style atmosphere that was the hallmark of his coaching tradition.

In 1968 Abe turned down a job offer to coach at Centenary College in Shreveport, Louisiana, telling *The Daily Oklahoman,* "It was an attractive offer, and one which I carefully considered. But Oklahoma City is my home, and my association with the city and with the university has always been pleasant. I intend to stay at OCU." [27]

— Chapter Twelve —

Wide-open Offense

I'd rather be a football coach. That way you know you can't lose more than 11 games a season.

Abe Lemons

ABE WAS POPULAR AS A SPEAKER AT COACHES' CLINICS AROUND THE country. He gave coaches the best of two worlds, his tremendous knowledge of the intricacies of basketball and the lighter side of life. He once told an audience of high school coaches in Tulsa, "This year I'm gonna show 'em my GMA offense—General Milling Around. That's what we run." [1]

Abe's love for wide-open offense came early in his coaching career. As an assistant to Doyle Parrack at OCU, Abe watched other teams open up their offense and drift away from ball-control. Abe's duty as Parrack's assistant was to mimic the next opponent's offense, which often was run-and-gun, or at least the 1950s version of that type of offense.

Abe had some definitive feelings about offense, "Some folks don't realize it, but it takes twice as much preparation to be a ball-control club...A wide-open game relaxes your boys more. There's not as much mental pressure on the kids. And a shooter needs freedom. It's a matter of necessity. You can't go giving a shooter all kinds of instructions about what to do with the ball. When I get a kid who can shoot, I like to leave him alone. I don't want to bother him with a lot of detail." [2]

Throughout his coaching career, Abe emphasized offense, telling a *Sports Illustrated* writer, "When you win, you gotta win with your offense, because you have to score more points than the other people. You can't tie, like in football. Show me a team that doesn't win with its offense and I'll show you a crooked scorekeeper." [3]

Abe Lemons and North Carolina State University basketball coach Jim Valvano, left, were two of the most sought-after speakers at coaches' clinics in the 1970s. Courtesy Oklahoma City University.

Abe was known in coaching circles for giving his players great latitude to use their skills and judgment. He disliked complicated maneuvers. He once quipped, "I don't care if a guy knows how to pivot. What good is it? Does he go downtown in a few years and say 'You wanna see a pivot?' What the hell good is it?" [4]

Abe tried to lull his opponents into believing that his teams were simply run-and-shoot clubs by making public statements such as, "We run what we call our Daylight Offense. The first guy who sees daylight after he crosses midcourt shoots." In reality, Abe's teams were highly disciplined and high scoring. He recruited good shooters and then built their confidence by allowing them to shoot when a reasonable shot was open. OCU stars responded, hitting near 50 percent from the field. Veteran Texas sportswriter Robert Heard said Abe's offense was not "run-and-shoot" but "run-and-score." [5]

Anyone who believed that Abe worked his players solely on offense was misdirected. Not a day went by that Abe did not instruct his players on defense. Norm Russell remembered defense occupying as much as 65-70 percent of practices during his years at OCU. [6] Abe believed defense was the hardest thing about basketball to teach. When one of his teams gave up a lot of points, he called his defense the Sieve Zone, "We leave our opponents so wide open, they get so excited they can't shoot straight." [7]

Abe's excitement about scoring more than the other team with quick baskets ran opposite to the thinking of many coaches who wanted to hold the ball. Abe knew holding the ball was not fair to the fans, "You may have a mangy team and feel like you have to hold the ball to win, but I don't like it...I'm not in favor of a 30-second clock or anything like that, though. Somebody came up with the idea of playing 'til one team gets 75 points. That sounds good, but some smart aleck would come along and hold the ball anyway, and you'd play all night and all day." [8]

Abe secretly wished that no one kept score in basketball. He just wanted his kids to play hard, learn the game, and have a good time. He once said, "My job doesn't depend on winning. We've had about four presidents at OCU and they've all said, 'Run a clean program and you've got yourself a job.' If I had to win to keep my job, I'd play Fairleigh-Dickerson [sic], Jayne Mansfield, Allegheny Subdivision, North and South Ontario, Marx Brothers College—anybody I could find." [9]

The Chiefs began the 1968-1969 season with All-American Rich Travis as the only certain starter. Abe recruited 6'6" Bob Villani from Kilgore, Texas Junior College, to help out in the rebounding department. Five players vied for the guard spot opposite Travis. Lettermen Joe Hayes, 6'3" from Columbus, Ohio, and Melvin Workman were pressed by transfer 6'0" J.S. McDaniel from Park City, Kentucky, and sophomores Bob Oleskevich and Jerry Gray. John Nelson, a 6'6" All-Stater from Wynnewood, Oklahoma, worked his way into a starting position. Abe also counted on Charles Wallace from Preston, Oklahoma, and Mike Wachob, a native of Westport, Connecticut, both 6'6", and 6'8 1/2" Willie

Rich Travis closed out his career at Oklahoma City University with 2,081 points, an incredible 26.1 per-game average over three years. Abe called Travis a player "with a perfect attitude and an unequaled desire for victory." Courtesy Oklahoma City University.

Watson from Clayton, North Carolina. [10]

Oklahoma City University lost to Texas Christian University in the season opener and then reeled off back-to-back victories over Nevada-Southern and Abilene Christian College. The Chiefs scored 113 points in the Nevada Southern game. OCU beat Texas Christian University and Georgia Tech at home but lost to Long Beach State and Loyola of Chicago on the road.

In the 1968 All-College tournament, OCU beat Tulane, lost a second round game to Louisiana State University, and was victorious over St. Bonaventure 81-71 in the consolation game. It was the heroics of "Pistol Pete" Maravich that led LSU to the win over the Chiefs. Abe thought Maravich may have been the best player he ever coached against.

In the second semester, Melvin Workman of Oklahoma City became the Chiefs' best defensive player in wins over Loyola of New Orleans, Southern Methodist University, Abilene Christian College, Arkansas, Denver, Centenary, Creighton, and Air Force.

In early February, during an 80-59 win over Centenary, Travis became OCU's all-time leading scorer when he took a pass from Charlie Wallace and drove in for a lay-up with 3:01 remaining in the first half. Travis finished the game with 25 points and a career total of 1,899, besting Hub Reed's record of 1,887 points. [11]

Against Denver, Travis hit a 17-foot jumper to push his career total points at OCU to 2,000, placing him in an elite group of college basketball players who had scored over 2,000 points by the late 1960s. The group included Oscar Robertson, Cazzie Russell, Bill Bradley, Elvin Hayes, Jerry West, Elgin Baylor, and Earl Monroe.

The Chiefs were 18-9 in 1968-1969, fueled by high scoring from Travis and Wallace, who scored almost 20 points per contest, and by the rebounding of Watson who grabbed an average of 14 rebounds per game.

In 1969-1970 the Chiefs returned to the friendly confines of Frederickson Fieldhouse on the OCU campus for their home games, a move approved by athletic department business manager and former star player Bud Koper. Koper had played pro basketball for the San Francisco Warriors for two seasons before a broken ankle put an end to his pro career.

Abe Lemons was happy after signing four Oklahoma City area players to national letters-of-intent in May, 1969. Left to right, Jim Lackey of Capitol Hill, Jerry O'Pry of Del City, Mike Polansky of Putnam City, and Larry Tribble of Midwest City. Courtesy *The Daily Oklahoman.*

Koper, Abe, and Paul Hansen had something in common in addition to serving together on the OCU staff. All of their offspring was female. Abe had two daughters and a granddaughter, Hansen had five daughters, and Koper had two daughters. [12]

With the loss of Travis, Abe turned to Villani, Nelson, and Wachob to anchor the team for the new season. Abe also depended on returning seniors Art Yancy, a 6'4" product of Quincy, Massachusetts, Wallace, Watson, and Hayes. Three juniors, Jim Stuber, 6'7" from West Orange, New Jersey, John Hoops, a 6'6" forward from the state of Washington, and 6'6" Archie Burtschi from Chickasha, Oklahoma, and one sophomore, 6'1" Bobby Hanes of Bowling Green, Kentucky, who averaged 28 points per game as a freshman, rounded out the squad.

The Chiefs won their first three games against Texas Christian University, Southern Methodist University, and Wisconsin-Milwaukee before dropping contests to Georgia Tech University and Texas Christian University.

Oklahoma City University was 4-2 going into the All-College after an impressive 101-94 upset of 11th-ranked Santa Clara on December 19. Wachob, playing in his first game of the season, scored 31 points and Wallace added 30 more.

The Chiefs were the host team for the 34th annual All-College tournament. OCU beat the University of Idaho 80-61 and was victorious in the semi-finals over Memphis State 72-58. However, All-American Calvin Murphy led his undefeated University of Niagara Purple Eagles over the Chiefs 87-75 in the All-College finals.

With only three days rest, the Chiefs headed west and lost a heartbreaking overtime game to UNLV 108-101 in Las Vegas. The next night OCU lost again, 112-80 against Long Beach State University in California. Long Beach State was coached by Jerry Tarkanian who later moved to UNLV and became one the country's best known college basketball coaches. From Long Beach, the Chiefs packed their bags and flew 2,000 miles to Alaska for four games in Anchorage and Fairbanks.

With a well-balanced attack, OCU swept through Alaska with two wins each against the University of Alaska and Alaska Methodist

University. The four wins actually did not count on the official record because the NCAA allowed only 26 games per season.

Abe had plenty of fun in Alaska. He stopped a taxi driver long enough for Frank Boggs to take his picture in front of a thermometer sign that indicated the temperature was 46 degrees below zero. Abe said, "When we get home, people will ask me why I ever brought my team up here. I'll show 'em this picture and tell 'em we came to practice freezing the ball." [13]

Abe was prepared for the Alaska winter. He bought thermal underwear, green hunting boots, and a stocking cap with slits for his eyes. Abe told a reporter later, "We went to Alaska once, and they made us honorary Alaskans. Then we went to Hawaii, and they made us honorary Hawaiians. Then we went to the Virgin Islands." [14]

John Nelson was a special player for Abe. Nelson confided in Abe that he had been recruited by 56 schools and many had offered him everything from new cars to clothing to cash for every game he suited up for. Nelson chose OCU and its genuine, legal offer of room, board, books, tuition and $15 per month for laundry money. [15]

After returning home to Oklahoma City, the Chiefs beat Southern Methodist University and Denver and continued their domination over the Arkansas Razorbacks. However, OCU cooled off and lost four consecutive games to Seattle, Denver, Hardin-Simmons, and Jacksonville. The two-point loss to Hardin-Simmons broke a 15-game home winning streak for the Chiefs. Villani's career-high 24 points was the only bright spot for OCU in the loss. Abe was livid at officials after a Hardin-Simmons player pinned a shot against the backboard. When no goal-tending call was made, Abe shot off the bench and was called for a technical foul. The two points at the charity stripe and possession of the ball allowed Hardin-Simmons to come back from a six-point deficit to win the game.

The Chiefs finished the season at 17-13, counting the four wins in Alaska. Wallace led the offense in scoring with a 23.2 per game average. Villani averaged 13.2 points per game in addition to clearing the boards eight or more times each game. Nelson averaged 9.7 points and 6.5 rebounds per game. Wachob, who led the team in scoring in the upset win over Santa Clara, averaged 12.6 points and

5 rebounds per game. [16] Watson was selected in the sixth round of the NBA draft by the Milwaukee Bucks.

The "Abe Lemons Show," a weekly televised visit with Abe, was broadcast in the late 1960s on KOCO Television in Oklahoma City. The program was produced by Bill Thrash and hosted by KOCO sports director Bill Allen. Later the show moved to WKY Television in Oklahoma City where assistant general manager Lee Allan Smith made arrangements for Thrash to produce the weekly telecast with Bob Barry as host. Smith invited University of Oklahoma football coach Barry Switzer to be a front-row guest in a live audience for Abe's first show on WKY.

The 1970-1971 Chiefs were young and inexperienced but opened the season with a win over UNLV at Frederickson Fieldhouse in December, 1970. Nelson was the only returning starter from the previous year. After the initial victory, OCU lost to Georgia Tech and Southern Methodist University, beat Texas Christian University and Miami of Florida but lost to Colorado and UNLV.

The Chiefs lost the opening round game in the All-College to Montana State University by a single point, then rebounded in the consolation bracket with wins over DePaul and Bowling Green for fifth place in the tournament. The Chiefs lost to Miami of Florida and nationally-ranked Jacksonville, led by All-American Artis Gilmore, on a road excursion to the Sunshine State.

At mid-season, the Chiefs' record stood at 8-9. OCU had a chance to even its record in a game against Tulsa. However, Tulsa won by four points and the Chiefs headed on a long road trip, losing to Loyola of New Orleans and Centenary.

Abe's forces could not get past Southern Methodist University and nationally-ranked Kansas in January but beat Centenary and Miami of Florida at home. In the Southern Methodist University contest, the Mustangs were leading 75-64 and went into a delay game. When an official failed to spot a turnover by Southern Methodist University, Abe roared off the bench and was hit with three straight technicals, automatic ejection. Referee Del Poss ordered Abe to leave the arena but Abe refused. The other official, Gene Barth, convinced Abe to at least leave the bench and sit on the first row with Southern Methodist University fans. A fan with a bandanna around his head and a string of beads around his neck sat next to Abe. Police had to intervene and force the hippie back to the student section. Abe said, "I couldn't tell if it was a student or a faculty member." [17]

The Chiefs hit the skids, dropping seven of their final eight games. Only an unexpected win over Air Force in the final game brought OCU to a 9-16 record, only the second losing season in Abe's coaching career.

Hanes missed the final eight games of the season after an emergency appendectomy. He was still the team's third-leading scorer, contributing 16.1 points per game.

One of the few promising developments of the 1970-1971 season was the play of 7'0" Norm Russell who averaged nearly 10 rebounds and scored 16.4 points per game. Russell grew up on a farm south of the tiny Kiowa County, Oklahoma town of Mountain View. He knew nothing but tractors and hay balers in the hot southwest Oklahoma summers until C.W. Sharp took over the coaching job at Mountain View High School in the summer before Russell's junior year. Sharp sent Russell to the OCU summer basketball camp. [18]

From the first time Abe and assistant coach Hansen laid eyes on Russell, they wanted him at OCU. Russell stayed extra weeks at the basketball camp for the next two summers, eating many meals at the Hansen home and flirting with the Hansen daughters. [19] Russell does not remember Abe actually coming out and asking him to attend OCU. Instead Abe and Hansen became close to Russell's parents who lived in a small house on their farm. "Sly," is the way Russell later described Abe's conversations with his parents, who did not have the financial means to travel in their 1962 Ford to see their son play basketball if he attended college at some far away school such as North Carolina or Stanford. [20]

Most of the nation's basketball powers expressed interest in Russell. UCLA coach John Wooden wrote Russell a hand-written note, inviting the Oklahoma lad to visit the west coast campus. After reviewing many schools, Russell narrowed the field to programs in the region, OCU, Houston, Oklahoma State, the University of Oklahoma and New Mexico. In the end, he chose OCU because of the respect he had for the team of Hansen and Abe and the closeness of Oklahoma City to Mountain View. [21]

Russell thought his career at OCU might be short-lived when in an early practice he hit 245-pound Willie Watson in the mouth with his elbow. Watson, a victim of severe overbite, lost blood all over the court as the trainer rushed him to a dentist. After extensive oral surgery performed by an orthodontist friend of Carol Hansen, Watson's teeth were restored and his overbite was gone. Russell had actually done Watson a favor. [22]

BELOW: Abe Lemons appeared on a wildlife television show on WKY-TV in Oklahoma City with host Don Wallace, left. Courtesy *The Daily Oklahoman.*

Russell's sophomore season turned out to be his best campaign at OCU. A highlight of his career was scoring 27 points against Artis Gilmore of Jacksonville. Before the game, Abe turned to Russell and said, "Watch out for him. You can't match up with him. He owns the lane." Russell accepted the challenge and blew away Gilmore most of the night. The only down side of gaining so much confidence in

LEFT: Abe Lemons paid an extra $10 and ordered a special Oklahoma license plate in 1970. Because he coached the Chiefs, he thought it appropriate that his tag say "Chiefs." But, when the tag came in the mail, "Chiefs" was spelled incorrectly, causing Abe to quip, "It's no wonder those guys are in the penitentiary." Courtesy *The Daily Oklahoman.*

BELOW: Abe Lemons has a big smile on his face as he watches 6'11" Norm Russell sign a letter-of-intent under the watchful eyes of his father, left, and high school coach, C.W. Sharp. Courtesy *The Daily Oklahoman.*

playing a great game against a superstar came when Russell decided to dribble around Gilmore and shoot from close in. Gilmore stuffed the ball back in Russell's face. The next time down the court Russell went back to the spot where he was shooting over Gilmore. [23]

Abe enrolled Russell in a karate class to make him tougher. Abe wanted Russell to have more confidence, suggesting, "He's such a nice guy. I thought if everybody knows he's a karate expert they'll leave him alone." Abe said he was considering allowing Russell to start out each game by giving a high kick and knocking out a ceiling light, "That oughta' make the opponents know what a vicious giant they faced." [24] Abe however had reservations about teaching Russell karate, "I just hope they don't break every bone in his body...I'd hate to have them hand me a shoe box and say, 'So solly, coach, here's your seven-footer.'" [25]

Russell was a finance major. During one game at half-time, Abe said one of the players was shooting eight for 12 for 74 percent. Russell corrected Abe, telling his coach that was only 66 percent. Abe smirked, "I sometimes wish I had my dummies back." [26]

After college Russell spurned the American Basketball Association draft and opted to attend OCU's law school. He successfully practiced law in Oklahoma City for many years after graduation and was appointed Associate District Judge of Kiowa County in 1998.

Abe took credit for landing one of his basketball players a job in the National Football League after the 1970-1971 season. John Nelson was spotted running sprints barefooted on the old OCU baseball field by Dallas Cowboys scout Cornell Green. Nelson, who was big, quick, and could jump over the roof of a car, played professional football for the Cowboys and the New England Patriots of the NFL. Nelson was also so strong that he could lift the front end of a Volkswagen beetle off the ground. [27]

The Chiefs wore new red, white, and blue uniforms in February, 1971. Abe had his players wear one blue shoe and one red sneaker. At Denver, a woman looked at the players' feet and said, "They look like clowns." Not to be outdone, Abe snapped back, "Wait 'til you see 'em play, lady." [28]

—Chapter Thirteen—

Let the Kids Play

You feel about a team like you feel about your own children.
A game is like when your child is in a recital. You just want 'em
to do what you've told 'em, not a bunch of other stuff. You just
hope they don't hit those sour notes, and then get off the stage.

Abe Lemons

ABE WAS NOT MUCH ON CURFEWS OR RULES FOR PLAYERS, ESPECIALLY
on road trips. Once in Miami, Florida, where the Chiefs were not
expected to have a chance win, he told the players to relax. Abe
recalled, "Well, sir, they went swimming every day, rode around 'til
2 in the morning—really had themselves a time. By the time the
game rolled around, the boys came dragging out onto the court,
their heads nodding. The game hadn't even started and they were
already asleep. At half-time, we trailed 60-46. But the final score
was 118 to 113, our favor. You never can tell." [1]

The reason Abe was against a team curfew was his feeling that it
was always his star that got caught. Earlier in his career, his star
Indian player Gary Gray had been caught out late. Abe said Gray
explained "the last time his folks went to sleep, someone ran off
with all their buffalo." [2]

Abe did have strict rules on the length of his players' hair. A
player once showed up for fall practice with long hair. Abe told him

the hair was okay but he could not be in the team picture. Another time Abe told a long-haired prospective player, "Where you been all summer? Oh, you just come in for the funeral?" When the player said, "What funeral?", Abe said, "Didn't your barber die?" [3] To a team manager who showed up with long, shaggy locks, Abe said, "Get it cut. But don't just go into the first barber shop and have it whacked off. Get some estimates." [4]

Abe was cognizant of the growing generation gap, "We coaches can't do some of the things we used to do," he said, "I don't mind long hair too much. I don't mind beards, and I don't mind miniskirts. I just don't like to see them on the same person." [5]

Abe was unconventional, to say the least, with how he ran his practices. He explained, "We don't do calisthenics. I used to do them at the end of practice, but I found out some of the boys were holding back, saving up for calisthenics. We don't run bleachers. I haven't had a boy who had to have a knee operation since we quit. We don't have any weights. We had a set, but somebody stole them. We figure we save about 20 minutes a day not lifting weights." [6]

Abe believed in allowing his players a certain amount of democracy. On an Alaska road trip in 1970, Abe asked John Nelson to go take a vote of the players to see if they wanted to practice. Nelson came back in five minutes and reported "a whole bunch of no's, a couple of don't cares, and one I can't." Abe said, "That settles it. I was gonna tell you, if you needed my vote to swing it, to put me down for a no." The Chiefs did not practice that day. [7]

To ensure that his players had fun, Abe would not allow them to sleep in their motel rooms all day on a road trip. Years before, when Gene Tsoodle was playing for the Chiefs, Abe rousted him out of his room in Miami Beach, Florida. Abe had other players throw Tsoodle in the water and told him, "Now you can go back to sleep or do whatever you want to, but at least in later years you can say you've been swimming in the Atlantic." [8]

Abe also had problems with some of the rules that tended to slow down basketball games. One of his ideas was, "Let's play the game without ever stopping for a free throw. Then, when the game is over, both teams will take their free shots. The PA announcer will say, 'Okay, the home team is now going to shoot 97 free throws, and then the visiting team will shoot eight,'" a reflection of Abe's feelings that his team was rarely treated fairly on the road. [9]

Abe thought the NCAA had become rule-crazy, "We got so many rules now it's scary. I guarantee you not one guy in the NCAA could pass a test on the rules. You ask 'em something and they gotta look it up." [10]

There was something different about the makeup of the 1971-1972 edition of the Chiefs varsity basketball team. Abe had heavily recruited from junior colleges and produced a volatile mix between farm boys and inner city kids.

The previous year Norm Russell had been the scoring star inside. Now Abe used sharp-shooting guards and forwards to lead his offense. Abe brought in 6'4" Ozie Edwards from Eastern Oklahoma State College where he averaged over 25 points per game. Tony Moya, a 6'5" transfer from Clarendon, Texas Junior College, and 6'4" Marvin Rich from St. Gregory's College of Shawnee, Oklahoma, bolstered the Chiefs prospects. The new shooters "never saw a shot they didn't like." [11]

Russell had difficulty with his change of roles. He respected Abe like a second father but his relationship with his coach was strained as he vehemently disagreed with Abe's selection of junior college transfers and the change of offensive strategy. Russell, who was selected as one of the nation's top 44 players to try out for the United States National team, was so unhappy with his new role that he talked privately of transferring to New Mexico for the remaining two years of his eligibility. However, Hansen talked him out of it and convinced Russell that his rebounding was a necessary ingredient for a winning year. [12]

Abe was tough on Russell and all his players in practice and in games. Russell became accustomed to the screaming, believing Abe's admonition, "When I quit screaming at you is when you need to worry. When I quit screaming, I've given up hope on you." Fortunately for Russell, Abe never stopped screaming at him. [13]

Oklahoma City University improved to 16-10 in 1971-1972 even though the Chiefs dropped their first three games to Texas

Christian University, Baylor, and Texas, and were 2-5 before beating Yale University in the Utah Classic. The Texas Christian University loss at home came despite the excitement created by a packed crowd, a newly painted Frederickson Fieldhouse, new cheerleaders and new broom girls, decked out in red and blue hot pants. Rich led the Chiefs with 29 points. Russell, in his new role as primarily a rebounder, scored only seven points. [14]

Rich and Edwards continued to pace the Chiefs' scoring as OCU beat North Texas State and Army in the first two games of the All-College after Christmas. However, the Chiefs repeated their bridesmaid role by losing to Eastern Kentucky in the All-College finals.

Between semesters, OCU beat San Francisco but lost back-to-back games to California and Baylor. After a loss to Abilene Christian College, the Chiefs came back the next night to beat Hardin-Simmons 102-100, in three overtimes, and began a 10-game winning streak, hitting at least 100 points on four occasions.

Rich, Edwards, and Russell began hitting everything they threw up as OCU beat the University of Texas at Arlington (UTA) twice, Loyola of New Orleans twice, Denver, Hardin-Simmons, Seattle, and Tulsa. In the Seattle game, Rich scored 30 points for the third time in the season and Russell added 29 points with a whopping 17 rebounds. Edwards was the number 35 scorer in the nation toward the end of the season with a 22.5 point per game average. Rich, at 22.1, was not far behind.

Hanes, the only senior on the team, broke into the top 20 in career scoring at OCU. Guard Mike Tosee harassed opposing guards with quick moves and steals and added over eight points per game in scoring.

In the middle of the second semester Abe agreed to play Oklahoma Christian College (OCC), a small-college powerhouse located in far north Oklahoma City. Some of the OCC players had bragged that their team was the best in Oklahoma and that the NCAA Chiefs could be beaten. After OCU hammered the Eagles by 40 points, 114-74, at the OCC gym, Abe commented, "Now you know. There is a difference between horses and ponies." [15]

Oklahoma City University's Ozie Edwards wins the battle of arms in a 1972 game. Courtesy *The Daily Oklahoman.*

Abe took his players to Hawaii for an exhibition game in February. It was a classic trip. Abe, always needing money to supplement his slim athletic department budget, accepted a substantial travel check from the University of Hawaii and then convinced commanders of the Air Force's Military Airlift Command to allow OCU players to hitch a free ride from the west coast to Hawaii. In exchange for the free passage, Abe agreed to put his players on the court in two-a-day exhibition games against Navy, Marine, and Air Force service teams. The Chiefs stayed at the Holiday Inn on Waikiki Beach for 10 days. They returned to Oklahoma City tanned and in great condition. [16]

In the summer of 1972 Abe was in Munich, West Germany, for the summer Olympics. He agreed to send letters to the *Oklahoma City Times*, reporting on his German adventure. The letters were hilarious. One epistle pointed out, "The one big observation I have made is if a country wanted to capture this place, don't bomb the fuel depots, factories, or forts. Bomb the breweries and bakeries. They could not last a week." [17] Using his Oklahoma humor, Abe wrote, "The best ticket is to the finals of the hammer throw. Now

LEFT: Taking time out for a friendly discussion, Abe tries to get the official word from referee Sturdy Wanamaker on just why he got a technical foul. Courtesy *The Daily Oklahoman.*

RIGHT: Marvin Rich of Oklahoma City University jumps high for another shot over the outstretched arms of Tulsa's Willie Biles, who was satisfied with his defensive efforts which held Rich to "only" 30 points in a January, 1973 game. Courtesy *The Daily Oklahoman.*

I know lots of folks in Oklahoma City and Walters will probably wonder why anyone wants to throw their hammer, but they do, and not only do they throw it, this is for the championship of the world, and I will be there." [18]

Abe had an idea how to make a million dollars. After UCLA coach John Wooden invited Abe to speak at a coaches clinic, Abe tried out his idea on a reporter, "I just figured out a way to make as much money as Wooden. This season, we are going to do everything exactly the same as usual. We will practice the same hours, go through the same routines, make the same road trips, stay at the same hotels. But we're gonna change one minor thing. We're not going to show up for the games. As you know, the penalty for forfeiting a game is two points. We'll lose all our games 2-0. When all the coaches look at the national statistics and see where OCU held everybody to an average of two points a game, then I'll write a book on defense and sell a million copies." 19

Abe was optimistic about chances for his 1972-1973 team to be one of the finest squads in the country. Beginning his 18th year as head coach of the Chiefs, Abe counted on 11 returning veterans, including four starters, and six new players.

Oklahoma City University opened the season with a one-point victory over the University of Texas at Arlington and then prepared for an in-state showdown against Oklahoma State in Oklahoma City's Myriad Convention Center. The Chiefs were accustomed to seeing OSU play a slow-down brand of basketball but the Cowboys had changed their strategy because of the new 30-second shooting clock instituted in the Big Eight Conference. As an independent, OCU was not bound by the rule. However, Abe, liking the idea of the Cowboys not holding the ball all night, agreed to be bound by the new rule.

Rich and Edwards hit 29 and 24 points respectively as the Chiefs beat a much taller OSU team 90-72. OCU won two games in successive weeks against Texas Christian University and beat California before heading to Austin to take on the University of Texas.

The Chiefs surprised Texas and beat the Longhorns 79-77. Paul Hansen had to run the team when Abe was ejected from the game for arguing with the officials.

In the All-College, OCU beat St. Francis College 109-81 but then fell to Long Beach State by two points and Florida State by 14 points. Abe was inducted into the All-College Hall of Fame.

Before the second semester began, Abe took the Chiefs on one of his patented, fun west coast trips. OCU went into the unfriendly fieldhouse at UNLV in Las Vegas and beat the Runnin' Rebels 81-73. Hansen again had to take over the team because Abe was kicked out in the first 45 seconds of the game. OCU player James Washington had a tooth knocked out during a collision with a UNLV player in one of the first plays of the contest. Abe picked the tooth up from the court, showed it to an official, and said, "This would be a foul in some places." Abe held the tooth up in front of a television camera, making his point that the referees had missed an obvious foul against Washington.

After the game Abe was greeted by a short, bald-headed man who owned one of Las Vegas' finest restaurants and nightclubs. Norm Russell remembered being escorted to the front table of the club, "Our elbows were on the stage. After a wonderful meal, here came some ladies who were dressed like the day they were born. It was too much for an Oklahoma kid from Mountain View." [20]

Abe and Hansen saw to it that their players received a cultural education during road trips. Once in Salt Lake City, Hansen rousted Russell out of bed and took him to hear the Mormon Tabernacle Choir. [21]

Continuing on their swing through the western United States, the Chiefs beat Puget Sound 76-75 and Abilene Christian College 100-93. In the second half of the season the Chiefs won big games against Tulsa and Air Force. Many considered Tulsa OCU's toughest opponent outside the All-College tournament. Tulsa was on top of the Missouri Valley Conference and was led by Willie Biles, the sixth leading scorer in the nation. However, OCU claimed the number seven and eight scorers in the country in Rich and Edwards. The Chiefs prevailed 100-96, hitting 54 percent of shots from the field. Lacy Lanier gave Abe what he had been looking for for years, "a shooting and scoring guard with basketball intelligence." [22]

The win was a career milestone for Abe. It was his 300th victory as a college basketball coach, placing him in the top 25 coaches of all time.

Oklahoma City University was 21-5 after the regular season. The team was in Atlanta, fresh from impressive victories over Georgia

State University and Georgia Tech University. Abe and his players faced a decision. Should they go to the prestigious NIT in New York City or accept a berth in the 16-team NCAA tournament? Many of the players wanted to go to the NIT but Abe and team leaders convinced the remainder of the team to accept the sure thing when an invitation to the NCAA came.

The Chiefs were sent to the NCAA tournament site in Logan, Utah, to play Western Athletic Conference (WAC) champion Arizona State. The OCU campus newspaper wrote, "OCU has been given a chance to play the best. Number One against a small school with nothing to lose. This is the chance the team has been looking for all year." [23]

After the 1973 season had concluded, Ozie Edwards was named to the Associated Press All-American team. Courtesy Oklahoma City University.

The Chiefs played a decent first half against Arizona State. But then disaster struck in the second half. OCU could not find the ball or the basket, prompting one reporter to write, "If air balls had counted one point the Chiefs would have won by 10." [24] OCU hit only 20 percent of its shots from the field in the second half. The Chiefs lost 103-78. All observers agreed that OCU played its worst game of the year and ASU played its best game of the campaign.

Abe was mad, sad, and disappointed in the season-ending loss. However, the silver lining was that if the Chiefs had won, they would have faced defending champion UCLA and its superstar Bill Walton in the next game.

Abe was saddest for his seven seniors, Edwards, Rich, Russell, Tosee, Larry Tribble, Jim Lackey, and Mike Polansky. He knew they had played their hearts out and deserved a better ending to a 21-6 season.

A month after the end of the season Abe was still depressed about the loss to Arizona State. While still in bed one morning, the phone rang. On the other end of the line was Dr. Ralph Schillings, president of Pan American University in Edinburg, Texas. Abe had known Schillings, a native of Seminole, Oklahoma, for years since Schillings had coached football at OCU.

Schillings asked Abe if he knew of anyone who might be interested in the basketball coach position at Pan American. Without thinking, Abe asked what the job paid. When Schillings said $28,000 to $30,000 a year, Abe said, "I'm interested." Schillings was shocked but invited Abe down to south Texas to talk.

Abe was an institution at OCU. He had spent most of his adult life either as a player, assistant coach, or head coach for the Chiefs. However, Abe had publicly complained that he had more responsibilities, and less pay, than any coach in the NCAA. He was making only $14,000 annually, after 18 years as head coach. And he was coach, athletic director, and head recruiter.

When Pan American offered to double his annual salary and provide plenty of money to fund a winning program, Abe said yes. It was now up to the Pan American Board of Regents. Abe and Betty Jo were at a coaches meeting in St. Louis when word came from Schillings that the board of regents had approved his recommendation that Abe be hired as the new coach at Pan American. Abe actually heard the news first from columnist Frank Boggs who asked Abe in a hallway in St. Louis, "You going to Pan American?" [25]

Abe then told Betty Jo they were moving to Texas. Betty Jo had no idea what Pan American was and Abe really was not sure where the school was. All he knew was it was time for a change.

Abe announced his resignation to a shocked gathering of Oklahoma City sports reporters. Paul Hansen, Abe's faithful assistant, was named to replace Abe as head basketball coach at

OCU. The announcement opened a new era in both Abe's and Hansen's life.

Several years later, Abe blamed his departure from OCU on lack of fan interest, telling a reporter, "How would you like it if nobody read your articles? How would you like to give a party, and nobody shows up? You get the best food and drink, and nobody shows up. That's the reason I left. Nobody cared. The last year I was there, we were a 20-game winner and went to the NCAA playoffs...I tried everything—the world's tallest team, the world's shortest team. We were all black. We were all white. We were Mexican, Indian and black. We were all locals. We tried everything to stimulate interest. I had all the freedom in the world but no money...After awhile you got tired of playing and nobody's sitting there watching. I tried not to think about it, but it was hard not to, especially when you were a big draw on the road and nothing at home." [26]

Abe's sentiments were directed to OCU fans, not the University and its students.

As Abe left OCU, Frank Boggs of the *Oklahoma City Times* wrote, "It probably is the fault of people like myself Lemons has made out to be such a comedian. He is a comedian, certainly. But sometimes we leave the impression his comedy routines overshadow his coaching ability. He still believes in stuff like integrity in these times when pressures steadily mount in collegiate athletics." [27]

— Chapter Fourteen —

Way Down South

There was not a lot of talking going on in the car
as we passed through San Antonio and headed farther south,
almost to Mexico. Had I lost my mind?

Abe Lemons

ABE AND BETTY JO HAD BEEN TO TEXAS MANY TIMES, BUT NOT AS far south as Edinburg. Moving from the culture of Oklahoma City to south Texas did not bother Abe but Betty Jo was upset at leaving family and the host of friends she had made in Oklahoma City during a period of 25 years. Abe thought housing in Edinburg was too high so the Lemons rented an apartment. Daughter Jan visited the south Texas town and decided to move back to Oklahoma City to finish high school at Northwest Classen.

Edinburg was strategically located near the town of McAllen in Hidalgo County, Texas. The southern border of the county was the Rio Grande River and Mexico. A short drive to the east was Brownsville and the Gulf of Mexico.

Abe was elated when he took over the head coaching and athletic director positions for the Broncs of Pan American University. For 18 years at OCU he had scraped the coffers each month just to make the ends of the athletic department budget meet. All the buildings on the Pan American campus were nearly new, the president of the school wanted a winning basketball program and was willing to give Abe all the money he needed to make that dream happen. [1] President Schillings' only admonition was that Abe run a completely clean program.

Abe hired Armando Robledo as the assistant athletic director and gave him the task of taking care of the business side of the Pan American program. That move gave Abe the freedom he had never had at OCU, the freedom to concentrate on teaching his players basketball, and not worrying about how to finance the next road trip. Bill White was Abe's assistant coach.

Abe did not feel a lot of pressure to win quickly at Pan American. He told the *Tulsa Daily World*, "Well, there's no booster club down here. They ain't gonna care whether we win or lose. There's too many other things to do around here. Why, there's white-wing dove hunting just 12 miles down the road." [2]

Abe tried to describe his new base of operation in the Rio Grande Valley, "This place isn't well known. We're 13 miles from Guatemala. We got to go 250 miles just to get on a highway. We have no newspapers. And on TV, the same guy does the news, weather and sports. He leaves the same map up because the weather never changes." [3]

Even though Abe was transplanted in what seemed to him like a foreign country, he did not lose his knack of spotting superb basketball talent. Marshall Rogers, a 6'2" guard, had written OCU wanting to transfer from defense-minded Kansas to a team with more emphasis on offense. The letter was forwarded to Abe who promptly invited Rogers to spend

ABOVE: Abe's naming of Armando Robledo as assistant athletic director to take care of the business administration of the Pan American program freed Abe up to spend more time on recruiting and coaching.

Abe, left, and assistant coach Bill White, right, pose with the Pan American basketball team. Courtesy Pan American University.

some time on the Pan American campus. The minute Abe saw Rogers, he knew he had something special. Rogers committed to play for Abe and moved to south Texas. It was a great move for Abe, Rogers, and Pan American.

Abe was somewhat familiar with Pan American because the south Texas school often played teams in Oklahoma. As soon as Abe hit town he began filling vacancies in the Pan American schedule with coaches he counted as friends.

Abe took over a Pan American program that had been placed on two years probation by the NCAA and had posted a dismal 4-22 record the previous season. Abe also inherited an incredible playmaker, 5'10" Jesus "Chuy" Guerra, Jr., who averaged 26 points per game in leading his Roma, Texas High School team to four consecutive district championships. He was awarded a full scholarship at Pan American and welcomed the brand of basketball Abe brought to the Broncs.

Abe described what it was like to have four Latin starters on his team, "If you don't think we have some great huddles. I get down there, and they give me no comprende this, no comprende that. Well, I got me a Mexican-American interpreter and got that comprende stuff down in a hurry." [4]

Abe would have been happy to win only three games in his first season, but the Broncs surprised everyone and posted a 13-9 record, including unexpected wins over Nebraska, West Texas, and Air Force. Because many teams had finalized schedules before Abe arrived, Abe filled out his card with games against Mexico City and the University of the Americas at Puebla, Mexico.

James "Jim" McKone, who retired in 1999 after 30 years as Pan American's sports information director, says the job Abe performed in his first year in south Texas was "the best coaching job I have seen in any sport, at any time, in 50 years of sportswriting." [5]

McKone, who began broadcasting Pan American games on KRIO Radio in McAllen, Texas, after Abe arrived, was so pessimistic about the team's chances in the new season, he told his wife he did not expect the Broncs to win a single game. [6]

After winning three games early in the season, Abe set his sights on five wins for the year. Fans turned into "mad dogs" as the win total kept rising. In the middle of the season, Pan American won five in a row, with Arkansas State and Hardin-Simmons among the victims.

McKone says it was a miracle that Pan American won any games in 1973-1974. In many games, only four of Abe's five players scored points. The fifth player, playmaker guard Don Cardenas, was not a great shooter and was told by Abe not to shoot more than once each game. Cardenas, who later graduated from medical school, disobeyed Abe in one game and shot an airball at the buzzer. However, the Broncs had held the ball for four minutes and Cardenas explained to Abe he had to shoot because he was trapped. Everything worked out because another Bronc player caught the airball and slammed it into the basket and the Broncs won the game. [7]

Bruce "Sky" King averaged 30 points per game for the Broncs. It was a school record and second best in the nation. King was 6'2" but weighed only about 150 pounds. Abe appreciated King's work habits, "Anytime we told him anything, he would work trying to do it." [8]

Because Abe had arrived so late at Pan American he really did not have adequate time to recruit for his first season. He literally took in players off the street. He said, "If they tell me they can play, I'll tell 'em to suit up. We need the bodies."

Abe used one player in an early season game without knowing the player's name. He called the player "Pizza Hut" during the game because he knew the kid had been fired by the local Pizza Hut for eating too much pizza, could not practice but two days a week, and had been showing up for home games. [9]

"Pizza Hut," whose real name was Arnold Vera, was shocked when Abe jumped up in the middle of the game and said, "Pizza, go get 'em." Vera entered the game, knocked down three baskets, pulled down seven rebounds, and turned the team around before fouling out. After the game Abe made a point to find out Pizza's real name. [10]

At a mid-season coaches meeting Abe downplayed his new team, "We're what is commonly known as a victim," he said, "When I got down there, everything was cleaned out, including the basketball team. I had only two players left. One they called 'Little Jesus' [Guerra] and he's a real tiger. The big center, Carlos McCullough, is 6'5" but we list him at 6'7"." [11] Abe pronounced Guerra's name as "gee-sus," rather than the correct Hispanic of "hay-suz."

Oral Roberts University pounded the Broncs 107-90. After the game Abe declared that Pan American was not yet in ORU's class. During the game Guerra complained about getting hit while he was trying to block a shot. Abe told the 5'10" Guerra, "Trying to block a shot? You can't see anything but their belt buckles out there." Abe said he had never seen so many big guys with such long arms as the players from ORU, "They just threw the ball up on the boards and ran right over us, that's all." [12]

Abe spent the off-season each year recruiting and speaking at basketball clinics. Ed Janka, a successful high school coach and head coach at John Carroll University in Ohio, invited Abe to a coaches' clinic in Cleveland, Ohio, in 1974. Janka, who in the 1980s and 1990s ran the nation's most successful coaches' clinics for Nike shoes,

Abe's faithful companion at Pan American was Lupe Garcia who drove Abe and his team in a GMC bus from the Rio Grande Valley to spots all over the continent. Abe always made Garcia, whom he called "Coach Garcia," feel like he was part of the staff. Once when Abe was named marshall of a big parade in Edinburgh, Garcia stood along the street as the marshall's car approached. When Abe spotted Garcia, he yelled, "Lupe, come ride with us!"

had first met Abe when Janka was a fifth-year senior and freshman basketball coach at Marquette University under head coach Al McGuire. Janka, raised in Chicago, was intrigued with Abe's slow speech and knife-sharp humor.

Janka recalls that Abe brought down the house with a story about a request several years before from the president of OCU that Abe recruit more white players for the Chiefs basketball team. Abe told the audience, "I did. The next year I recruited Robert White, James White, and John White." Janka said coaches were "falling out of their chairs" at Abe's stories. [13]

It was not long until Abe's enthusiasm and his wide-open, high scoring offense won the support of Pan American fans. The fieldhouse on the Edinburg campus seated more than 5,000 people, much larger that Frederickson Fieldhouse on the OCU campus where Abe had played his squads for more than a dozen seasons.

By Abe's second season at Pan American, basketball fever hit the campus. The fieldhouse was packed for every home game. Anticipation of a championship caliber team in 1974-1975 ran high all over south Texas. Newspapers picked up the pace in covering Broncs games after a 78-60 pounding of Southern Methodist University to open the season. One paper said, "Who ever heard of little Pan American beating up on Southern Methodist University?"

Abe had four blacks and one Mexican-American in his starting five. With tongue in cheek, he said, "We need a little racial balance here. I'm thinking about getting a Chinese faculty adviser." [14]

Hopes for the new season were tempered after a two-point loss to Texas Christian University. However, Pan American won its next 20 games in a row, including two exhibition games against Mexican teams that did not count on the official record. The Broncs moved into the Associated Press Top Twenty. The team's ranking at number 15 was, and still is, the highest ranking for a Pan American basketball team.

Abe, with sunglasses and a new cigar, waits for Frank Gifford to hand him the microphone at a coaches' clinic in 1974.

Abe's big guns were Rogers, Julies Howard, King, and Guerra. After Guerra brought the Broncs back from what looked like certain defeat in a game against Lamar, one reporter wrote, "Guerra is Pan Am's 'glue man' at guard...He is the spark plug of the Broncs team, coached by a man who knows exactly what he has at all times, and who knows how to use what he has at all times." [15] Guerra scored 20 points in the mistake-laden Lamar game in which Marshall Rogers was held to only 16 points.

During the 20-game win streak, Pan American beat Tulsa, Arkansas State twice, Lamar, and Texas A & I. In one of the games against Arkansas State, Abe thought his team was defeated when Pan American was down by five points and Arkansas State had the ball. Rogers' three baskets in 33 seconds pulled out the game. The 6'2" freshman Cris Garcia passed the ball to Rogers who sank the final shot at the buzzer to carry the Broncs to a 71-70 win. [16]

On a road trip through Georgia, Abe's squad outscored Georgia Southern 110-83 and beat Georgia State and Georgia Tech. Newspapers in Atlanta, Georgia, referred to "Pizza" Vera as a "chubby sub" after Vera hit the winning basket with one second left on the clock in the Georgia Southern game. Abe spouted off, "Tomorrow, they're gonna call him a chubby starter." [17]

Poker was a favorite sport of Abe and sports information director McKone on road trips. McKone says his greatest thrill during Abe's time at Pan American was not on the court in some big game, but "was when I won $2 in nickel-dime poker with four queens when Abe was already eyeing the pot with his four tens." [18]

Abe used his contacts in Hawaii to take his team to the island paradise and promptly beat up on the University of Hawaii in a two-game series. Pan American trailed at half-time of the first contest in Hawaii. Abe took Gilbert King aside and griped at him for only scoring four points in the first half. King had been averaging 24 points per game and was having an off night. Abe said, "King, you're stumbling around against Japanese about that tall [holding a hand belt-high]. If we get beat, it's your fault. You're not holding up your end." [19] Other team members chimed in with Abe. King was so incensed he scored 24 points in the second half and Pan American won by five.

After the season's second loss, to Air Force, the Broncs completed their schedule with victories over Denver, Southern Mississippi, and Trinity. Abe partially blamed the new tartan surface at Air Force for the loss, saying, "You couldn't hear the ball bounce, not a bucket of air in the whole state...They weren't good ballplayers. They had white sidewall haircuts and looked country and held the ball on us and cut us to pieces. They just took us to the cleaners." [20] The loss to Air Force ended a 10-game road winning streak in five states and knocked the Broncs out of the Top 20.

Because Pan American was still on probation from past NCAA violations, there was no post-season invitation.

Pan American fans loved the high-scoring of the Broncs who hit the century mark in seven games in 1974-1975. The Broncs had a season high of 121 against Mexico, with 119 points against Texas A & I and 111 against Trinity. Former Oklahoma State coach Henry Iba was the color commentator for the television broadcast in the Trinity game.

Abe was asked after the Trinity contest if he would ever schedule a game against Paul Hansen's OCU team. Abe replied, "I don't see any merit in it. You play people for a reason. I'm packing them in now. If we were to beat OCU it wouldn't help Paul any and if they beat us, so what?" [21]

Pan American became the nation's leading independent basketball power in 1974-1975. Rogers finished the season as the ninth best scorer in the nation with 26.7 points per game. King was the sixth-best rebounder in the country, averaging 13.3 rebounds per game. [22] As a team, the Broncs' 22-2 record, with a .917 winning percentage, ranked third nationally behind Indiana and Louisville. Pan American's scoring average of 87 points per game was 18th in the nation, just seven points per game behind leading North Carolina State. [23]

Abe immensely enjoyed the season, packing the Broncs fieldhouse with standing room only crowds of more than 5,200 screaming fans for the last six home games. Abe got thrown out of only one game in his second season at Pan American. It is more accurate to say that Abe threw himself out of the game against Denver. His team was down by eight points with a few minutes left in the first half when Abe was called for his second technical. He began leaving the court when the referee said, "Abe, you've got only two fouls." Abe said, "Yeah, but you know and I know I'm gonna get another one." Abe told reporters later that his only regret was that he had not taken a heavier coat to Denver, saying, "That dressing room was like ice." [24]

After his second season in the Rio Grande Valley, Abe compared Edinburg with his former job at OCU, "It's summer all year long here. You can cat fish, golf or go to the beach. We can't run people off here. Guys flunk out and stay here to work. Kids can swim before a game, then play in an air conditioned gym. Coaches can golf and pick grapefruit and oranges off the trees. Besides that, I run a clean program. Everybody knows that at my place they're playing with a straight deck. Up there [in Oklahoma], everybody was just waiting for the Big Red [University of Oklahoma football team] to kick off." [25]

Abe said he missed Oklahoma "but only until the first of the month when payday comes." Abe said coaching in south Texas was almost like being retired, "Not a lot of people around. Sometimes I think I'm on Gilligan's Island." [26] Abe filled his time with appearances on his own television show, wrote a newspaper column, and sat beside his swimming pool a lot, watching the world go by.

Pan American's president gave Abe sufficient funds to host an annual golf tournament in south Texas. The tournament gave much-needed national publicity to Pan American and Edinburg and gave Abe the opportunity to renew friendships with many of the nation's leading coaches. Oklahoma City Lincoln Park Golf Course professional U. C. Ferguson and columnist Frank Boggs were invited to the tournament. Boggs reported to his readers, "The crowd around the breakfast table was pretty good because after a couple days the coaches attending Abe Lemons' golf tournament realized that nobody hides jalapeno peppers in a bowl of cereal. The siesta never was meant to be a time of rest but merely something to do while waiting for the fire truck to show up." [27]

By 1975 many of the veteran basketball coaches in the country such as Rupp, Iba, and Allen had retired. Abe found himself and Joe Vancisin of Yale as two of the nation's veterans. Abe was respected throughout the ranks of the nation's college basketball coaches and was elected vice president of the 1,400-member National Association of Basketball Coaches (NABC). Duke University coach William E. "Bill" Foster was the President of the NABC and jokingly said he did not feel exactly secure knowing that Abe was his vice president.

The NABC, with Joe Vancisin as its executive director at national headquarters in Branford, Connecticut, held its annual meeting at the NCAA Final Four and sponsored numerous coaching clinics. Foster observed Abe at those clinics, "Abe was equally witty and wise. He was good for the game of basketball. Everyone expected to be entertained, but within the entertainment was much philosophy about coaching and working with players to get the best out of their ability. Abe had a lot of deep stuff to offer coaches." [28]

Foster, who coached at Duke, Rutgers, Utah, South Carolina, and Northwestern, and is now a basketball consultant for the Big XII Conference, remembered an NABC coaches clinic at Kutsher's Country Club in Monticello, New York. Abe, who was not known for his skill as an operator of any kind of equipment, was using a film projector to show coaches a game film. Abe somehow threaded the projector backwards. When the film started, with the images reversed, Abe was quick to remark, "When's the last time you saw five left-handers play another team of five left-handers?" [29]

As an NABC board member, Abe was asked to chair a committee to look into requiring coaches to submit to lie detector tests when questions of recruiting violations arose. Abe was disturbed over apparent cheating among college coaches. He was mad at the NCAA for apparently only picking on the small programs, saying, "Well, they got Doane, Livingston and Pan American. They've cleaned up all the big ones." Before leaving OCU, Abe had filed a complaint with the NCAA over recruiting methods of the

University of Oklahoma. The NCAA returned his letter marked "insignificant." Abe recognized that the NCAA would not take just one coach's word to begin an investigation.

Abe was disgusted that at coaches meetings, discussions centered around cheating and scandals, not basketball as it had been in the past. Abe blamed so many rules for the confusion, "Rules are so numerous and often so complicated that many are broken in good faith. Testing of coaches would concern whether or not a player has been given an automobile, extra cash, the big stuff."

Abe volunteered to take the first lie detector test if the proposal was passed by the NCAA. Abe's idea was that conferences should administer the lie detector tests each year on a volunteer basis. Abe thought, "If one coach does not volunteer to take the test, eyebrows would lift in his direction."

Abe met with Abb Curtis, former supervisor of officials in the Southwest Conference, who had administered lie detector tests to two officials who failed and were banned from the conference for life. After much study, Abe's idea was dropped by the NABC for the time being. Years later, the Southwest Conference accepted Abe's suggestion and used the polygraph in investigations of illegal practices.

Life was laid back for Abe in south Texas. He often found solace playing golf or fishing in some nearby stream or lake. He even occasionally missed practices. When a player asked Abe if he could miss practice too, Abe replied, "No, because I'm the boss, and you're not." [30]

Abe's third, and final year at Pan American was a super success. The Broncs finished the season at 20-5 with Rogers leading the country in scoring with a 36.3 per game average. Abe paid tribute to his star, "He had a great burst of speed and was great on the stop-and-go. I can show you a film where he got 38 points and you can't find them on the film, he got them so quietly." [31]

Guerra completed his career at Pan American by breaking every assist record in the book, topped 1,000 points in his four years, and was named an Academic All-American with a 3.4 grade point. Guerra later returned as coach of his high school alma mater and was elected in 1998 to the Texas Association of Basketball Coaches Hall of Fame. [32]

Abe said Guerra, as the quarterback of his basketball squad, was the most unselfish player he had coached in his first quarter century. In his senior year, Guerra averaged nearly 12 assists per game with a single game high of 20.

In 1975-1976, Rogers' blistering scoring pace was supplemented by King's 23.3 and Guerra's 13 points per game. The Broncs beat Texas Christian University, Arkansas State, Rice twice, and Denver. The second Rice win came in a 95-66 thumping of the Owls in the championship game of the Senior Bowl tournament in Mobile, Alabama.

After Rogers scored 58 points in a 124-90 win over Texas Lutheran College, he told Abe it was the first time in two years his back did not hurt. Questioned by Abe as to what he meant, Rogers said, "I hurt my back at Kansas when they kept me stooped over, trying to play defense all the time." [33]

Rogers actually had a chance to score 60 points in the game. He intercepted a pass at the top of the key with time running out and dumped the ball off to King who scored. Abe asked Rogers why he did not score himself. Rogers said, "Gilbert [King] has never gotten 40 points before." Abe replied, "You've never gotten 60, either." Rogers said, "Coach, I never even thought about that." [34]

Pan American won its last eight games of the season, the final three victories over schools in Hawaii. However, the 20-5 record did not garner the team an invitation to the NCAA tournament or the NIT. Abe was hostile, saying, "I guess we could have gotten in if we lost a few more games," an obvious reference to post-season bids handed out to Oregon, Kentucky, and St. Peters, all with 10 losses, and Niagara with 11 games in the loss column.

Abe charged that independent teams were overlooked in the NCAA post-season tournament selection process. He pointed to Oral Roberts, North Texas State, and Florida State, all with six losses or less, who also were overlooked. With Abe's team left out of the post-season field, Abe landed a spot as a color commentator for television broadcasts of NCAA games.

Abe's only losses in 1975-1976 were to Texas Christian University, Mississippi, Arkansas State, UNLV, and Hardin-Simmons.

In January, 1976, Abe was honored as Senior College Coach of the Year by the Texas Sports Writers Association. Abe accepted the accolades of the writers at a banquet in Dallas and told the audience that he was against raising the baskets above ten feet, which some coaches had suggested, "I say we should cut a hole in the floor and put the ball through it. That way, everybody will want to recruit midgets, not the big guys. I can see myself now, recruiting midgets." Abe bent down and cupped his hands around his mouth, and continued, "Hey, little fellow, can I offer you a car?" [35]

In April, Abe took over as president of the National Association of Basketball Coaches. He called himself "El Presidente" in honor of the tacos he ate for breakfast every morning. With the prestige of the position and his wit, Abe became one of the most sought after banquet speakers in the land.

Life was good for the Lemons family. Abe was a folk hero, the leader of one of the best independent basketball programs in the country. Betty Jo had made a new circle of friends and was enjoying her role in the valley. Then came a call from Darrell Royal.

Chapter Fifteen

Burnt Orange

Texas offered to send a plane to Edinburg for me,
and that showed me something. Before,
someone had always come for me in a pickup truck.

Abe Lemons

DARRELL ROYAL WAS THE FASTEST MAN ON THE UNIVERSITY OF
Oklahoma football team in 1946 and won All-American honors as
the Sooners' quarterback three years later. He grew up at Hollis, not
too far from where Abe entered the world in southwest Oklahoma.
In 1957, at age 32, Royal crossed the Red River and became head
football coach at Oklahoma's arch-rival, the hated University of
Texas (UT). After two decades as one of the most successful football coaches in the land, Royal assumed full-time duties as the Texas
athletic director.

Football was king at the University of Texas. The Longhorn basketball program lagged far behind football in attendance, interest, and
quality. Royal turned to Abe to bring Texas basketball to a higher level.

Abe and Royal had been friends since 1941. They met when
Royal traveled from Hollis to Weatherford where his brother and
Abe were students at Southwestern State Teachers College. Both
men had followed each other's careers and had often visited at

coaches meetings and Oklahoma sports events. Both were "honest as the day is long," products of a small Oklahoma town and the morality instilled by the Great Depression.

Back to the phone call. After missing each other for several days, Royal and Abe finally made contact. Royal said he would like to talk to Abe about becoming the new Texas basketball coach. Abe had always wondered what it would be like to coach at a major school. Not one to have to think about a decision for ten days, Abe took about four seconds and said, "Yeah, Darrell, I'll come up there and talk to you about it." [1]

The University of Texas needed a basketball face-lift. The Longhorns had losing seasons in six of the previous nine years under coach Leon Black. In 1975-1976, Texas was 9-17 overall and 4-12 in the Southwest Conference. Royal was unhappy with the state of the program and was willing to offer Abe a five-year lucrative contract, to lure him away from Pan American.

Abe talked to Betty Jo who left the decision to her husband. When Pan American President Dr. Schillings told Abe he would soon retire as head of the university, Abe's mind was made up. He was going to the University of Texas.

Royal explained why he picked Abe, "He had won great respect from fellow coaches. Although he approaches coaching differently from most, he's effective...I just felt like he was the tonic we needed to get our basketball situation moving." [2]

Royal recognized that Abe would be good copy for the press and Texas basketball could use the free promotion. Royal told a reporter, "He's not a con man, a promotion man. He's an excellent basketball coach in addition to having personality and humor...There's a lot of depth to 'ol Abe that will go right past you if don't stay close to him. I believe he can conduct a first class program without overwhelming everyone around him. He's not the type who would want basketball to be bigger than the University of Texas." [3]

In March, 1976, when Abe's acceptance of the UT head job was announced, he immediately became the king of Austin press conferences. Sportswriters had to pull out their dictionaries to accurately reflect the tone of Abe's first meeting with reporters while wearing his new orange coat. Among the quotes attributed to Abe that day were:

"I won't say Betty Jo is happy about the move [from Edinburg to Austin], but she's had everything packed and sitting by the back door for two days, and right now she's reading the dictionary trying to learn English again."[4]

"Aw, there are good things and bad things about all jobs. Main thing that worries me about this one is having to get three fingers cut off so I can give that hook 'em Horns sign. I'm gonna offer my left hand. It will screw up my golf grip, but I'm not playing good anyhow." [5]

"I'm looking forward to working at a place that has its own school song. For 21 years, I've coached teams that didn't have one. All I could do was stand around and hum." [6]

"My salary is about the same. I made over $10,000 [at Pan American] on a TV show. But Darrell [Royal] told me I can now charge more for speaking fees. I may make $2,500 every time I tell a few of my stories. Yeah, I'm in the chips now." [7]

"I won't hang on to teach hopscotch if I don't get the job done. A lot of players want to come here, but you're not going to get your blue-chippers just because it's Texas. You still have to recruit them. Once you get the program built up, all you need is one or two blue-chippers a year. People have a tendency to want to be part of a winning tradition." [8]

"If you have a reputation as a fast gun, you always wonder if you could do it down the road...what it would be like at a prestigious place. I've never had to answer to a commissioner, wear patent leather shoes and say, 'Yes, sir' and 'No, sir.' So I don't know how that'd be. I saw a sign in Austin on a car window. It said, 'The University.' Whether you like it or not, people know what that means. They sure as hell don't think of Howard Payne." [9]

Abe wondered how big he could make basketball at the University of Texas. Years before, Rice University coach Don Suman had given Abe some advice about Southwest Conference basketball. As Abe took over his new job, Abe remembered Suman's words, "If

University of Texas athletic director Darrell Royal, left, and Bob Knight, University of Indiana basketball coach, congratulate Abe on being named head coach of the Texas Longhorns. Courtesy University of Texas.

football wins at your school, you can win. If football loses, you can lose. If football loses and you win, you have a problem." [10]

As soon as Betty Jo was settled in Austin, Abe took off on a recruiting trip. Texas had 11 players returning from the previous year but had lost its only double-figure scorer, Dan Krueger, to graduation. Abe told reporters he needed "a wild guy, somebody that's stung by a bee." [11]

Abe initially did not have any luck signing players from the state of Texas to attend UT. Many prospective players thought UT was only a football school and they would be lost in the shadow of the football program. Abe was not dismayed, telling a reporter, "We didn't get the people we are after, but it's like asking a girl to go to the dance with you. If you don't get the date you're after, you don't just don't go. You try to find someone else, and that's how people get discovered." [12]

Abe always looked for rare individuals. He thought such players made the world go round. He liked a 6'1" center whom nobody wanted, a 5'8" guard who weighed less than 150 pounds. He said, "I like a wild horse that just tears up the gym. I like people with unusual characteristics that you can calm down and help make something of. My ideal starting five would all have nicknames, like 'The Adding Machine,' 'The Helicopter.'" [13]

On a recruiting trip to California Abe spotted Ron Baxter in a high-school all-star game against a Russian team. The 6'4" Baxter was the co-player of the year in Los Angeles high school ranks at Dorsey High School and was a recruiting plum for Abe who called Baxter "a quality player." [14] Abe had such success in the next few years pulling good players out of California, Texas A & M coach Shelby Metcalf called Texas "The University of California at Austin." [15]

Baxter liked Abe's style of coaching from his first visit to the Austin campus. Baxter said, "He doesn't come on like a coach. There was none of this 'You'll have breakfast at 7 and go such and such at 8 and talk to so and so at 9. He said, 'What do you want to do? What do you want to see?'" [16] Baxter chose UT over other schools because Abe convinced him he could be part of a building program. [17]

One of the first persons Abe met in Austin was Frank Erwin, a successful lawyer who exerted major influence on programs and policies of UT. For many years Erwin served as chairman of the UT Board of Regents. Abe met Erwin at the Quorum, a restaurant near the UT campus that served as a gathering place for celebrities and athletes. Erwin "bled orange," never missed a Longhorn sporting event, and offered to help Abe make Texas a national basketball power.

A major part of Royal's plan to rejuvenate Longhorn basketball was the construction of the new 35 million dollar Frank Erwin Special Events Center, an elaborate basketball facility that seated more than 16,000 fans. Abe knew he had to produce a winning attitude among his players quickly to fill the larger facility. Abe said, "If we do our part, the Super Drum's [Erwin Center's nickname] gonna be a basketball showcase. The best way to have one is to have a winning team…That's why I'm here. If I don't do it, somebody else will be here. I'm not naive enough to think they'll keep me around because I'm a good ol' boy." [18]

Abe presented Frank Erwin with a plan to establish the Burnt Orange Club, a basketball booster club, to revive fan interest in the Longhorns. Erwin helped Abe negotiate his way around legal barriers to the sale of alcoholic beverages on state property. Erwin knew his way around the university power structure and worked out a situation which allowed fans who became members of the Burnt Orange Club to buy food and drink in the Burnt Orange Room and mingle with players and coaches after games. Erwin also was able to convince university officials to set aside special parking for Burnt Orange Club members near the Erwin Center.

The Burnt Orange Club was an immediate success. Fan interest in Abe and his players mounted as talk of the new season became the subject of morning coffee and donut sessions at hangouts and cafes all over Austin.

The creation of the Burnt Orange Club was revolutionary in basketball promotion circles at UT. Before Abe arrived in Austin, about 30 basketball supporters had paid $35 annually for membership in a booster club. Of the old booster club, Abe said, "These guys pay $35 a year and want to tell you how to coach. Why should I pay any attention to them?" Abe, however, said he would listen to $5,000 donors to the new Burnt Orange Club, saying, "If a guy gives five grand, I won't just listen, I'll do whatever they suggest." [19]

Erwin became Abe's mentor in the field of politics. Abe had never been forced to play politics to a great degree in his previous positions. However, things were different at UT. Abe answered to his athletic director and university vice presidents he had never even heard of.

Abe had two assistant coaches. Barry Dowd, a native of Dallas, lettered three years at UT in basketball in the 1950s and was a highly successful coach in the Dallas high school system. He was head coach at the University of Texas at Arlington for 10 seasons before becoming Abe's chief assistant. One of Abe's first calls after accepting the UT head coach job was to Dowd who had become close friends with Abe as a member of the board of directors of the National Association of Basketball Coaches. [20]

The other assistant coach was Steve Moeller, a Cincinnati, Ohio, native, who was serving as an assistant coach at Rice when he was hired by Abe. Moeller attended Otterbein College and coached four years in high school ranks in Ohio, including two seasons at his alma mater, Cincinnati Colerain High School.

Abe began fall drills in the old UT fieldhouse, Gregory Gym, which held only 7,000 people and had been in use since 1931. About Gregory Gym, Abe quipped, "They have so many lines painted on the floor we can't find out-of-bounds. They came in the other day and painted another volleyball court in the middle. Now we can't find center jump." [21]

The first practice was a rude awakening for players like Ron Baxter who believed Abe to be a run-and-gun, offense-minded coach with little structure in his teaching. Baxter was a little loose on the court and Abe grabbed his shirt, saying, "Hey, kid, when I point to a spot, that's where I want you to go." [22] Baxter, who played later in the Continental Basketball Association (CBA) and became a successful computer company sales representative, recalled, "From the moment he grabbed my shirt, I knew this man was all business in practice. He might have said some funny things to loosen us up, but he demanded my attention every moment in every exercise. I knew if I wanted to play, I had to go all out in practice." [23]

Dowd recognized he was working for a basketball master on the first day of practice when Abe said, "Pick out the worst five guys you see out there and run a defense against my five guys." Dowd recalled, "From the moment we began practice, I saw why Abe had been so successful. His coaching logic was 'Keep it simple.' He was the best practice coach in basketball. He meticulously taught the players every specific move and spot. As an offensive coach, he has no peer. He saw things other coaches didn't see. He didn't write them down. They were all in his head." [24]

Reporters gathered around Abe after a late September practice in Gregory Gym to glean from his sayings. The reporters were not disappointed. Abe was at his best in explaining how he would coach at Texas, "I coach the first team, whether it's seven or eight or 10 men. Not another soul, assistant coach or anyone, is allowed to even talk to them. They're mine. I referee every day, and our first team has never lost a game. I don't ever want the second team to win. Some of the little darlings would get the idea they ought to be playing. I never substitute just to substitute. The only way a guy gets off my team is if he dies...I play my regulars. And they'd better not get tired. If one of them says he's tired, I suggest he can rest by staying on the defensive end of the court a couple of possessions. Nobody has ever taken me up on that." [25]

Abe explained to Dowd why he did not like to substitute, "What you have to understand is that if I take somebody out, I gotta put somebody else in. Who do I play?" Dowd looked down the bench, understood what Abe was saying, and never mentioned the word "substitution" again. [26]

As the first game of the season approached, Dowd was concerned that Abe had never sat down and explained to him his specific assignments as assistant coach. Abe would always say, "We'll talk about it," but never did. Dowd and Abe developed a special brand of silent communication during their first few weeks in Austin, sharing an apartment before their families made the move.

Dowd had many responsibilities, including service as Abe's chauffeur in the new Lincoln Towncar leased for Abe by UT supporters. Dowd handled most of the administrative details of the basketball team, leaving Abe time to calculate maneuvers to beat the next opponent. Riding around Austin in the shiny Lincoln, Dowd, given the nickname "Pencil," for all his administrative work, used the CB handle "Lemons-aide." [27]

Dowd later followed Abe as president of the National Association of Basketball Coaches, the youngest president of that group, and was head coach and athletic director at East Tennessee State University, associate athletic director at Oklahoma State University, and is presently athletic director at Arkansas State University.

Abe looked to Baxter and Jim Krivacs, a sophomore transfer from Auburn who had sat out the previous year at Texas, to anchor his first Longhorn entry into the tough Southwest Conference. Krivacs had starred at Southport High School in Indianapolis, Indiana. Abe was impressed with Krivacs' work habits in practice, saying, "If you give him a choice of a week in Acapulco or a week of practice, he'd take practice. If you live in the building [gym] like he does, you're going to get better. Lot of guys don't realize that. They think they're gonna have a vision one night and just play better. It don't work that way." [28]

Abe did not know much about the talents of the rest of his squad. He had not bothered to look at films of the previous year's games in which a totally different brand of basketball was played under Coach Black. Abe explained, "I wouldn't know anything about what they could do for me. I'll just throw a basketball out on the floor and see what we have." [29]

In addition to Baxter and Krivacs, Abe picked Johnny Moore to be his guard, his quarterback, "the man I talk to." Abe sincerely believed that a coach could not talk to every player during a critical time-out. He always chose one player to pass along words of instruction to. Then the player could tell the rest of the players. Abe rationalized, "And they take it better coming from him."

Abe's philosophy about player instruction during timeouts was straightforward, "You can tell a player one thing and he might remember it. You tell him two things and he'll forget 'em both." [30]

Moore, who had been recruited by Leon Black and had never heard of Abe, thought briefly about leaving UT after Black was removed as head coach. Moore feared Abe would bring in his own group of players with him to Texas. However, Moore took the word of athletic director Darrell Royal, that Abe was a player's coach and knew basketball as well as anyone in the coaching business, and decided to give Abe a chance. [31]

Other players who made up Abe's initial Longhorn squad were Rich Parson; Michael Murphy; Tom Nichols; Ovie Dotson; John Danks; Henry Bauerschlag, Jr.; and Jan Robert Handley.

Before the season began, Abe changed the official program that was sold to fans at basketball games. In the past, only a simple, one-page sheet with the names and numbers of players was handed out. Abe copied the method the Texas football coaches used to produce a quality printed program and contracted with J. Nells Thompson to coordinate the project. Abe and his coaching staff sold the advertisements and wrote the copy for the program, in return for half the profits. The coaches who worked on the program were compensated for their time and the remainder of the profit went to the Burnt Orange Club. The university kept money from the actual sale of the programs at games.

University auditors later looked at the program-production scheme and decided that it did not fit internal auditing guidelines at UT. For awhile the programs were not even allowed to be sold inside the Erwin Center. Abe never understood why he received so much heat for producing a professional program for basketball fans when the football leadership at UT was operating in the exact same manner to print programs for home football games.

Practice was fierce for Abe and his new players. Abe told the team that he customarily played only eight or nine men. That promise caused heated practices in which players ferociously competed against each other to make it to the top eight or nine in Abe's mind. [32]

Jim Krivacs explains how Abe's practices were so intense, "There was no job security. There was a fear, a healthy fear, that we played under. I knew that if I didn't give 100 percent in practice and in games, I could be replaced in a minute. That fear caused me to play hard." [33]

Abe won the loyalty of his players by sticking up for them in a fight over space in the athletic dormitory. Before Abe arrived, UT basketball players were relegated to the basement of the oldest dorm, Moore-Hill. Abe lobbied athletic director Royal and negotiated a move upstairs for his players, away from the noise of the washers and dryers in the Moore-Hill basement. [34]

It was an emotional night for Abe as he brought his players out onto the floor at Gregory Gym for his first game as head coach at Texas. The opponent was Oklahoma State, coached by Jim Killingsworth.

The game marked the beginning of a new era in college basketball. The ten-year ban on the dunk had been removed and just minutes into the game, Gary Goodner dunked the ball into the basket and the crowd roared. Texas beat the Cowboys 74-73 in overtime and Longhorn fans talked the next day all over town about the new brand of basketball that would sweep Austin and Texas fans everywhere.

A few days later Oklahoma University came to town and beat Abe's Longhorns 60-56. Then Texas beat Wisconsin-Stout and the University of Southern California (USC) before leaving for its first road game against Mississippi State.

The NCAA, in allowing dunks in games, still prohibited dunks during pre-game warmups. When a Mississippi State player dunked the ball in the pre-game, he was assessed a technical foul. Abe thought the official was crazy for calling the foul and protested in an unusual way. When Texas was awarded two shots from the foul line for the Mississippi State infraction, Abe asked for a volunteer. Krivacs, normally a nearly 90 percent free throw shooter, volunteered. Abe told Krivacs to shoot with his back to the basket. When the official saw what Krivacs was doing, he asked him about it. Krivacs said, "Oh, that's the way I always shoot free throws." Krivacs missed and Texas lost the game by two points, 91-89, in overtime.

The next road game was just as tough. Abe took his team to Oklahoma City to play OCU. Hundreds of Abe's friends, former players, and a few hecklers showed up to see OCU beat Texas by a single point 66-65.

The Longhorns were 3-3 when they flew to Providence, Rhode Island, to play in the Industrial National Classic. Texas split the two games played in the classic, losing to Providence and beating Rhode Island. Before the Providence game, Abe overheard a Texas player tell Longhorns assistant coach Barry Dowd that some of the guys on the team were saying Texas could not win that night. Abe tried even harder to instill confidence in his players. They lost the Providence game but bounced back the following night to beat the taller and stronger Rhode Island. [35]

The Longhorns opened up conference play at Texas A & M on January 4, 1977. Texas was cold at the free throw line, hitting only five of 19 charity tosses while the Aggies hit 12 of 15. It was the difference, and Texas lost 68-59, spoiling Abe's debut in the Southwest Conference.

Abe called the loss "a damned disgrace. We had one guy [Gary Goodner] miss eight free throws tonight. Is that some kind of conference record?" [36] What made Abe so upset was the fact that

Goodner had hit four of five free throws in the previous game against Rhode Island. During the A & M game Abe went to the scorer's table and complained, "Can't you make them quit calling fouls on the Aggies? We're playing right into their hands by going to the free throw line." [37]

Abe was anything but complimentary of his players, "If you think this bunch was good, you should see the ones we left at home." [38] Abe continued, "That's embarrassing, scoring like that. I'm supposed to have high scoring teams, and we got beat scoring in the 50s...I never saw a team that hated practice like this one does. They think I'm a rookie, that I came in on a load of peaches. This hurts my reputation, night after night. I wouldn't mind getting beat if it was 110 to 95." [39]

Abe did cool down in the post-game press conference to brag on Goodner and Parson for "working like hell," and on Moore and Krivacs, "First time both guards have had a bad game." [40]

Asked for a final comment on his first conference loss, Abe opined, "It was a disgrace. It was awful...I need fresh blood. These guys baffle me. They're probably in there now wondering where we're going to eat. I guess we better put the little darlings on the bus and take them home." [41]

Abe's methods were difficult for the UT players to learn. However, once the team learned his style, they were off and running.

Abe was even tougher than usual on his team in the next few practices. He stung one player with his words, "Look, I know you couldn't guard a dead man, but at least you could move around and squeak your shoes a bit and fake it." [42] Abe never apologized for his tart comments during practice or in the middle of a game. He knew if a player quit because of his comments, instead of getting mad and trying harder, the player would probably quit in the fourth quarter when the going got tough. [43]

The massive coverage of Abe in the press brought paying patrons to the Gregory Gym. More than 7,800 fans, far above the fire-marshal sanctioned capacity of 7,000, jammed into the gym to watch the Longhorns lose a second consecutive conference game to Baylor 75-73.

Two nights later, Abe challenged his team that was preparing to take the court against Texas A & M, telling them, "I haven't said a good word about you since I came to town, but since people are filling up the place, don't you think you should give them something back?" [44]

The Longhorns responded and gave Abe his first conference victory 87-73.

Ron Baxter (12) drives the lane as Jim Krivacs, left, watches carefully. Courtesy University of Texas.

Abe was vindicated in the victory over A & M for playing 6'7" senior Rich Parson at center. Fans had booed the slow, awkward, poor-shooting Parson in previous games. However, against the Aggies, Parson scored 17 points and grabbed 12 rebounds. Parson worked hard and Abe thought he had earned a starting berth. Abe was right.

After the game Abe had his first kind words for his Texas team, "They've been eating like Notre Dame. But you know, there's something about this bunch I really like." [45]

Krivacs scored 21 points in the win over the Aggies, prompting Abe to say, "It's about time he woke up. He's been drivin' me crazy, actin' like a zombie. He looks at the wall five hours before a game." [46]

Even though Texas won the game and officials called far fewer fouls on the Longhorns than the Aggies, Abe still complained. He told referees Paul Galvan and Arlan Staub they had called a poor game. Abe rationalized his behavior, saying," If you don't complain about it when you win, they don't pay any attention to you when you lose." [47]

Austin was buzzing over the Longhorns' success. It was the first time in history the fieldhouse had been sold out for two consecutive games. Abe was proud of the jam-packed gym. "You couldn't have got a midget in there. I don't know what they're going to do if we get any people who can play. They'll probably go crazy," he said. [48]

Texas lost to Southern Methodist University by one point at Dallas, 74-73, when Moore missed a long shot at the buzzer. Abe continued to have near-heart attacks as Goodner hit only a third of his free throws. Goodner was fouled with six seconds on the clock and had a chance to tie the game with a free throw. He shot an air ball and Southern Methodist University won. After the game Abe said, "I was hoping he'd lay down and play hurt." [49]

Back at home the Longhorns beat Texas Tech 73-72, the first victory over the Red Raiders in 18 tries over nine seasons. Texas then lost to the two best teams in the conference, Houston and Arkansas. Houston's All-American Otis Birdsong poured in 43 points for the Cougars.

Abe's team was dealt a severe blow in late January when Goodner was declared academically ineligible for making an

"Incomplete" in an 8:00 a.m. geography class. Three days later, Arkansas, led by Ron Brewer, Sidney Moncrief, and Marvin Delph, crushed Texas 86-58. Abe said of Arkansas, "They had us outclassed at every spot. They're the best team the Southwest Conference has had in a long time...How do you beat them, unless they get the bubonic plague?" [50]

Abe was sad to see Goodner leave by way of ineligibility. He had seen real progress in Goodner's play since fall practice began. Abe bragged on his remaining players, especially rail-thin guard Krivacs, the Longhorns' best long-shot shooter. Abe said Krivacs was so skinny "he looks like he just came off a death march." [51]

A reporter for the *Houston Chronicle* conducted an in-depth interview with Baxter about Abe's coaching techniques. Baxter gave a glowing account of his new coach, "He's the best sideline coach in the nation...He cut me up pretty good in practice [referring to Abe's tart tongue used with his players] for not moving down the baseline when I was inbounding against a fullcourt press, and he told me I couldn't get open if a dead man was guarding me, and that I couldn't hit the basket with a shotgun." [52]

Baxter was appreciative of Abe's relationship with his players, saying,"There's no curfew, not even on the road. It's all up to you...Before the games, he'll come in and tell a few jokes and that's it. Then, before we go out again, he'll just remind us of the things we need to remember...You can't believe everything he says. Sometimes he talks to just talk. We understand that. He'll say a lot of things just to get everybody together." [53]

Texas won its next six games over Rice; Texas Christian University twice; Centenary; Baylor, in two overtimes; and Southern Methodist University.

Texas Tech broke the Longhorns winning streak at Lubbock, 87-69. Abe was enraged by the officiating of Denny Bishop. Abe declared Bishop would never again call a game in which he was participating. After Ovie Dotson of Texas was whistled for his third personal, Bishop turned and called a technical foul on Abe who swore all he was doing was telling his players to get a little more physical. A minute later, Bishop called a technical on UT assistant

Barry Dowd who was counting, "One thousand, two thousand, three thousand, four thousand," pointing out to the officials that Tech players were staying in the lane longer than the three seconds allowed by rule. Bishop said Dowd was trying to intimidate him.

After the game Abe accused Bishop, who had played college basketball for the University of Houston, of ignoring Tech's coach Gerald Myers who "was off the bench on roller skates all afternoon and nothing was called on him." [54] Abe could not figure out how Bishop could hear the mutterings of Dowd with 5,500 fans screaming their lungs out. Abe said the technicals, which resulted in four points for the Red Raiders, lost Texas the game.

Dowd and Abe coached well together. Betty Jo accused Dowd of being able to read Abe's mind. Abe hardly ever verbally told Dowd what he expected him to do as his assistant coach. As Dowd said, "It just happened. Without him telling me anything, I just knew what he wanted me to do, what part he wanted me to play in the whole scheme of things." [55]

After losing to Houston, the Longhorns prepared for a return match with Arkansas, at Fayetteville. When Abe discovered the game had been picked for a weekly Southwest Conference television broadcast, he said, "The guy who thought of that ought to be in a rubber room." [56] Arkansas had won the first meeting with the Longhorns by 28 points. However, at Fayetteville, Abe's troops cut the margin, losing by 12, 73-61.

On his first trip to Fayetteville, Abe began a hate-hate relationship with Arkansas fans and Razorbacks coach Eddie Sutton. Abe told John Schill, the host of Abe's weekly television show on KTBC-TV in Austin, "We changed planes three times and we were still 50 miles from Fayetteville. I got to Alaska easier than that." Abe revealed that because several of his players had had viruses, he told them to "cough on the Arkansas guys. Maybe it'd keep 'em off of us." The Filling Station, a popular Austin restaurant, was the sponsor of Abe's television show for the first season.

Abe accused Arkansas fans of poor sportsmanship, saying, "It's amazing why grown people come to harass young men. There's got to be a flaw in a man's character to do that." [57]

Abe blamed the loss to the Razorbacks on uncalled fouls. Longhorn Rich Parson caught an elbow from Razorback Jim Counce that broke Parson's nose and no foul was called. Krivacs pointed out the error to the official who promptly called him with a technical. Texas did not go to the foul line once in the first half. [58]

Texas closed out the regular season with a 90-51 victory over Rice, giving the Longhorns an 8-8 mark, good enough for a tie for fourth place in the conference.

Texas won a spot as a host team for the first round of the post-season conference tournament, which Abe did not like, "We play 16 games to see who wins it, then turn around and play a tournament to see who loses it." [59]

Several Texas players were still ailing with bad colds. Abe said, "We're all hackin' and coughin', really decimated. But we gotta keep poking 'em to stay out there. If it was a war, we could surrender, but we're obligated." [60]

Texas lost to Baylor 72-70 in the opening round of the Southwest Conference tournament and Abe's first season at the helm of the Longhorns was over. His team posted a 13-13 record. Athletic director Royal and Texas fans were happy with the improvement over the previous decade and the excitement generated by Abe's antics both on and off the court. Abe said he was tired, he had never had to work this hard at coaching before.

After the season the *Austin Citizen* sent reporter Candy Lowry to interview Betty Jo about her life as wife of the UT head basketball coach. In a feature article, the newspaper reporter described the Lemons' home, "The Lemons' kitchen overlooks a sitting room hung with family photographs and decorated with overstuffed chairs and a hooked rug done by Betty. 'I like this part of the house because it's so homey,'" she [Betty Jo] said, 'Also, I can cook and visit with Abe and my girls when they're home.' She [Betty Jo] can also listen to music (a stereo intercom is installed near the oven), or she can sit at her kitchen desk and re-read the sign that hangs there: 'When you get lemons, make lemonade.'" [61]

A Tribute by Darrell Royal

of Abe:

first met Abe Lemons over 50 years ago when I was visiting my brother at a small college near our hometowns in southwestern Oklahoma. We were both a long way from the University of Texas, then.

Our paths would cross from time to time after that. In 1976, basketball was beginning to make an impact in the Southwest Conference and we at the University of Texas were in need of a coach to take us to that next level. We were opening a new building and I knew we needed someone who could win on the court and be popular with the fans.

Abe had had all of that success with Oklahoma City University and he was doing a great job at Pan American University. He had been a winner everywhere he had been and I have always believed that "winners win."

So I called Abe who called me back from a truck stop. He agreed to become the UT basketball coach and was exactly what we needed at the time. In his second year, our first in the new arena, he took a team that had an unlikely bunch of heroes and won the National Invitational Tournament in New York City.

The next year we sold 15,500 season tickets for an arena that seated 16,200. Abe was a local and national celebrity. His teams were fun to watch play and his homespun philosophy captured the fans.

The most impressive thing about Abe is that he has never changed. Success did not spoil him. He was always a maverick and he was honest to a fault. He would fight for his kids and fight for what was right, even if his position was not popular with the powers-that-be.

As his boss, I always appreciated Abe's loyalty. Once I had to call him into the office when he called an official a dirty word in a post-game argument and our college president, a lady, got a letter about it.

I flipped the letter toward Abe and told him I needed to talk to him about it. He dutifully read the letter, looked up sheepishly, and said, "Darrell, I guess chicken —— doesn't look very good in print." That was the only time I ever had to call him down.

There was a fierce competitor in Abe. But when you listened to him, you heard a man who had the game of basketball in perspective to the real game of life.

The highest compliment you can pay a person is call him your friend and Abe Lemons is my friend. And I were going into a fight, he would be the first guy I would want on my side.

—*Chapter Sixteen*—

A Dream Season

You can say something to popes, kings and presidents, but
you can't talk to officials. In the next war, they ought to give
everybody a whistle.

Abe Lemons

ANY TIME ANYONE WOULD LISTEN, ABE TALKED ABOUT SORRY
officiating and cheating in recruiting. He said, "The referees get
smaller and the players get bigger. We play the cleanest of anybody
in the league, but it just doesn't pay off. We're going to have to get
some bullies. It's turned into a wrestling match, and we can't win."
[1] Abe threatened to send his players to karate class, blaming league
officials for not insisting that games be called closely, "You can tag,
hold, hack. We need to take a couple of lessons. I'm not complain-
ing, but I think we need to learn a few little tricks." [2]

One thing was sure. Abe got over his anger at officials quickly
after a game. Irv Brown, a veteran referee who worked six national
championship games in his career, said Abe was one of those
"When it's over, it's over" kind of guys. Brown put Abe in the same
category with Al McGuire of Marquette, Bob Knight of Indiana,
Hank Egan of Air Force, and Don Haskins of the University of

Texas at El Paso. Of Abe, Brown said, "He'll listen to you. Abe's knows what's going on at all times."

Abe quickly learned that Texas fans wanted more than just a game. As a natural-born promoter, Abe won the hearts of the Texas faithful by spicing up the extras at games. He said the biggest roar he ever heard in the dressing room was at half-time when someone won a trip to Acapulco by hitting a shot from midcourt. [3]

Abe went on a one-man campaign for honesty in recruiting in the Southwest Conference. Darrell Royal approved Abe's recommendation that polygraphs be used to investigate recruiting infractions. Abe was disgusted with cheating everywhere he looked, "You go to recruit a kid, and he has holes in his shoes. Next time you see him, he's wearing a $300 suit. To me, that's suspicious...Or you go to the gym to practice on a road trip and the parking lot looks like a new car agency. Some of our players at Pan American had cars, but they wouldn't start." [4]

Abe disliked the lack of camaraderie and the hypocrisy he saw overtaking the coaching profession, "The under-the-table dealings are worse than ever. Everybody's getting into it. They call some guys great coaches, but look how they get their players...Nobody believes those things happen in college basketball. One coach in the Southwest Conference reports another for cheating, and everyone wants to know who the dirty rat was that turned him in." [5]

Abe admitted that he had turned in coaches whom he suspected of misdealing on the recruiting trail, "I don't mind being a spy. Hell, yes, I've turned guys in, but they always knew about it. I told them about it beforehand, and it wasn't for anything Mickey Mouse. They can fly parents in for games. They can fly the kid home. It's the things like money and cars that has to stop." [6]

Abe's philosophy on competing in big-time sports was simple, "It's a sad day when people think that if you try to do something especially good, you can't be honest and do it. You try to be straight, run a clean program, and somebody down the road is cheating, trying to put you out of business. But if you yell, you're the one who is scorned." [7]

Abe had a successful off-season of recruiting in the spring and summer of 1977. One player he missed was 6'9" Freddie Cowan of Union County, Kentucky. Abe thought he had a lock on Cowan until Cowan scored 34 points in a state tournament game and drew the attention of every recruiter in the country. Abe ultimately lost Cowan to the University of Kentucky.

Abe spent a lot of time in the off-season on the banquet and coaches' clinic circuit. Nike consultant Ed Janka, who set up many of the clinics at which Abe was a guest, explained the impact that an Abe Lemons appearance made on coaches, "We had high school and college coaches, some of the most well-known in the country, who would stop what they were doing to listen to Abe and Jim Valvano [head coach at North Carolina State University] speak. The two were classics, best friends, maybe the last of the 'cowboys,' that breed of coach that would say exactly what was on their mind. When Abe and Valvano appeared on a program, there was standing room only and no one left until the last story had been told."[8]

Abe's secretary at UT was Ronda Lands who was hired by him in an unusual interview. After a preliminary screening by assistant coach Dowd, Lands was ushered into Abe's office. He kept working and she just sat there, quietly. After five minutes Abe announced Lands had the secretary's job because "you don't chat much." Lands called Abe "an eagle among men."[9]

The Longhorns moved into the new Frank Erwin Center for the 1977-1978 season. The 16,000-plus seat arena was a Cadillac among basketball centers in the country. It was called "The Super Drum." Abe was impressed, "It's a pretty classy place, you know. They've even got rugs on the walls [to improve acoustics]. I guess they're there if you want to walk up the wall. I've walked up a few myself."[10]

Abe had Krivacs and Baxter back for his second season at Texas. He also recruited Tyrone Branyon, a 6'7" forward from Cypress, California Junior College and native of Cushing, Oklahoma. When assistant coach Dowd was dispatched to California to watch Branyon, he reported back to Abe, "Picture a big, slow white kid who shot from his hip and couldn't jump. He had 27 points, about

14 rebounds and was the MVP of the tournament." Abe said, "Sounds like my kind of player." [11]

Abe had increased awareness of the Longhorns basketball program by speaking to alumni groups and civic clubs from one end of Texas to the other. Often he appeared with UT football coach Fred Akers.

The Longhorns' success in basketball attracted all kinds of people and changes in the program. In previous seasons the second-string cheerleaders showed up for basketball games. Success meant the first-team cheerleaders took over.

A group of spirit dancers, called the Luvs, began performing during timeouts. The scantily-clad girls drew much attention, not all good. When a fan complained that the girls were performing suggestive dances, Abe received a letter from UT vice-president Jim Colvin. Abe was less than diplomatic in his answer to Colvin:

Dear Dr. Colvin, I have not seen the Luvs dance, but will make it my personal concern to do so. In the mean time, what about the cheerleaders at football games, where one of the male cheerleaders hoists the girl cheerleader over his head, holds her up by the foot with the other hand on her ass and she lifts the other leg high in the air and shows her crotch to the crowd. This should be investigated. If you wish to disband the Luvs, you will have to talk to the athletic director and explain why to the student newspaper.[12]

The season opener was against the University of Southern California in Los Angeles. While in California Abe and his players met Jaclyn Smith and Cheryl Ladd, two of the stars of the hit television show "Charlie's Angels." Abe was not impressed, "What the hell. They'd be just average on the UT campus." [13] Abe may have won the hearts of the undergraduate females on the Austin campus with his comments, but his basketball team fell short, dropping the opener to USC by a single point 65-64. Abe was proud of his team for an incredible effort in a losing cause.

The Longhorns returned to Austin and hosted the University of Oklahoma. Texas beat the Sooners 83-76 and began a phenomenal streak of 25 straight victories in the new Erwin Center. After the win over Oklahoma, season ticket sales went through the roof and attendance in the new arena steadily climbed. Texas averaged more than 9,000 fans per game in the 1977-1978 campaign. Attendance would be even better the next year. [14]

Texas avenged the previous season's controversial loss to Mississippi State by winning at home 83-69. Louisiana State University was the Longhorns' third victim in the early season. Mike Murphy, a 6'8" hometown boy from Austin, hit three field goals and had five rebounds in the win over LSU. Abe said, "Murphy's been hiding in the woods but he woke up last week [he had five points in the Mississippi State game] and he came alive this week. He's not on fire yet, but he's smoking a little around the big toe." [15] Unfortunately, Murphy ended up playing in only 17 games and scored just 36 points for the year.

Abe took his team into enemy territory, to Stillwater, Oklahoma, for a December game against Oklahoma State. Texas surprised even itself with a 21-point victory over the Cowboys 108-87.

"We were on a mission," Krivacs recalled 20 years after the dream season, "We wanted to win a national championship and Abe made us believe we could. Everything may have looked funny to supporters who sat in the stands watching practice but there was nothing funny to the players who went about practice with a passion. We were a short and skinny team who couldn't jump, but we won because we had chemistry and Abe knew which five players to have on the floor in any situation." [16]

Texas easily outscored Alaska and Centenary the next week. Then the Longhorns raised their record to 7-1 with a 88-71 whipping of OCU, the best start for a Texas team since 1948.

The Longhorns accepted an invitation to play in the Milwaukee Classic in Milwaukee, Wisconsin. In the first game Texas was matched up against Army, coached by young Mike Krzyzewski. The Longhorns narrowly escaped with a one-point victory, 74-73. Abe lauded Coach K, "You will never look good playing Army. If anybody could spell his name, the Army guy [Krzyzewski] would be coach of the year." [17]

Texas hit only 32 percent of its shots in the championship game of the Milwaukee Classic against Marquette University. Marquette was the defending national champion and beat Texas 66-65, snapping the Longhorns' eight-game winning streak.

One bright spot in the Texas loss was the play of Tyrone Branyon who came off the bench and landed five long-range field goals. Branyon was the fifth starter that Abe had been looking for. The Oklahoma native became the Longhorns' top inside scoring threat even though he did not exactly look like a top athlete. During one game television commentator and former coach Al McGuire told Abe that Branyan reminded him of "those guys you see at the YMCA, playing with their underwear showing." [18]

Gary Goodner played tough under the boards for Texas in the game against Marquette. However, Goodner was no match for Marquette's 6'10", 250 pound Jerome Whitehead.

Back in Texas, the Longhorns manhandled Texas Christian University 90-41 in Fort Worth, one of the worst defeats of the Horned Frogs in history. Back home in the Super Drum, Texas beat Texas Tech and won at Houston. However, for weeks Abe and his staff had been looking forward to the January 14th game against Arkansas in Austin.

The Razorbacks were 14-0 and ranked third in the country. Abe told reporters the day before the game that Arkansas could not be beaten. He later said the reporters should not always believe everything he said.

Secretly, Abe built the confidence of his players to a new level. Johnny Moore led the Longhorns onto the floor with the look of a fanatic. In fact, the whole Texas team played like never before and upset Arkansas 75-69.

Krivacs was the heart and soul of the Texas basketball team. Skip Bayless of the *Dallas Morning News* paid tribute to Krivacs who had, in high school, run third in the balloting for "Mr. Indiana Basketball," a title close in prestige to the governor's job in Indiana. Bayless wrote, "You can search many a playground and all-American team before you'll find a more remarkable success story.

Disney should do the movie...At age 14, the little Hungarian kid decided that if he couldn't beat the black kids dominating basketball, he'd join 'em. He rode his bicycle into inner city Indianapolis and played with black players." [19]

Austin sportswriter Robert Heard called Ovie Dotson a "free spirit" from San Antonio who thrilled Super Drum fans with two-handed dunk shots. When Texas clearly had a game in hand, the home crowd would chant, "Ovie, Ovie, Ovie," until Abe would put Dotson in. [20]

Texas beat Rice 78-64 in a game in which Owls coach Mike Schuler made 99 substitutions. The Austin crowd enjoyed the wholesale substitutions so much the fans began calling for new players to enter the lineup. Abe said, "All they needed were clowns to make it a circus." [21]

The Longhorns pulled out a 79-77 overtime win at Texas A & M and beat Baylor, Southern Methodist University, and Houston. Texas trailed for much of the Houston game. Two of the Longhorn starters were sick and another two were injured. Somehow, Texas pulled out a 73-72 victory, the fourth win in a row by five points or less. Branyon finished with 16

Ovie Dotson became a fan favorite in Austin. Abe said Dotson was probably his most valuable player, "His spirit, his character, is much of our driving force. If I had a son, I'd like him to be just like Ovie. However, since Ovie's black, I might have some explaining to do if my son was just like him." Dotson later played for the Harlem Globetrotters. Courtesy Harlem Globetrotters.

points and 10 rebounds. He hit six of eight free throws, telling a reporter after the game, "I had to make those free throws. If I didn't, Abe might never play me again." [22] The Longhorns brought their season record to 17-2 and were the darlings of the national media.

Next the Longhorns ran into a revenge-minded Arkansas team in Fayetteville. This time the Razorbacks won 75-71. As usual, Abe was mad at the officials. Warned not to say anything bad about the striped-shirts in a strong letter of reprimand from conference officials, Abe quoted a Houston player who had said that Arkansas had quick hands and officials had slow eyes. Arkansas, ranked second in the country, hand-checked brilliantly on defense, a maneuver Abe knew his team could not compete against.

Johnny Moore's number 00, the same number he wore while a Texas Longhorn, was retired in 1998, after Johnny's 10 seasons in the National Basketball Association. In 1985, Moore was felled by a deadly infection. For months, he was plagued by excruciating headaches and terrible nausea. Doctors told him he might go blind and lose the use of his limbs, and possibly die. However, Johnny came back and slowly his health returned to normal. Courtesy San Antonio Spurs.

Longhorn Johnny Moore was blunt in his post-game comments, "They [Arkansas] hold you on the weak side and don't let you move the ball. I can't blame them because they always get away with it...But poor officiating like that detracts from the game." [23]

When Texas went to Houston to play Rice, Owls' fans remembered Abe's comment about "clowns" in the big-time substitution game in Austin earlier in the year. Hundreds of Rice students showed up in clown costumes. Abe was not rattled, saying, "I've seen wharf rats bigger than some of these clowns." When Texas won the game 102-86, Abe said he took no offense by the actions of the Rice crowd, "They had a good time, not as good as they hoped to have however." [24] A United Press International photographer took a photo of Abe standing in front of a Rice fan decked out in his clown suit. The UPI photo appeared in newspapers across the country.

After a 90-66 thumping of Texas A & M, Texas was upset by Baylor 79-77, dropping the Longhorns a half-game behind Arkansas in the race for the Southwest Conference crown. Abe blamed poor lighting for his team's lackluster performance in the Heart O' Texas Coliseum in Waco, "I thought they were having a seance. We ran in pairs just to keep the spiders from eating us." [25]

Abe congratulated Baylor on the win, "It's too bad Baptists don't drink in public. It would be a nice night for them to celebrate." [26]

The Longhorns beat Texas Tech but still trailed Arkansas in the conference standings. No one really gave Texas a chance to tie Arkansas for the Southwest Conference regular season crown because Arkansas' final game was against Houston. However, the Cougars upset the Razorbacks, giving Texas a chance to beat Southern Methodist University and win a co-championship.

In a priceless moment in Texas, and broadcasting history, Abe opened his weekly television show after the Arkansas loss to Houston lying down with his hands folded across his stomach while organ music played in the background. As the camera panned to his head, Abe opened his eyes, raised up on one elbow and said, "We're not dead yet." [27]

Texas accepted the challenge and beat Southern Methodist University 82-74 to share the Southwest Conference title with Arkansas. The win assured Texas of a bye in the post-season tournament.

The Southwest Conference tournament was played on the University of Houston's home court at The Summit in Houston. The Cougars upset Arkansas to face the Longhorns in the tournament finals. Houston beat Texas 92-90. Abe griped, "We'd like to play this thing in Austin sometime. We'd like to stay at home and sleep in our own beds. I think playing in Houston made the difference the last two nights." [28]

Conference officials listened to Abe's complaints about the obvious hometown advantage for the University of Houston. Eight months later, the conference voted to move the tournament in 1980 to San Antonio, where no conference team would have a home-court advantage.

Abe also complained about referee Paul Galvan who was only about 5'6". Abe said referees should be taller, "so they could see what's going on." Galvan later quit officiating in the Southwest Conference and Abe was widely given the credit for Galvan's departure. [29]

Passed over by the NCAA, Abe took his 22-5 Longhorns into the NIT first round action in Austin against Temple University.

Texas beat the Owls 72-58, in Abe's 400th career victory, to earn a second round game against Nebraska. The Longhorns won the Temple game despite playing the worst first half of the season. In a radio interview after the game, Abe pleaded for someone to call in to volunteer for rebounding duties. "I don't care if you're 3-foot-2," Abe cried.

Tournament officials had mistakenly promised both Texas and Nebraska that they could host the game. Abe loudly refused to go to Lincoln, citing the personal promise of the president of the NIT that Texas could host the game. Abe explained the dilemma to athletic director Darrell Royal who said he saw no way for Texas to refuse to go to Nebraska. Abe simply replied, "What about a man's word?" referring to his conversation with the head of the NIT. Two members of the UT Board of Regents, university president Dr. Lorraine Rogers, and Longhorn supporter Frank Erwin backed Abe and urged him to stand his ground.

When Abe forced the game to be played in Austin, a member of the Nebraska board of regents suggested Nebraska should break athletic ties with Texas. Abe quipped, "I didn't know we had any." [30]

Texas topped Nebraska 67-48 and won the right to travel to New York City for the NIT final four. The Longhorns were pitted against Rutgers University. When told that Rutgers coach Tom Young had suggested that Texas played only offense, Abe told his team that it was time to show some defense. Texas did, and beat Rutgers 96-76, advancing to the NIT championship game.

During a practice at the NIT, Georgetown University head coach John Thompson watched Ron Baxter work out. Thompson said, "Who's the fat kid over there?" Abe said, "He's my star."

Abe was the toast of the New York press. He told a news conference, "I had two eggs for breakfast this morning and the bill was $4.95. I want to see the chicken that could lay $4.95 eggs. It would have to have a fancy little umbrella and a gilded nest." [31] Before Abe arrived back in Austin, some Texas fan sent him three chickens who promptly messed all over the top of his desk.

Ron Baxter took some heavy kidding from New York writers about his weight. Some said he weighed 250. Another said he looked like he had a ball under his jersey. Baxter responded and scored 26 points in the NIT championship game as Texas beat North Carolina State 101-93 to take the NIT crown, a first time honor for any Southwest Conference school.

The Longhorns had early leads of 20-9 and 36-23 before mounting a 54-39 half-time advantage. The second half was more of the same, "more fast break lay-ups for the Longhorns and more heartache for Norm Sloan whose team wasted strong performances from Tiny Pinder and Hawkeye Whitney." [32] The game was actually not as close as the final score indicated. Abe emptied his bench and North Carolina State scored the last seven points to narrow the final margin.

Krivacs and Baxter were named co-most valuable players of the 41st National Invitation Tournament. The two Longhorn stars combined for 59 points in the title game. University of Texas President Dr. Lorraine Rogers was so happy that she ran up to Abe immediately after the game and kissed Abe on the mouth. North Carolina State coach Norm Sloan said if Texas had been in the

LEFT: Abe, left, and Duke University basketball coach Bill Foster, right, became great friends as successive presidents of the National Association of Basketball Coaches. Foster is now in charge of Big XII Conference basketball. Courtesy Bill Foster.

BELOW: Abe gives the "hook 'em horns" sign as the final buzzer signaled the Longhorns victory in NIT championship game. Courtesy University of Texas.

NCAA tournament, the Longhorns would have won it all. Sloan complimented Abe's team for "great discipline, great execution, ability to take whatever the other team gives, and particularly the great shooting." [33]

Abe told a *New York Post* reporter, "We chewed up the full-court press like chicken fried steak." The reporter wrote about the post-game news conference, "Lemons smiled and puffed on a cigar that looked as though it had been in his mouth since last October. His audience was laughing again. That's the kind of NIT it was. Lemons making us laugh, and the Longhorns making him proud." [34] Abe's Longhorns completed the 1977-1978

BELOW: Longhorn Ron Baxter cuts down the net after the University of Texas defeated North Carolina State 101-73 in the finals of the 1978 NIT at Madison Square Garden in New York. Courtesy Associated Press.

dream season at 26-5, 14-2 in the Southwest Conference, one of the best records in the country. Abe summed his team, "People thought we were a ship of fools, a McHale's Navy. But we had discipline. People knew what they were doing." [35]

John Danks echoed Abe's assessment of the NIT win over North Carolina State, "We outsmarted them. We'd play for awhile, stop and talk about what the opponent was doing, then we'd do the opposite. They pressed us. When they did that, it was like we were rubbing our hands together like evil scientists. We were saying, 'These idiots played right into our hands.'" [36]

Danks called Abe a genius, "He wasn't the most technical coach you ever saw, but when it came to the human condition he was an expert. He knew how to get inside people's heads, good or bad. Nobody could match wits with him. If he wanted to burn you down, he knew which button to push. But if he wanted to build you up, he knew how to do that, too." [37]

Krivacs, now a successful Florida-based sports agent, looked back at the dream season, "Abe's brilliance was incredible, but it was camouflaged by how funny he was. He had people dying laughing on the sideline, but it was serious business to us...Everybody we played against was bigger, faster, stronger and quicker. But that's not what winning is all about. We had a smarter coach." [38]

The high-leaping Dotson, who played seven years with the Harlem Globetrotters after starring at UT, gave Abe all the credit for the dream season. "Abe always believed it was a players' game. He took the losses, we took the wins. He treated us like men...His big deal was 'Can you win in life?'" [39]

Assistant coach Dowd said Abe had no equal when it came to offensive basketball, "He'd tell a kid, 'Stand there. You'll get a shot,' and sure enough, they would. I've seen scorers through the years since then and I'd think to myself, 'If he was playing for Abe, he'd be getting 40 a game.'" [40]

In April, 1978, Abe and Duke University coach Bill Foster were named national co-basketball coaches of the year by the National Association of Basketball Coaches.

The NIT victory gave Abe a boost in press coverage around the nation. A United Press International dispatch from New York called Abe "one of a kind." The UPI reporter wrote, "His endearing southern drawl, dry wit and homespun frankness have placed him in high demand for public appearances around the country...He can time a joke with the best of them, or stun you with his candor...The reason is obvious why Lemons is so popular. He can be coarse, abrasive, uppity and shocking, or he can be friendly, confiding, sincere and lovable. And when he's in top form, really sharp, he can combine all those characteristics into one, leaving you to decide for yourself...Hollywood should have a place reserved for Abe Lemons." [41]

Chapter Seventeen

Abe and Eddie

I never could take some fat slob yelling at me from
behind the bench. Those little old ladies dressed in school colors
from head to toe, with their jugular veins sticking out, yelling
obscenities at the players and coaches. I wonder if on the way
home from the game they jump into a phone booth and come
out wearing a housecoat and serving tea.

Abe Lemons

A GOOD SCREENWRITER IN HOLLYWOOD COULD PROBABLY TAKE
the exchanges between Abe and Eddie Sutton, coach at Arkansas,
Kentucky, and now Oklahoma State, and craft a best-selling movie.
The rivalry between Abe and Sutton began while Abe was at Texas
and Sutton was at Arkansas.

Abe alienated himself from many citizens of Arkansas with his
comments about the state, and in particular, the city of Fayetteville,
where the University of Arkansas was located. Abe once told his
players the day before Texas met the Razorbacks, "Here's the deal.
The guy who plays the worst has to stay in Fayetteville for a week.
We'll vote on it if it's a close call. We'll get you a hotel room, paid
for in advance." [1]

Abe had a glimmer in his eye when reporters asked him about
going to play at Fayetteville, "We'll probably have to parachute in

there. Their airport's not much." [2] Abe said if someone moved from Oklahoma to Arkansas, the IQ of both states would go up.

Frank Boggs observed the Abe and Eddie jabs and counter-jabs down through the years. Boggs wrote, "Lemons forever has kept up a steady outpour of anti-Arkansas one-liners. He and Sutton are two of the best in the business, but they don't go out and eat enchiladas together. Abe, in the past, has suggested the visiting team be given ropes, so everybody could swing into the Fayetteville area, a la Tarzan, and keep the mud off their shiny shoes." [3]

The rivalry between Abe and Sutton was not always humorous. After a 1979 Arkansas win in Austin when Sutton became offended at the way Longhorn John Moore set himself to take a charge, Abe jumped in the middle of the fray. A newspaper account was vivid, "With the sprig of hair that dominates his [Abe's] forehead dancing all over his face, [Abe] threatened to do bodily harm to the Arkansas coach. 'I'll rip his Sunday clothes,' was one of the few lines that could be reproduced in a newspaper." [4]

After a Texas victory over Arkansas, Abe was invited to speak at a function at which the majority of fans were from Arkansas. An over-cautious building manager stopped Abe at the door and warned him that the people inside were hostile. Abe was unafraid and said, "Well, I once went into a place in Calcutta you couldn't stick a rat into. I've worked in a slaughter house. I've been lots of places. I'll give it a try...The place is packed with school kids. They see me and they freeze like they've seen Lucifer." [5]

The Arkansas legislature entered the fray between Abe and Sutton in March, 1979, when a tongue-in-cheek resolution honoring Abe was introduced. The resolution praised Abe for speaking so highly of Arkansas, for showing goodwill toward the Razorbacks, and for doing his utmost to promote Arkansas and its image. The document even declared Abe to be an honorary citizen of Arkansas. The resolution failed 93-0. Abe took the legislative action in stride, "I would not have accepted Arkansas citizenship anyway. I could never be that low." [6]

Years later, after the intense heat of Abe and Sutton's rivalry had cooled, Abe showed up at a roast of Sutton in overalls and a wig similar to Sutton's hairstyle at the time. After Abe and Indiana coach Bob Knight bombarded Sutton with "an array of insulting remarks," neither was invited to a reception at the Arkansas governor's mansion. [7]

Abe's feelings were not injured and the venerable Abe even had a few kind words about Sutton and his coaching ability, "Eddie's really one of the better coaches to come around. He's really good." [8] Abe even admitted that deep down he liked Arkansas fans, saying, "I just stirred them up to hype the game."

However, those "feel-good" comments were nowhere to be found as the 1978-1979 basketball season began for the Texas Longhorns. Most observers predicted the new version of the Longhorns could not perform as well as the previous season. Abe thought the prognosticators might be right after Texas lost its first game to Long Beach State 76-71.

The Longhorns rebounded and scored a record 148 points, taking frustrations out on Northern Montana, who scored only 71 points in the one-sided affair. Abe's squad beat Oklahoma State and BYU but lost to Oklahoma and San Francisco before beginning the tough Southwest Conference schedule.

The Longhorns beat Texas Christian University but lost a road game at Texas Tech. Then Texas won at Houston, at tough Barnhill Arena in Fayetteville, Arkansas, at Rice, and pounded Texas A & M, Houston, and Baylor at home. Arkansas returned the favor by beating Texas in Austin.

Texas reeled off five conference wins in a row in February against Texas Christian University, Rice, Texas A & M, Baylor, and in overtime against Texas Tech. In the last regular season game, the Longhorns fell to Southern Methodist University in Dallas and prepared for the Southwest Conference tournament in Houston.

Texas beat Houston in the first game of the post-season tournament but fell one point short in a 39-38 slow-down second round game against Arkansas.

Invited to the NCAA round of 32, Texas was beaten by Oklahoma 90-76 in a first round game in Dallas. The final numbers looked good for Abe's third season at Texas. The Longhorns were 21-8 and tied for the Southwest Conference title at 13-3.

The 1979-1980 Texas Longhorns team. Courtesy University of Texas.

Abe had made an unprecedented impact upon UT basketball in his first three seasons. His won-loss record was 60-26, the winningest percentage of any UT coach to that point.

The Longhorns drew an average of 15,885 fans to home games in 1979-1980, fourth best in the nation. The increase of more than 6,000 fans per game over the previous season was tops among major college powers. Texas became one of the most televised teams in the region, their games picked up by both the networks and cable systems such as ESPN and Madison Square Garden.

Johnny Moore left school early and was drafted in the first round of the NBA draft by Seattle who promptly sold him to the San Antonio Spurs. When Moore was cut from the Spurs squad before the season began, he called Abe who counseled him to return to school. Abe gave Moore a job as a graduate assistant coach the next season before Moore again tried out for the Spurs. The second time Moore won a position on the team and played for the Spurs for ten years. [9]

Few fans considered the 1979-1980 Longhorns to be a contender in the Southwest Conference. Local newspapers predicted UT would lose about as many games as they won and finish in the middle of the pack in the conference.

Ron Baxter was the only returning starter for Abe. Senior John Danks and sophomore Henry Johnson, a 6'6" forward from Los Angeles, had substituted well the prior year, but Abe was puzzled how the two would fit into the latest Longhorn club.

After two weeks of practice, Abe told reporters to expect an up and down year, that his team could beat anybody one night and lose to anybody the next night.

Texas opened strong with victories over Northwestern Louisiana, Harvard, Biscayne, Hardin-Simmons, Murray State, and San Francisco. After a mid-season slump, the Longhorns finished with a 10-11 record in the regular season and sole possession of third place in the Southwest Conference.

Baxter claimed seven school records in his senior season, including all-time leading scorer and rebounder. He was third in the conference in scoring with a 17.9 per game average and was a consensus first-team all-conference selection.

Danks, known for his all-out style of play, was the team's second leading scorer at 15.7 points per game and sparked the squad as a starter.

Young players gave UT fans something to look forward to with their performance in 1979-1980. Freshman LaSalle Thompson, a 6'10" post man from Cincinnati, Ohio's Withrow High School, made Abe look good as a recruiter. Thompson had been one of the nation's most sought-after high schoolers the previous spring. In his first year Thompson led the Southwest Conference in rebounding with 292, was third in field goal percentage at .558, and 17th in scoring at 12.8 points per game.

Fred Carson, a 6'1" guard from Springfield, Ohio, was a sophomore and became Abe's point guard. More of a shooter in high school, Carson made the transition well and quarterbacked the Longhorn team effectively.

Johnson nailed down a starting berth at mid-season and solidified the Longhorns down the stretch. Ken Montgomery, a 6'6" forward from Indianapolis, Indiana Meridian High School, transferred to Texas after a year at North Carolina State and played in 27 of UT's 30 games.

Abe and the Longhorns were riding high at the end of the season after two conference wins over Texas Tech and Rice. In the Southwest Conference post-season tournament played at San Antonio's HemisFair Arena, Texas beat Houston by 20, 67-47 in the first game, then dropped a disappointing two-point game to Arkansas 64-62.

The strong performance in February earned the Longhorns an invitation to play in the NIT. It was Texas' third trip to post-season tournaments in Abe's four years at the helm.

Texas hosted the first game at Erwin Center in Austin and beat St. Joseph's 70-61 but was upset by Southwestern Louisiana 77-76, even though Baxter scored 24 points. However, the year had turned out to be better than expected. The Longhorns finished the season at 19-11.

In January, 1980, Darrell Royal retired as UT athletic director and was replaced by longtime Longhorn assistant coach and athletic department aide Bill Ellington. A new era in UT athletics began as Ellington hired T. Jones as assistant athletic director and Dr. L.O. "Tom" Morgan, a chemistry professor, replaced J. Neils Thompson as chairman of the UT Athletics Council. Morgan, a native of Oklahoma City, and his council oversaw all intercollegiate athletic matters at UT.

With Royal gone, Abe sensed problems in communications with the new UT athletic department administration. The Longhorns often received shoe samples from different manufacturers around the country and Abe allowed his players to wear the free shoes. The Athletics Council complained and Abe was forced to stop the practice. Also, the Athletics Council refused Abe's request for pay raises for his assistant coaches. And Abe began a running battle with Ellington over the use of the Erwin Center for practices. Abe was livid when Ellington kicked the basketball team out of the facility to allow the new women's volleyball team to practice on the main court.

A distraction for Abe's leadership of the UT basketball program was a grand jury investigation in Austin in 1980. The panel was called to look into allegations that Johnny Joseph, known to Abe as a local real estate developer, was a big-time gambler and that UT sports events were tainted by Joseph's influence. Amid rumors that UT officials were accepting money from Joseph at the Quorum Restaurant near the campus, Abe volunteered to take a lie detector test. Abe testified briefly in front of the grand jury whose investigation fizzled quickly. Abe's only explanation of his involvement was attributed to the media, "They had to have a big name involved to make the story newsworthy. I knew Joseph because he, and a thousand other guys, hung out at the Quorum, a popular spot for sports and political celebrities. There was never nothin' to the rumors." [10]

Abe began planning the 1980-1981 season with new staff help. John Danks, the four-year letterman, became a student assistant coach while completing his degree requirements. Paul Johnson was named part-time assistant coach while working toward a masters degree at UT. Johnson came to Texas after two years as head coach at Natchez, Mississippi High School.

For the tenth year, Bill Little, the Assistant Sports Information Director, handled the play-by-play for Longhorn basketball on a far-reaching radio network, anchored by KVET Radio in Austin. Fans across the Southwest and Great Plains could hear Texas game broadcasts on powerful stations WBAP in Fort Worth and WOAI in San Antonio.

Abe fielded a young team again in 1980-1981. He had to find replacements for Baxter and Danks who had accounted for 44 per cent of the Longhorns' scoring the prior season. Three starters, Thompson, Carson, and Johnson, joined junior college transfers 6'7" Daryl Bushrod, from Henderson County, Texas Junior College, and 6'6" Virdell Howland from Tyler, Texas Junior College.

Abe was forced to depend upon three freshmen to play a lot of minutes in the new season. What a recruiting class it had been! Mike Wacker, a 6'8" 220 pound forward from San Marcos, Texas, considered by many the top high school prospect in Texas, had averaged 22 points per game in high school and was on *Parade's* All-America team. His father was head football coach at Southwest Texas State University.

Wacker, who had played for a high school coach who was extremely structured in his approach to the game, was at first frustrated and did not understand Abe's concept. Wacker's frustration ended suddenly one afternoon during practice when something just clicked in his brain. Wacker said, "It finally hit me. It was so simple. Abe didn't tell me where to go and where to play. He told me to ask myself, 'Where's the defensive guy?' Abe pounded it into my head to read the defender and go where the defense wasn't." [11]

Bobby Harris, a 5'9" guard, averaged 26 points per game at Columbus, Ohio South High School, setting a city record with 50 points in a game. The third freshman Abe looked to for contribution was Ray Harper, a 5'11" guard who scored more than 3,000 points in his career at Bremen, Kentucky High School. He made Kentucky's All-State team his final two seasons in high school.

Harper, who coached his Kentucky Wesleyan College Panthers to a NCAA Division II national basketball championship in 1999, remembered the "deep" advice Abe gave him as 19-year-old freshman at UT, "Abe told us 'Don't embarrass yourself, don't embarrass your family, and don't embarrass the school" [12]

The new basketball campaign started off badly when the Longhorns were upset by the University of the Pacific 78-77, despite 19 points and ten rebounds from Ken Montgomery. Abe was hit with a critical technical foul with four minutes left in the game, resulting in a four-point play. The Longhorns started basically a no-guard offense with a starting lineup of Johnson, Howland, Montgomery, Wacker, and Thompson.

Fans were less than enthusiastic about the prospects for the young season. In an exhibition game against the University of Windsor, Canada, only 6,254 fans showed up at the Erwin Center. Sportswriter Randy Riggs called the crowd "wildly unenthusiastic." Abe said the fans were downright dull, "I'd say that was one of the dullest things I've ever been associated with. There are highs and lows in dull. This was a high dull." [13]

After defeating Biscayne University, largely on the strength of Thompson's career-high 30 points, Texas' offense got untracked and produced 101 points in a win over New Mexico State University. Montgomery, who Abe had said was slow and "couldn't steal a ball off a dead woman lying on the floor with violets on her chest," [14] scored from everywhere on the court and hit a career-high 34 points. Darryl Bushrod was upset with playing time and left the court at half-time, got dressed, and exited the arena. Abe said, "Kids are going to be kids. They have problems just like us adults. If he shows up, it's fine." [15]

Texas steam-rolled Long Beach State 92-67 with Johnson's 30 points as the high-water mark of the game. The lack of a spectacular team was evident to one reporter who wrote, "Abe isn't working with a cast of thousands, exactly, but it's becoming clear he does have his fair share of offensive weapons." [16] The newspaper account of the game referred to the fact that three different players had led Texas in scoring through the first three games of the season.

The Longhorns hit the century mark for the second time in the season with a 103-82 victory over North Texas State University. Henry Johnson was pumped up for the game because former Texas star Ovie Dotson visited the Longhorn locker room before the contest. Johnson said, "It fired me up. When I saw him, I wanted to show him I appreciated what he did for me in the past, and that this team will carry on." [17]

The conference season began with Texas losing to Texas Tech 89-79 in Lubbock. After the Longhorns were blasted by Texas A & M by 29 points, Abe told a reporter that he was already looking at next year.

In January, 1981, Abe was sick about his team's 5-7 record and even sicker about the Longhorns' 0-3 record in the Southwest Conference. On top of those illnesses came the point in the schedule when Abe loaded up his team and headed for Fayetteville, Arkansas, to take on the Razorbacks and coach Eddie Sutton.

The Nike shoe company contracted with an Austin television station to produce a film about the conflict between Abe and Sutton and picked the January 12, 1981, game to document the rivalry. Cameras followed both coaches for the week before the big game that was slated for national television. Abe bemoaned the fact that Arkansas was undefeated in conference play and his Longhorns had not even played anyone close in the first three conference games. Arkansas had lost only five games in Barnhill Arena in seven years and had won 21 consecutive games that were televised nationally. Abe candidly told the press his team did not have a chance to win.

The Nike television special played up the lack of success of Abe's latest team, "This is not an easy time for Abe. The losses continue to mount. There's no sign of improvement in his team and local fans are putting on the pressure. So off the court, Abe spends time with friends, friends who don't care about rebounding or scoring or winning or losing." [18] The camera showed Abe having breakfast with some of his non-basketball friends at an Austin restaurant across town from the UT campus.

Some Texas newspapers began to question Abe's leadership of the Longhorns. The *Fort Worth Star-Telegram* wrote, "Those rumblings from Austin, Abe Lemons' detractors say, are the sounds of the foundation of the Texas basketball program buckling." However, Abe said the bedrock of the program remained firm, "The biggest tendency is to change your system when things go wrong. But you can't let society wash you out. The best farm is gonna have a bad year." [19]

Abe took his players into Fayetteville with one goal in mind, make them loose and ready to play. The Razorbacks controlled the opening tip and sank their first shot. However, the hostile crowd did not rattle the Texas players and the Longhorns soon found themselves with a five-point lead at half-time. In the dressing room, Abe warned the players about overconfidence and reminded them what a great team Arkansas had.

Texas maintained its lead throughout the second half. Abe could see his players beginning to believe they actually could beat the Razorbacks. Sutton threw a full-court press at Texas with four minutes to go. His players responded with two steals and suddenly the game was tied. But Arkansas fouled Wacker with ten seconds to go and Wacker sank both ends of the one-and-one. When the second shot fell through the basket after hanging on the rim for what seemed like a short eternity, Abe breathed again.

It was a stunning upset, one which Abe did not see, especially since Arkansas star shooter U.S. Reed was dribbling toward the basket with only a few seconds left. After the game, Abe told Randy Riggs, "I just closed my eyes and when I heard the final buzzer and nobody yelling, I knew we were okay." [20]

Losing seasons always bring out verbal snipers who take pot shots at the man in charge. The spring of 1981 was no different. Abe had fired assistant coach Steve Moeller, who had headed up recruiting for the Longhorns, the previous September. Abe said the two men were just not compatible. Moeller called Abe a negligent recruiter and both blamed each other for the program having five unfilled scholarships. Abe announced he and assistant coach Dowd would be spending more time on the recruiting trail. Abe was frustrated with the jabs he took in the press but went about his business trying to win more conference games and prepare for the post-season tournament.

The Longhorns completed the regular season schedule with a ten-point road win over Rice and then beat Rice 58-44 in the first game of the Southwest Conference tournament. Conference observers were baffled as Texas jelled and upset Texas Tech 66-58. Thompson, picked the day before the tournament begin as the center on the All-Southwest Conference team, scored eight straight second half points to overcome a Red Raider seven-point lead. Texas moved on to a semi-final game against Arkansas. Again, the Longhorns were given little chance of winning. Every newspaper in the conference had picked Arkansas and Houston to meet in the title game.

Abe told his players before the game that it was time for people to sit up and take notice of Texas, that only they stood between victory and the sea of doomsayers waiting back in Austin. The Longhorns sent Arkansas packing for home early, beating the Razorbacks 76-73. Abe was literally speechless after the game. He was beaming with pride of his players who never quit in what many thought was a hopeless situation.

With the win over Arkansas, the Longhorns faced powerhouse Houston in the conference finals. Conference player of the year Rob Williams poured in 37 points and the Cougars burst the Longhorns' bubble in a 84-59 runaway. Texas hit only 42 percent from the field while Houston sank 61 percent of its tries.

Sportswriter Bill Sullivan saw hope rising from the defeat. He wrote, "So forget Saturday night, and remember that no one would have figured these people [Texas] would be here in the first place. Forget crying about the refs...When it was over, Texas came away with a future. At the end of a season of ups and downs, the past few weeks proved that Abe Lemons' team has one after all. The future is LaSalle Thompson, and two more years of one of the best big men in America. It is Mike Wacker, who came on these past weeks to help turn a nightmare of a season into the promise of better things to come. The future is Fred Carson, who overcame a horrible start to establish himself as a very respectable major college guard, and Ray Harper, another player who should only get better with age. The future is an improved Ken Montgomery and a more relaxed Virdell Howland." 21

Texas closed out the season at .500 at 15-15.

Views

of Abe:

Abe Lemons; witty, clever, magnetic, compassionate, humorous, entertaining, emotional, caring, concerned; a man with tremendous ability, insight and integrity. Which description fits him best; which is more important? The answer is probably all of the above.

ABOVE: Abe was the big laugh-getter at a roast of Houston Astros owner Don Sanders in November, 1993, at the River Oaks Country Club in Houston. Left to right, Abe, baseball great Nolan Ryan, and Sanders. Courtesy Houston Astros.

The first time you meet Abe and the last time you are with him - it's all the same. You are awed with his strengths and enthusiasm. He has a magnetic personality and his stories are wonderful. You try to remember them all, but can not.

I sometimes think that I've been around him so much that I know his homilies by heart - know exactly what he is going to say - but he always surprises me with something new.

I first met Abe in Houston at a Texas-Rice basketball game in 1978. Texas won. Since that time we have developed a friendship and relationship that is priceless. My trips and travels with Betty Jo and Abe over the years have been as important and meaningful to me as anything I've done.

Of the hundreds of hours I have spent with Abe I only remember one time where he was speechless. Since 1982 Abe has been a major participant in the annual Nolan Ryan Celebrity Golf Tournament held each year at Columbia Lakes, located outside Alvin, Texas, Nolan's hometown. The proceeds of this tournament go to support the Alvin Junior College baseball program. Our group each year included me, Nolan, Abe, (yes, he was the celebrity) and another person. In 1991 the now Governor of Texas, George W. Bush was our fourth.

The format each year is a scramble. The 14th hole is a par 4 with a lake in front of the green. We played Nolan's drive and were about 120 yards out. Abe steps up and hits his shot in the middle of the lake. George W. steps up and hits his shot 2 feet from the pin, turns to Abe and says, "Abe, the difference in your game and mine is that while you were growing up and picking cotton in Oklahoma, I was hitting golf balls at the country club." Not a word was uttered from Abe.

Picking cotton in Oklahoma, coaching basketball teams, winning 599 games and being idolized, respected and admired by so many of us—that's not bad!

—*Chapter Eighteen*—

Ruffling Feathers

After one of my stars, John Nelson at OCU, played lousy in
a game in which he had the flu, and scored only one point, I
told him, "You scored one point more than a dead man."

Abe Lemons

AFTER FIVE YEARS AS HEAD COACH AT THE UNIVERSITY OF TEXAS,
Abe had proven he could be the leader of a big-time basketball program. He was 94-52 in five seasons at UT and ran his career win-
total to 458, seventh best among active coaches in the nation. He
was respected by his peers in the coaching profession and was
selected Southwest Conference coach of the year.

Abe was successful off the basketball court as well. He was the
most sought after speaker in college athletics, the most often
quoted coach, and his weekly television show during the season was
aired by many stations outside Texas.

The only rough spots in Abe's road of life were inside the athletic department at UT. From his early days in Austin, Abe had ruf-
fled the feathers of a major Longhorn supporter and former regent,
Wales Madden, an Amarillo, Texas lawyer. The feather ruffling was
totally unintentional. When he first arrived in Austin, Abe and
assistant coach Barry Dowd had divided a stack of letters that had

accumulated in the coaching office, letters from alumni and supporters recommending potential recruits. Madden was upset because Abe, the head coach, passed his letter off on the assistant coach.

In the fall of 1981, Abe discovered that Madden, now a member of the UT Athletics Council, had not only opposed a raise for Abe the previous season, but had actually recommended Abe be fired. On top of the problem with the Madden relationship, Abe had to learn the methods of a new athletic director, DeLoss Dodds, a former athletic director at Kansas State University and assistant commissioner of the Big Eight Conference.

It seemed as if Abe was called upon again and again to defend his laid back relationship with his players. When questioned by an Austin reporter during fall drills, Abe said no one should question the fire that burned in the hearts of his players, "I don't use things to make something painful. You don't have to stick your hand in the fire to know it's hot. When you see my teams play, I think they give you full effort. They play hard, they work hard, they hurt when they get beat. They're happy when they win. But they aren't a rah rah team. They're not much on turning the lights out, lighting a candle, sitting there playing the Marine anthem, all that kind of stuff. That's a bunch of malarkey. You play for yourself, you play for the team, and if somebody else can help with that, fine. People will accept you if they know you're giving them a true effort." [1]

The media recognized Abe's tenuous relationship with the new UT athletic department administration. Jeff Ketner wrote in the November, 1981 issue of *Austin City Magazine*, "Although Lemons is quick with the one-liner, he's also learned that sometimes his remarks do not sit well with a publicity-conscious UT administration, that his tongue can get away from him. In a one-on-one interview, the Lemons wit is more subdued, his remarks less risky, as if to make sure that the tape recorder will not betray him. Responding on the spur of the moment—in practice, after a game, during a controversial call—Lemons will let fly with his full arsenal. But in a more formal setting, he measures his words carefully, speaking slowly, punctuating his sentences with puffs of cigar smoke." [2]

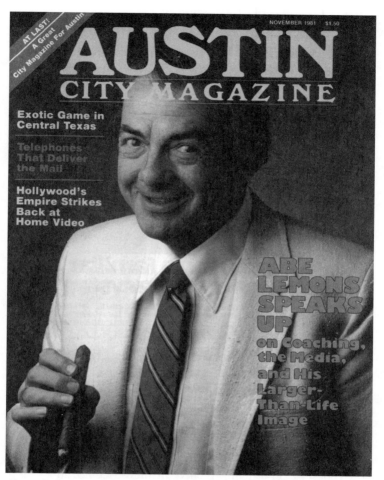

Abe made the cover of the November, 1981, issue of *Austin City Magazine*.
Courtesy Amag Group.

In the interview with *Austin City Magazine*, Abe summed up the keys to his success, "You've got to have good people to operate with. It's like a racehorse. If you don't have a good horse, you can't win the race. Then if you get a good horse, you have to have a good jockey. Then you have to have a good trainer. A coach is a lot the same way. You got to get the team, you have to train them, you have to get them ready to play. And if you do your best, you have a chance of winning." 3

Abe gave his UT players a cultural education to accompany the basketball knowledge he was striving to impart to them. On road trips, Abe's wide circle of friends visited the Longhorns in the dressing room. In Houston, future hall of famer Nolan Ryan gave a pep talk to the team before a game. On a trip to Boston, to play Harvard, Abe made certain the players rode the subway to the game. In southern California, before playing USC, actor James Garner, a native of Norman, Oklahoma, made an appearance in the Longhorn dressing room and Abe took his players to the movie set where the television show "Charlie's Angels" was being taped.

The 1981-1982 Longhorns were not given much chance of a successful season by media prognosticators. *The Sporting News* did not list Texas in its top 84 teams in the nation. However, Abe never read the polls and never voted for his team even though he cast weekly ballots in the United Press International poll.

Texas began the season with expected wins over Hardin-Simmons, Colorado, Drake, and Biscayne. Then the Longhorns caught fire and scored 108 points against Iowa State; beat Harvard, in overtime; Drake, again; Xavier of Ohio; Texas Tech; and Southern Methodist University.

At 10-0, and as one of the few unbeaten major college teams in the country, the Longhorns still had not broken into the Top 20 in either the Associated Press or United Press International polls. National sportswriters apparently reasoned that the Longhorns had not played anyone and would surely lose to Southwest Conference powerhouses Houston and Arkansas, games scheduled in the next few days. However, Texas moved to 19th in the Associated Press poll shortly before the Houston game.

Abe was as relaxed as he had ever been, enjoying a great season. *The Dallas Morning News* sent a reporter to Austin to observe Abe. The scribe wrote, "Abe was the picture of peaceful contentment as he lay on an old sofa in the coaches' dressing room. Stretched out full length, feet crossed, hands locked behind his neck, he looked like he didn't have a care in the world as he gazed dreamily at the concrete ceiling...He was enjoying the rare, fleeting luxury of unblemished success. He savored it like a good smoke." [4]

Abe tried to explain the phenomenal year his team was having. In the off-season, Abe had scored heavily on the recruiting trail, winning the signings of James Tandy, a 6'1" guard from Kentucky, who despite his size, could dunk the ball with both hands; Carlton Cooper, a 6'4" high flying prospect who led his Paris, Texas, high school with 23 points per game the previous season; Jack Worthington, a 6'2" ballhandler who started at guard as a freshman; and James Booker, a 6'5" California junior college transfer with a 41-inch vertical leap, prompting his California coach to label Booker "Skywalker."

"He spends more time on the floor than a rug." Abe said of Worthington. "He's the quickest player on the team. He's daring. He's reckless, the kind of player I like." [5]

Abe was pleasantly surprised with the play of walk-on Dennard Holmes, a 6'4" sophomore swingman from Westinghouse High School in Brooklyn, New York, and veteran Ray Harper, later, after graduating from UT, the basketball coach at Kentucky Wesleyan University.

Abe had his own idea why Harper, at only 5'11" and not very fast, was such an outstanding player, "He looks like he oughta' be pullin' a red wagon. But Harper is smart, nerveless, and outstanding passer and, when he's hot, can flat bomb the basket from 30 feet. He plays best under pressure." [6]

With a bench full of talent, however, it was the play of center LaSalle Thompson and forward Mike Wacker that led the Longhorns to their best start in history. Both players were ranked among the top 20 rebounders in the nation.

Abe took his club to Houston to play the 12-1 Cougars, led by Nigerian import Akeem Abdul Olajuwon, a 6'11" sophomore-scoring machine, and guard Clyde Drexler. Texas stunned Houston 95-83. Wacker led all scorers with 32 points, hitting 14 of 15 chances at the free throw line. Thompson was matched up against Olajuwon and limited the Nigerian star to one field goal and six rebounds. It was the worst game of Olajuwon's career at Houston.

Abe took the victory in stride, telling a dressing room throng, "I used to lose sleep over losing. Now I can't sleep trying to figure out why we keep winning." 7

With the Houston win, Texas moved into the Top 20 in both the Associated Press and United Press International polls. Abe was wary of reporters who had picked up their criticism of his coaching methods, especially his yelling at players during practices and games.

Abe, left, has a smile for his star rebounder Mike Wacker. Courtesy University of Texas.

Abe was 59 years old but felt good. A Dallas newspaper summarized the growing criticism of Abe, "Lemons' critics view him as a man who has grown increasingly sour and grump and set in his ways after 26 years in basketball. While he may know the game inside out, they say he doesn't project the 'image' expected of a coach representing the state university. They complain about his lack of tact and diplomacy. They cringe at his seemingly insensitive attitude toward his players." 8

Abe went about his assigned duties of preparing the Longhorns for a televised contest against his arch-rival Arkansas Razorbacks who were ranked in the Top 20 and favored over Texas, even though the game was to be played in Austin.

Before the largest crowd ever to see a regular season Southwest Conference basketball game, 16,401 at the Erwin Center, Texas crushed Arkansas 87-73, the worst conference defeat for Eddie Sutton in his first eight years at the Razorbacks' helm. Thompson scored 32 points, hitting 12 of 14 field goal tries, sank eight of nine free throws, grabbed 13 rebounds, blocked six shots, and even had two steals.

The win over Arkansas vaulted the Longhorns to fifth in the United Press International coaches' poll and seventh in the sportscasters and writers Associated Press poll, the highest rankings ever enjoyed by a Texas basketball team. In fact, it was the last time UT was ranked in the Top 10 nationally. *Sports Illustrated* named Thompson the magazine's college player of the week. In the two games against Houston and Arkansas, Thompson scored 53 points and pulled down 24 rebounds.

Thompson continued his rampage against opponents as Texas beat Texas Christian University 105-88. Thompson had 31 points and 19 rebounds against the Hornfrogs. On national television, on ESPN, three days later, the Longhorns beat South Carolina 88-71. With top-ranked North Carolina's defeat, Texas was one of only three unbeaten major-college basketball teams.

Tragedy struck the Texas basketball fortunes in Waco, Texas, on January 26, 1982, when Mike Wacker went up for a tip-in during a game against Baylor. Wacker came down on his right foot and planted his left foot when he heard a sickly crack before crumbling to the floor. Wacker required extensive surgery on his right knee. His season was over. On top of the terrible loss of Wacker, Abe's Longhorns lost their first game of the season to the Bears, 69-59, even though Abe missed the game. He was in Oklahoma City at the bedside of his ailing 73-year-old brother, Bud, hospitalized for removal of an aneurysm in his left leg. Abe listened to the second half of the game driving back to Austin. It was one of the toughest moments of his life.

Texas suddenly found itself without its second leading scorer and rebounder. Wacker had averaged 15.2 points and 9.3 rebounds per game in the Longhorns' first 14 victories of the season. Abe said of Wacker, "He's a coach's dream. If you could draw up a picture of a guy you'd want to coach, he'd look at lot like Wacker." [9]

Abe began the search for a replacement, hoping to find the right chemistry that had propelled Texas to its winning heights. Seldom-used 6'6" senior Ken Montgomery replaced Wacker in the starting lineup and played admirably. However, the special chemistry Abe was looking for never came.

After college, Wacker became a successful assistant basketball coach at the University of Texas at San Antonio and head coach at Judson-Converse High School in the Houston, Texas, area.

The Longhorns lost a tough, overtime game to Texas A & M, 71-69, were embarrassed by Rice 80-49, and struggled in a 69-56 win over Southern Methodist University at home. Abe was frustrated as he boarded his team on an airplane headed for a much-anticipated rematch with Arkansas at Fayetteville.

Texas had a chance to win the game with 51 seconds remaining when Holmes missed a second free throw after tying the game. Montgomery had the ball and began stalling for a final shot. Abe was yelling for a time-out to set up a final play when Montgomery was called for traveling with 24 seconds remaining.

In overtime, the Longhorns turned the ball over on their first six trips down the court and lost to the Razorbacks 62-55. The game was marred by a scuffle on the court in the closing minutes and an ugly incident after the final buzzer had sounded. Abe stormed out onto the court and yelled at Arkansas' Darrell Walker for punching Texas guard Ray Harper.

On the way to the dressing room, Arkansas fans spit on and threw ice and soft drinks on Abe and his players. Texas publicist Doug Smith was punched in the stomach by a Razorback fan. Two Texas players went into the stands and a well-meaning Razorback fan wrestled Abe into the Texas dressing room to prevent further brawls. [10]

The Texas press corps renewed its attack on Abe. One writer said there was no excuse for Abe's behavior, asking, "How can a coach discipline a team when he cannot discipline himself?" [11] Abe's players backed him completely, lauding him with their appreciation for sticking up for them in the face of a brawling Barnhill Arena crowd.

Abe filed an official complaint with the Southwest Conference office. Al Witte, the Arkansas faculty representative to the conference, lashed out at Abe saying the Texas coach "could benefit from consulting with trained and skilled people who have expertise in clinical psychology." [12] Abe shot back a veiled reference to Witte's family, scoffing, "I knew a family of Wittes. The brothers were named Half, Nit, and Dumb. I don't know if he's any kin to 'em or not." [13]

After the Southwest Conference investigation, Barnhill Arena officials made security changes. The opponents' dressing room was moved to another part of the arena and access from the court was roped off. Plain-clothes security guards were also posted and the public address system used by the pep band leader to incite the students was dismantled. Arkansas athletic director Frank Broyles urged fans to treat the visiting teams as their guests. [14]

With Wacker out of the Texas lineup, opposing teams concentrated on getting the high-scoring and high-rebounding Thompson in early foul trouble. The ploy worked more often than not and Texas hit the skids, losing to Houston and Texas Christian University. After a win over North Texas State, the Longhorns lost their last five games of the year to Baylor, Texas A & M, Texas Tech, Rice, and Baylor, again, in the Southwest Conference tournament at Waco.

What once was a 14-0 season for a rising Texas squad had plummeted to a 16-11 final record. Weeks before the Longhorns had been fifth-ranked in the nation and led the Southwest Conference. After the Wacker injury, Texas was 1-10 in the conference, finishing in a tie for seventh place.

The only bright spot of the final half of the season was the splendid play of Thompson who became the first Longhorn basketball player to lead the nation in an individual NCAA category. Thompson averaged 13.5 rebounds per game, slightly more than Olajuwon of Houston.

On March 10 Abe received a call that athletic director DeLoss Dodds wanted to see him in his office. The conversation was short. Dodds said, "I've got bad news for you. You're fired." Abe was shocked. He looked around the room and thought Dodds might be talking to someone else. Abe asked Dodds, "Why?" Dodds simply said, "Our basketball program needs new leadership and new direction for the future." [15]

At a news conference Dodds refused to answer questions from reporters as to the specific reasons Abe was fired. Dodds would speak only in generalities, "It's a simple statement of fact that we need new leadership. We need to get a course for the future and continue to progress, nothing more or less than that." [16] Dodds said UT would honor Abe's $52,106 annual salary for the two remaining years on his contract. However, UT went back on its promise and refused to settle, requiring Abe to remain on campus to draw his salary.

Mike Wacker learned about Abe's firing while walking on crutches across the UT campus. UT football quarterback Donnie

Legend has it that Abe taped a sprig of mistletoe to his back side as he left Deloss Dodd's office after his firing. *The Daily Oklahoman* cartoonist Jim Lange immortalized the moment in this 1999 cartoon drawn especially for this biography. Courtesy Jim Lange.

Little saw Wacker and said, "Hey, I just heard they fired Abe." Wacker felt guilty about his season-ending injury and thought he personally was responsible for Abe's loss. However, Abe never for a moment blamed Wacker for Dodds' action. [17]

Abe's comments after his firing were reserved. He grinned and said, "Maybe I was a little too crusty for Texas officials." [18] Many years later, during the writing of this book, Abe reflected, "I loved the Texas job, as did my family. With a little help, it would have been easier. I woke up Texas basketball and the wonderful fans. It was a great time, fun for all. It's strange when a handful of people behind closed doors can judge you even without a hearing. Watch out for the one with a smile and an invisible knife. Some people in the tower worry about chicken manure when there are elephants in the yard." [19]

A very wise man once said that history is the best gauge of how a person performed at a particular task. Almost two decades after Abe was fired as the Longhorns' head coach, sports historians point to the Lemons era at Texas as the greatest years of UT's basketball history. Abe and his teams drew large crowds to Erwin Center. Texas averaged more than 9,000 fans per home game in Abe's last season. The following year, under new coach Bob Weltlich, the per-game average dropped sharply to 3,956.

A glance at the latest UT basketball media guide drives home how successful Abe was at attracting fans to home games in Austin. The 15,885 fan-per-game average in 1978-1979 stands as tops in Texas, and Southwest Conference, history. The 14 home games in 1978-1979 drew 222,400, unsurpassed in a single season at the Erwin Center. Even when coach Tom Penders led the Longhorns to successful seasons in the 1990s, Erwin Center attendance records set during Abe's regime in Austin stood firm.

Abe Lemons was good for University of Texas basketball.

Chapter Nineteen

Back to OCU

Yeah, I'm happy to be back in Oklahoma City. Marco Polo had to come home eventually. I've never been unhappy unless it was when I was pickin' cotton. Anything is a move up from that and carrying a syrup bucket to school.

Abe Lemons

ABE WAS UNEMPLOYED FOR THE FIRST TIME IN 30 YEARS. HE WAS mentioned as a prominent prospect for the head coach job at the University of New Mexico. And his friend, North Carolina coach Dean Smith, promised to help him land the top spot at the University of North Carolina at Charlotte. Abe was depressed over his firing at Texas and rebuffed advances from officials at both schools.

Abe and Betty Jo lived on one of Austin's finest golf courses, Onion Creek, so Abe spent much of his time playing golf. However, his life had been spent studying and coaching basketball, and the time off from coaching caused him to miss the game greatly. Abe called the 1982-1983 season his "redshirt year."

As UT basketball faltered in a big way the year after Abe was fired, the Texas press corps lamented their loss. A story on the sports pages of *The Houston Post* is a good example, "For the Longhorns, the firing of Abe has been a self-inflicted wound...There is no mystery to

RIGHT: Wearing an "I love OCU" button, Abe and assistant coach Harry Masch are introduced to the media at an April, 1983, news conference in Oklahoma City. Left to right, Betty Jo, Mrs. Masch, Abe, and Masch. Courtesy *The Daily Oklahoman.*

BELOW: Paul Hansen, left, and Abe had begun their long journey as college basketball coaches 32 years before this photo was taken in 1987. Courtesy *The Daily Oklahoman.*

the firing. He did not fit someone's image of a Texas basketball coach. He cracked too many jokes, did not seem to treat his job with the seriousness of a coroner, and his clothes often had a rumpled look, suggesting that he had been up all night working on a case with Columbo...Following in the wake of Abe Lemons is like riding in the back of a flatbed truck with a loudspeaker on top. People step off the curb to get closer to the sound...All Abe Lemons has ever done is win, though not always in a conventional way." [1]

In early 1983, Oklahoma City University President Jerald C. Walker sent word to Abe that OCU was very interested in the veteran coach returning to lead the Chiefs. Walker dispatched athletic director Arnold Short and Bud Sahmaunt, both former players for Abe at OCU, to Austin to convey a simple message to Abe, "You have lots of fans in Oklahoma City and we want you back as our coach." [2]

Oklahoma City University basketball was in shambles ten years after Abe left for Pan American. Paul Hansen had coached the Chiefs successfully for six seasons before moving on to Oklahoma State University and the University of Science and Arts at Chickasha, Oklahoma. Then OCU began four losing seasons in a row, was placed on two years probation by the NCAA for recruiting violations, and had fired coach Ken Trickey after two years. The Chiefs were actively searching for a replacement for coach Lonnie Nichols who was in the middle of OCU's worst season ever.

The Chiefs were down to seven men because of players quitting and the team's two leading scorers flunking out of school. An embarrassing Associated Press dispatch told of three Chiefs fouling out in a game against Evansville, leaving only four players on the floor. During the stretch, OCU suffered its worst loss in history, a 46-point defeat at the hands of Oklahoma. [3]

The Chiefs ended the 1982-1983 season at 4-22 and coach Nichols saw the handwriting on the wall. In fact, Abe had already been secretly hired before the end of the season. Nichols, taking his fate good-naturedly, had been answering his phone "Coach

Lemons' office" for weeks. In April, OCU officials announced Nichols was being replaced by the 60-year-old Abe Lemons.

Oklahoma City University also revealed plans for the Chiefs to drop out of the NCAA and compete against smaller colleges as a member of the National Association of Independent Athletics (NAIA), established in 1937. OCU became a member of the Midwestern City Conference (MCC) with Oral Roberts University, Loyola University of Chicago, Xavier University, Butler University, St. Louis University, and the University of Evansville, Indiana.

Abe, with 474 basketball wins to his credit, was enthusiastic about his return. So were sportswriters around the country. Many of them showed up in Oklahoma City to write feature stories about the legendary Abe.

The Denver Post's Shelby Strother wrote, "The long, obnoxious cigar stops the conversation. Its fire is out. Abe Lemons, a little bit Will Rogers, part Red Auerbach, some snake-oil peddler, pauses to re-light...It's been more than a year since he was unceremoniously bounced from his job as coach of the Texas Longhorns. Nothing's been very funny since then. But in April, he agreed to return to Oklahoma City, which is where all the Abe Lemons genius and madness and fun began 32 years ago." [4]

Abe reflected on his year without a job in basketball, "Whenever I would talk to another coach, I didn't feel on equal ground. A team can play without a coach, but ain't no coach who can coach without a team...Yep, that's the loneliest, most pitiful, damn awfulest sight in the world. A coach without a team." [5]

The OCU faithful, especially athletic director Arnold Short, who had starred for Abe as a Chief years before, were thrilled to have Abe back at the helm of the basketball program. Former OCU and OU coach Doyle Parrack was proud of Abe's accomplishments, "He is a master blender of control and fast break basketball. No one in history can utilize the type of players he has been given in a particular season better than Abe. He's one of the best coaches ever." [6]

Abe did not like the head coach's office under the stands at Frederickson Fieldhouse on the OCU campus and opted for a much smaller office, closer to the basketball court, saying, "I want to be close so I can see the guys go back and forth. I like to know when they're practicing and when they're just jackin' around." 7

An astute observer of Abe's antics was athletic department secretary Birdie Duniphin, who had starred as a girls' basketball player in her hometown of Newcastle, Oklahoma. She loved her job, talking to famous coaches like Bob Knight of Indiana who frequently called Abe. She remembers about the only time Abe was extremely upset was when someone in street shoes walked on the polished basketball court. Abe would mutter under this breath, "Don't they know any better than that?" 8

Even before Abe's first season in his second stint at OCU began, rumblings from his years at Texas haunted him. *The New York Times* quoted UT law professor Charles Alan Wright who said Abe "scoffed" at the notion of his players maintaining a firm academic background and that most of Abe's players never graduated from college.

Abe was understandably shaken by the accusations of Wright, an esteemed law professor who had once represented President Richard Nixon during Nixon's Watergate troubles. Wright, who had met Abe only once, informally at a UT reception, was completely off target with his remarks and later apologized to Abe. The absolute truth of the matter was that Abe emphasized the importance of learning to every player he ever coached. If players did not attend class according to university rules, they did not play for him. And, most of Abe's players earned their degrees and made significant contributions to society.

Abe brought a Texan with him to be his assistant at OCU. Harry Masch was a University of Texas graduate who built Lanier High School in Austin, Texas, into a basketball power in the 1970s. Masch was coaching at Tyler, Texas High School when Abe tapped him for the job in Oklahoma City.

Two UT basketball players, Jack Worthington and Dennard Holmes, starters on Abe's 1981-1982 Longhorn squad, also made the journey across the Red River to join Abe at OCU. The two players had to sit out a year before their eligibility was reinstated for participation as a Chief.

Even though Abe was back in Oklahoma, he was still good copy to sell newspapers in Texas. The *Austin American-Statesman* dispatched a sportswriter to Oklahoma City to report on Abe's transition. The next day, Abe's new life was featured in a light-hearted story:

The crowd cheers. The team, clad in blue and white sweats, dashes out of the locker room. An announcer yells: "Here come the Chiefs!" As OCU takes the floor, the band strikes up a version of "Sweet Georgia Brown." Finally, out comes Abe Lemons. Dressed in a black pinstripe suit and modest red and black tie, he has the look of a dapper, gray-haired outlaw. He appears much thinner than he did during his UT days; a new gray mustache adds a nice touch. His manner is very calm and unhurried, even on the OCU bench. For once, he does not seem in a hurry to go anywhere. At age 62, Abe has inherited a team that was one of the worst in college basketball last season. [9]

Abe had a major rebuilding job to perform at OCU. Early in the new season, his two top scorers were both freshmen, 6'0" guard Steve Wiedower, a high school All-American from Greenbriar, Arkansas, and 6'4" forward Marvin Owens, a high school All-American from Cleveland, Ohio. Abe's best all-around player was senior Dan Davis, a 6'6" forward from Plano, Texas, by way of Lon Morris Junior College in Jacksonville, Texas.

Davis first met Abe when Abe was recruiting scoring sensation Jaime Pena at Lon Morris. Pena did not want to see Abe and slipped out a locker room window, leaving Davis to meet Abe. When he returned to OCU, Abe was delighted to see Davis was ready to play for him his senior year. Davis had missed a season because of an ankle injury.

Davis remembers that Abe talked more about life some days than about basketball, "He never came down hard on the players even when we messed up. If we missed class, he calmly warned us that it would catch up with us later in life. He told us that running extra laps wouldn't punish us, but missing class would hurt us later when we got out into the real world."

Davis, who became the Chiefs' third-best scorer in 1983-1984, recognized Abe's philosophy of fielding a team. Davis said, "If you could score, you could play for Abe." [10]

Other players available for Abe's new team were George Clayton, a 6'2" senior from Columbus, Ohio, where he was an All-Stater; Les Crockett, a 6'4" sophomore All-Stater from Denver, Colorado; Brannon Craig, a 6'9" senior from Houston, Texas; and Thomas Ryer, a 6'4" junior from New York City, who became the Chiefs' leading rebounder.

Oklahoma City University launched the second Lemons' era with a win over the Southwestern Kansas State Moundbuilders, lost to Texas Tech, beat Hardin-Simmons, dropped a contest to San Diego State, and then beat Long Island University.

By December 18, the Chiefs won their fourth game, matching the previous year's total. Wiedower scored 28 points as OCU throttled Hardin-Simmons 74-60 in the last game to be played that season at Frederickson Fieldhouse. The Chiefs were slated to play their remaining home games at the Myriad Arena or the State Fair Arena.

Attendance at OCU home games the previous season had barely topped 1,000. With Abe again at the helm, the Chiefs began averaging more than 4,000 fans per game, even though the 13,000-seat Myriad looked very empty only one-third full. OCU athletic director Bud Sahmaunt and Abe hosted a monthly Blue-White luncheon during the season for OCU boosters. It was a time for Abe to report to the OCU faithful about the progress of his team. [11]

Struggling, with a losing record, the Chiefs put it all together in late January and beat conference-leading Xavier University 71-70. It was the first win for OCU since beating Texas-San Antonio in the All-College in December. Dan Davis, who after graduation attended the Oklahoma City University Law School and became a successful Oklahoma City lawyer, told a reporter that players had had to make a transition from the coaching methods of Nichols to

Abe, "Getting mentally prepared for Coach Lemons' ways was tough at the beginning, but once we got it down, he's the easiest coach to play for." [12]

Abe used several strategies to generate enthusiasm for the OCU basketball program. He began a talk-back session with fans and players after each home game. He told fans that his office was always open to anyone interested in the Chiefs, and he kept that promise. He told his players that he wanted their time as a student-athlete to be fun, the happiest time of their lives.

The Chiefs' loss to Detroit University was costly in personnel. Ryer suffered a gash above his right eye. Senior Jones Richmond received a broken nose and Wiedower was knocked to the floor head first and had to be taken to a local hospital. A bright spot for the Chiefs was Owens' best performance of the season, a career-best 24 points and 10 assists. Owens was inspired by a pre-game pep talk from former Chief All-American Rich Travis who lived in Michigan and attended the OCU-Detroit game. [13]

It was Abe's "death" that created the most stir for the Chiefs while in Detroit. Abe received a phone call at 1:30 a.m. from a reporter who was checking out the rumor that Abe had been killed in an automobile accident. Abe was funny, even in the middle of such a shocking request about his status. He denied the rumor and said, "I know I'm not dead. One reason is when you die, you don't go to Detroit, you go to Fayetteville, Arkansas." [14] Abe kiddingly said when he called Betty Jo to report that he was still alive, she had a mixed reaction. [15]

In early February, the Chiefs posted a stunning victory over St. Louis University 64-60. OCU out-rebounded the Billikins 40-30. When Dan Davis was flagrantly fouled by St. Louis star Darryl Anderson, who was ejected, the Chiefs began a run that gave them a 29-28 half-time lead.

Davis had his best game of the year against Oral Roberts University in a game played in Tulsa. However, Davis' 21 points were not enough as the Chiefs lost to the Titans 92-83. Abe called the game "the worst-officiated game of the year." Two questionable calls late in the game sealed the Chiefs' fate. [16]

OCU lost its final two games to Southwest Missouri State University and Oral Roberts. The Chiefs finished with an 8-18 record, only the third losing season in Abe's career.

After the season Abe hit the recruiting trail. He faced stiff competition in Oklahoma against coaches Billy Tubbs at the University of Oklahoma, and Abe's former assistant, Paul Hansen, head coach at Oklahoma State University. In April, Abe was elated when 6'7" Tim Boynes announced he would attend OCU.

Views

A Tribute by John Wooden

of Abe:

I have known Abe Lemons for many years. After all, we were once young basketball coaches together.

Abe had a brilliant coach's mind. He could coach defense as well as anyone. Because his teams were high-scoring, Abe was often criticized for not teaching his players defense. However, any student of the game could watch Abe's players on the court and know that a master had taught them how to defend.

Abe always had an unusual relationship with his players. They knew he meant business when outlining a strategy in the closing moments of the game. Abe's players respected him greatly because they knew he cared for them like a father.

I wish all coaches in America cared for their players like Abe Lemons did.

ABOVE: John Wooden won more national NCAA basketball championships than any coach in the history of the game. His University of California at Los Angeles (UCLA) Bruins excelled under Wooden's leadership. Courtesy *The Daily Oklahoman.*

— *Chapter Twenty* —

More Rebuilding

Behind all of Lemons' lines is a wily hoops fanatic. Let me
tell you, the country-bumpkin stuff is all con.

Sportscaster Dick Vitale

MOTORISTS IN OKLAHOMA CITY WERE TREATED TO AN UNUSUAL
billboard in the fall of 1984. A caricature of Abe, dressed in a red
tie, blue tails, and a red, white, and blue stovepipe hat, pointed his
finger at passers-by, saying, "I want you." The billboards were part
of the OCU promotion effort to bring large crowds back to Chief
basketball games.

Abe saw promise in returning four starters from his 1983-1984
team but recognized he still had much work to do to bring OCU
basketball to the heights he had taken the program years before.
Lack of size continued to be Abe's problem as he surveyed the
returning starters Les Crockett, Thomas Ryer, Marvin Owens, and
Steve Wiedower who had broken the Midwestern City Conference
scoring mark with 348 total points the previous season. None of
Abe's starters were taller than 6'4".

Between seasons, Abe and assistant Harry Masch had signed several taller players. Tim Boynes was 6'7", John Heath was 6'8", Chip
Zumer was 6'9", Thad Murphy was 6'7", and Wayne Montgomery
was 6'6". [1]

University of Texas transfers Denard Holmes and Jack Worthington were also new faces to help Abe's 1984-1985 team. Worthington gave OCU a dependable point guard.

"General" Abe kicks off the 1984-1985 season. Courtesy *The Daily Oklahoman.*

Before the season began, the Chiefs lost Tim Boynes, the Oklahoma City freshman who had shown tremendous potential in pre-season workouts. Boynes withdrew from school and quit the team without talking to either Abe or assistant coach Masch.

The Chiefs began the season winning five of their first team games, then lost eight in a row and 13 of the final 14 to wind up the regular season at 6-19. OCU was blasted by Loyola of Chicago in the Midwestern City Conference (MCC) post-season tournament at Tulsa's Mabee Center.

The season was one of Abe's darkest in 30 years of coaching. Starters Steve Wiedower and Denard Holmes quit the team in the middle of the season and junior college import Calvin Grigsby was declared ineligible. Abe was forced to discipline players by relegating some to the bench and canceling others' tickets for road games. And the Chiefs were plagued with injuries. Abe just wanted to forget about the year and begin recruiting a new group of youngsters. [2]

Abe was excited as fall practice began for the 1985-1986 season. For the first time since he had resumed the head coach responsibilities at OCU, he could look down the bench and see 12 potential starters. Abe's team was still not big, with Zumer, 6'7" junior Joe Shidler, and Murphy the only Chiefs above 6'4". However,

RIGHT: Even though Abe was well into his sixties, he still had fortitude left to show his displeasure to officials. Courtesy *The Daily Oklahoman.*

LEFT: Abe explains a fine point of the game to Chiefs forward Chip Zumer during a 1985 loss to St. Louis University. Abe had found Zumer working as a cashier at a Happy Foods convenience store in Oklahoma City. Courtesy *The Daily Oklahoman.*

Abe visits with former coach and television sportscaster Dick Vitale, left, in Oklahoma City in 1986. Courtesy Oklahoma City University.

Abe expected leadership to come from senior Crockett and Luther Burks, a 6'2" junior, from Sapulpa, Oklahoma, who played good defense, rebounded well, and took effective shots in the paint.

The Chiefs began the season in a new conference, the Sooner Athletic Conference (SAC), comprised of OCU, Bethany Nazarene College (later Southern Nazarene University), Oklahoma Baptist University (OBU), Oklahoma Christian College (OCC), Phillips University, and the University of Science and Arts of Oklahoma. The SAC was assigned to District Nine of the NAIA.

Oklahoma City University was on fire to launch the 1985-1986 campaign, winning its first 12 games and scoring more than 100 points in four of the wins. A tenacious pressing defense limited opponents to hitting only 40 percent of their shots in the first half of the season. Guard Luther Burks led the Chiefs scoring attack with able assistance from Lavelle Wilson, Calvin Grigsby, and Tommie Bolden. Thad Murphy became the top rebounder.

By late January, 1986, the Chiefs were ranked number one among Oklahoma NAIA teams and second nationally with a 16-1 record. The only blemish was a loss to Southwestern Oklahoma State University, a team that OCU had beaten twice already in early season play. Sportswriters thought only David Lipscomb College of Tennessee was a better small-college basketball team. Abe was back on top.

Abe had added players at the semester break. Muhammad Akbar was a 6'6" transfer from Oklahoma State University where he had led the team in scoring and rebounding before being dismissed for academic reasons. David Simmons, a 6'7" senior from North Carolina, and Mark Baltimore, a 6'3" sophomore transfer from Pratt Junior College in Kansas, added strength to Abe's already vastly improved team.

Abe won his 500th game as a college basketball coach in a 74-64 game against Southern Nazarene University. He was presented the game ball and Oklahoma Governor George Nigh proclaimed a day of celebration sponsored by the OCU Alumni Association as "Abe Lemons Day" in Oklahoma.

The Chiefs' toughest opponent in the 1985-1986 season was the Oklahoma Christian College eagles. The Eagles beat the Chiefs twice, the second time on a last-second desperation shot. Abe was incensed by what he thought was an unfair call that cost OCU the game. In the noisy Frederickson Fieldhouse, Burks dunked the ball after a whistle had blown to stop play. After a

Luther Burks was the leading scorer for the Chiefs in 1985-1986. Courtesy Oklahoma City University.

long discussion among officials, Burks was assessed a technical. The call resulted in a four-point turnaround and was the difference in the game. [3]

The Chiefs saved their best game of the year for a rematch with OCC in the District Nine playoffs. OCU avenged the two heartbreaking, one-point losses earlier in the year to thrash OCC 93-69. However, the Chiefs met top-ranked Southeastern Oklahoma State University in the District Nine finals. The Savages, led by future NBA star and world-renowned celebrity, Dennis Rodman, beat OCU 84-61. The Chiefs shot only 39 percent from the field and Rodman had 19 points and 19 rebounds. [4]

Abe's third season back at OCU had been an outstanding success. He was named co-coach of the year in the SAC, along with OCC coach Dan Hays. Bolden and Burks were honored as OCU's representatives on the All-District team. Burks was named to the second team and Bolden as Honorable Mention of the NAIA All-American team.

From scratch, Abe had built a team that finished 26-5, the winningest team in OCU history. Consistently ranked in the NAIA top ten, the Chiefs fell to 13th in the final poll. Burks scored a team high of 670 total points with a 21.6 per game average. Bolden was the second leading scorer with 510 points.

In the summer of 1986, many of Abe's friends gathered in Oklahoma City to honor Abe's accomplishments and OCU athletics. From Nashville came Mae Boren Axton, Abe's childhood mentor. Paul Hansen, Abe's former assistant, and then coach at the University of Science and Arts of Oklahoma in Chickasha; North Carolina State coach Jim Valvano; TCU coach Jim Killingsworth; and University of Southern California coach George Raveling all paid tribute to Abe.

At a banquet at the Marriott Hotel in Oklahoma City, Valvano said, "This man [Abe] has had more impact on coaches in this country...We have had clinics at coaches' meetings that nobody showed up to, but when word got around that Abe was going to speak, the place would be packed." [5]

Hansen took a good-natured jab at Abe, "People keep asking me how I could be an assistant to Abe for 18 years. I tell them, it was easy, I didn't listen." [6] Mae Axton said, "I've known Abe since he was a teenager, and he still acts like one." [7]

Abe added some height to his 1986-1987 Chiefs. Senior guards Bolden and Burks returned after standout junior seasons. They were joined by center Joe Shidler and seniors Lavelle Wilson and Calvin Grigsby.

The Chiefs were absolutely unbelievable in the new season, breaking every winning record in state collegiate basketball history. OCU won 34 games in a row, was 19-0 at home, 11-0 on the road, and was ranked number one among America's small colleges for most of the years. Ten times the Chiefs scored more than 100 points, with a high of 140 points against hapless University of Dallas.

The Chiefs closed out the regular season with a 137-100 win over Panhandle State University and was seeded number one in the NAIA national tournament. The Chiefs easily handled first-round foe Northwood Institute of Michigan 101-66.

Oklahoma City University had the opportunity to become only the second undefeated champion of the 50 years of the NAIA tournament. But number 16 seed Georgetown College of Kentucky stood in the way. The Chiefs, who had been unstoppable from the outside with deadly shooting and tough inside, were neither. OCU lost to Georgetown College 67-64 at Kemper Arena in Kansas City, Missouri.

Nine seniors anchored the super club of 1986-1987. Burks was named the SAC's most valuable player and led the league in scoring with an average of 20.4 points per game. Sixth man Muhammed Akbar was second in scoring at 13.6 points per game, followed by Bolden, substitute David Simmons, and Lavelle Wilson. Burks and Wilson were selected to the conference all-league first team while Simmons was named to the second team. Akbar and Bolden were honorable mention. Abe was named SAC coach of the year.

It was the first time in Abe's career that his team had gone unbeaten through an entire regular season. The Chiefs rewrote the OCU record book in several categories, most points in a season,

3,183; most field goals, 1,253; highest field-goal percentage, 55.2; and most game points, 140. The team also set all-time records for total free throws, assists, and steals.

Graduation decimated a majority of Abe's team after the 1986-1987 season. Lawrence Gradnigo, a 6'4" forward, was the only

BELOW: Rich Dozier was a second generation OCU Chief. His father played for the Chiefs in the early 1950s. Courtesy Oklahoma City University.

INSET: A caricature of Abe on the cover of the 1987 OCU basketball media guide. Courtesy Oklahoma City University.

player returning from the year before. Abe looked for help from sophomore Rich Dozier; Steve Morris; Greg Miles; 5'10" redshirt guard Charles Weekly; 6'0" guard Byron Woodward, a transfer from Trinity Valley, Texas Junior College; 6'7" forward John Gaines from Danville, Indiana, Junior College; and Lawrence West, a 6'7" forward from the University of Nevada-Las Vegas. Two true freshman, 6'2" Clayton Moore from Oklahoma City and 6'7" Mike Berry from Lawton rounded out the squad.

Oklahoma City University went international when Abe signed 6'5" Juan Carlos Gonzales from Cali, Colombia. Gonzalez averaged 19 points per game for the Colombian national team in the Pan American games.

The Chiefs won their first five games of the new campaign. The fifth win came over the University of Dallas Crusaders who had lost 65 straight games coming into the matchup with OCU. Weekly led all scorers with 27 points, followed by Morris and Miles who scored 24 points each.

A 43-game regular season winning streak came to a sudden halt when OCU was beaten by Southwestern College of Texas in the first round of the Fort Hays State College tournament in Kansas.

When West, 6'5" junior Jay Griffin, and Woodward, all transfers, became eligible in the second semester, the Chiefs received much-needed help in scoring and height. Griffin was named second team All-District and led OCU in scoring.

The Chiefs finished fifth in the SAC in the regular season then beat Northwestern Oklahoma State University to reach the semifinals against Southern Nazarene University (SNU). In a game played at SNU's home court, OCU lost 101-85. Griffin led the Chiefs in scoring with 22 points while Woodward and West threw in 16 apiece and Morris contributed 10. OCU finished the season at 19-12.

Abe and assistant coach Masch put together a team of primarily young, untried players for the 1988-1989 season. Returning starters Steve Morris, Rich Dozier, and Charles Weekly joined transfers Tim Griffin and Andre Jenerson on the Chiefs' squad that had a serious lack of height.

The season was a tough one for Abe and Chiefs. The team fought adversity and often came within one shot or one free throw from winning a close fought contest. In the season finale against Oklahoma Baptist University (OBU), the Chiefs were ahead and had the ball. When Griffin's shot bounced out, OBU rebounded and tied the game with a three-point shot as the buzzer sounded. After two difficult overtime periods, the Chiefs lost 137-134, completing the season at 12-14.

Oklahoma City University officials were proud of their decision to move from the NCAA to the NAIA. Not only did the school save approximately $500,000 in annual costs, OCU had developed interesting rivalries in its first four years of competition in the NAIA with OBU and Oklahoma Christian College.

Views

A Tribute by Nolan Ryan

I treasure my friendship with Abe Lemons. Whether it is on the golf course or just sitting around telling war stories, my time with Abe is always pleasurable. Abe is genuine, truthful, and very funny. He can make me double-up in laughter with stories of his family, players, and wonderful life.

Abe is blessed with a basket full of friends and a wonderful wife. Betty Jo has stood with Abe through thick and thin. When the laughter of life has died away for the day, Betty Jo is there as a loving wife and incredible mother for their girls.

Abe treats his friends like family. I have no doubt that any favor I asked of him he would agree to do in a minute. That is why I am honored to call Abe Lemons my friend.

ABOVE: Nolan Ryan, one of baseball's greatest pitchers ever, shouts at the home plate umpire for a strike during a 1990 game against the Oakland A's. Courtesy *The Daily Oklahoman.*

— Chapter Twenty-one —

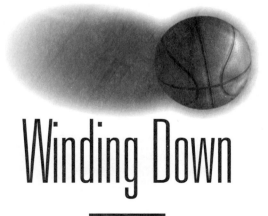

Winding Down

Anytime my team was under .500, I invited Abe to speak at a
banquet. He could make 'em forget about my lousy season.

Coach Bill Foster

ABE ENTERED HIS LAST BASKETBALL SEASON AS A COACH IN THE FALL
of 1989 as the fifth winningest active coach in America. His 579
victories in 33 seasons were surpassed only by Clarence Gaines at
Winston-Salem College, Dean Smith at the University of North
Carolina, Jim Phelan at Mount St. Mary's College, and Norm
Sloan at the University of Florida.

The 1989-1990 season was Abe's 25th year as head coach at
OCU. He had taken his teams at OCU and Texas to eight NCAA
tournaments and three NIT appearances. But coaching was still the
same to Abe as it had been when he stepped on to the court as the
young coach of the Chiefs in 1955. He wanted to win and he
worked his players hard to accomplish that lofty goal.

Abe publicly said he had "no definite plans" on whether or not
he would retire. But privately, as the long season progressed, he and
Betty Jo talked about this campaign being his last.

Abe officially announced his forthcoming retirement in January,
1990. The end of an era drew the attention of national media,

including producers of NBC's *Assignment America*, which aired reporter Bob Dotson's review of Abe's career. Dotson knew Abe from his stint as a newsman at Oklahoma City's WKY Television.

Seniors Charles Weekly, Andre Jenerson, and Rich Dozier formed the nucleus of Abe's last Chiefs team. But it was junior Tim Griffin who was OCU's season scoring leader, at 17.6 points per game, as the Chiefs were 16-12 in the regular season.

Abe was honored by cheering fans attending the "Abe Lemons Appreciation Night" at the Chiefs last home game at Frederickson Fieldhouse against Midwestern State University. OCU won the game 106-93, Abe's 598th victory. The elusive 600-win mark was very close.

Before the game against Midwestern State, OCU President Dr. Jerald Walker and well-wishers presented Abe and Betty Jo with dozens of gifts, including walking shoes, a big screen television, and life-time tickets to OCU games. Abe took the microphone and thanked Chiefs fans for their support and said he was glad he had been introduced as a "living legend." Abe quipped, "Lately, I've been wondering about that." [1] Holding

Abe shouts instructions to his team during his final game. The legendary coach fell one game short of 600 wins. Courtesy *The Daily Oklahoman*.

up the life-time tickets, Abe said, "I should probably trade these in for a bottle of Geritol." [2]

Abe, left, is congratulated at a retirement party by Henry P. Iba, Paul Hansen, and Glen Boyer, February, 1990. Courtesy Oklahoma City University.

Abe won career-win number 599 with a District 9 first-round playoff win over Phillips University. All that stood in the way of Abe reaching victory number 600 was his old NAIA nemesis, Oklahoma Christian College (OCC).

On March 2, 1990, Abe coached his final basketball game, unfortunately a one-point loss to OCC. The legendary career of one of basketball's greatest coaches and gentlemen was over. Abe's final career record was 599-343. As he walked out of the dressing room after his last game, Abe sighed, and told a friend, "Let's go fishin'. I need something to do." [3] Abe told a reporter, "Damn referees, I'll miss them less than anybody." [4]

As Abe's retirement was still good copy for sports pages, John Rohde, a sportswriter for *The Daily Oklahoman*, called several of the top basketball coaches in the country to get their words of wisdom on Abe stepping down. Rohde wrote, "Getting other basketball coaches to discuss Abe Lemons was a breeze. Told Lemons was the topic, coaches returned telephone calls within minutes." [5]

Rohde talked to Jerry Tarkanian, coach at the University of Nevada-Las Vegas, who said, "He's the greatest, he's really the greatest." [6] Dean Smith at the University of North Carolina said, "He could do what every coach wishes he could do, have his players be relaxed and play hard. I don't know anyone who did that better." [7]

Jim Valvano of North Carolina State, considered to be along with Abe, one of the funniest and most sought after banquet speakers among the nation's coaches, said, "Abe was a treasure to college basketball. He had the ability to put the game into its proper perspective. It's a game. It's to be enjoyed. It's not life and death." [8]

Indiana University's Bob Knight said Abe was the funniest man he had ever met, but "He always has passed himself off as being some kind of country bumpkin. If you really know Abe, that's the furthest thing from the truth." [9]

Abe left OCU basketball in great shape. Darrel Johnson, a graduate of Putnam City High School in Oklahoma City and for five years the head coach at Oklahoma Baptist University, was named to replace Abe. After two seasons, OCU hired Tulsa, Oklahoma native and former Oklahoma State University star Win Case as head coach. Case led the Chiefs to a national championship in 1994 and repeated the feat two years later, the fourth NAIA national crown for the Chiefs in the decade. Abe was one of Case's biggest supporters and often dropped into Frederickson Fieldhouse just to see how his old haunt was holding up. OCU women's coach Kent Stanley led the Lady Chiefs to an NAIA national championship in 1999.

In September, 1990, Abe was inducted into the Oklahoma Sports Hall of Fame

Abe was presented an honorary degree, Doctor of Humane Letters, by OCU President Dr. Jerald C. Walker May 5, 1990. Courtesy Oklahoma City University.

LEFT: Abe, left, and former University of Oklahoma football coach Barry Switzer were two of the inductees into the Oklahoma Sports Hall of Fame in 1990. Courtesy *The Daily Oklahoman.*

RIGHT: Abe is joined by several of his former players at a 1993 OCU alumni reception. Left to right, Bud Sahmaunt, Larry Jones, Abe, Harry Vines, and Dewayne Hunt. Courtesy Larry Jones.

along with former University of Oklahoma football coach Barry Switzer, the late wrestling coach at Oklahoma A & M, Ed Gallagher, and baseball great Johnny Bench, who grew up in Binger, Oklahoma.

Bench, who spoke before Abe, said he was so proud of his hometown of Binger that he used "Binger" as his son's middle name. OCU athletic director Bud Sahmaunt followed Bench and tried to be serious in introducing Abe, comparing him to the greats in the history of athletics and human endeavor. However, Abe completely destroyed the effectiveness of the serious presentation when he walked to the microphone, looked over at Bench, and said, "I'm sure glad you didn't grow up in Bowlegs, Oklahoma." [10]

After retirement Abe had more time to hit a golf ball on Oklahoma City area golf courses. Courtesy *The Daily Oklahoman.*

In 1992, Abe was the guest on Roy Firestone's "Up Close" interview program on ESPN. It was a half-hour of merriment, with Firestone bending over double when Abe responded to questions with one-liners, some well-known, some brand new. Firestone asked Abe to explain the difference between doctors and basketball coaches. Abe said, "Doctors bury their mistakes. We keep ours on scholarship. I'd like to go to a doctor who lists his won/loss record on the door, like lost four tonsillectomies and saved 42, then you kinda know how you're gonna do." [11]

Don Sanders, one of the owners of the Houston Astros baseball team, and Abe's longtime friend, founded the Abe Lemons Endowed Scholarship, in 1994. Fund-raising dinners added money to the program to help OCU men's basketball and baseball players who had exhausted their scholarships to finish their degrees.

Also in 1994, OCU retired Abe's No. 55 jersey at a benefit auction. Texas basketball coach Tom Penders was on hand to rib Abe and raise money for the OCU athletic department.

Abe was honored in November, 1994, when he was inducted into the University of Texas Longhorn Hall of Honor. More than the usual showed up for the gala at Austin's Hyatt Hotel, wondering what Abe would say with the man who fired him at UT, athletic director DeLoss Dodds, in attendance.

Bill Little, the UT sports information director, wisely put Abe as the last speaker. Early in his remarks, Abe read from the cover of the program, "To be eligible to receive the award, the recipient shall possess or shall have possessed in addition to outstanding ability in a sport or sports, other qualifications such as sportsmanship, character, and integrity, and be one who has brought great distinction to the University of Texas." [12]

Abe looked up at the audience, with that trademark dead-serious look, and said, "Makes you wonder how in the hell I got fired." [13] One reporter wrote, "Surprised and delighted, the crowd exploded in whoops and applause. Dodds did not participate." [14]

Oklahoma City University began an annual early-December basketball tournament in 1995 and called it the "Abe Lemons-Paul Hansen Tournament of Champions." The Jim Thorpe Association created an "Abe Lemons Award," to be presented each year to the member of the Association's executive council who "demonstrated the same qualities as Lemons-working to preserve Oklahoma's sports heritage while giving his time and talents to numerous sports organizations." [15]

In the summer of 1997, Abe was named to the Oklahoma Coaches Association Hall of Fame. University of Missouri basketball coach Norm Stewart could not attend the induction ceremonies in Tulsa, but wrote Abe, "I have learned a lot of basketball and other things about coaching and life in general from you and Betty." [16]

By 1998, Abe was slowed by Parkinson's disease, a degenerative neurological disorder most often marked by tremors and slow movement. The disease was named for James Parkinson, who in 1817 first described its symptoms. Abe, with his usual light-hearted outlook on life, said, "It's not so bad. I finally have rhythm." [17]

Abe and Betty Jo returned to Austin in February, 1998, for a reunion of the 1978 team that won the only national basketball title of any UT squad in history. The team was honored at halftime of the UT-Colorado basketball game. After the game, Abe held a group of UT supporters spell-bound in the Burnt Orange Room for a half hour, spinning yarns of yesteryear. Michael Pearle, covering the event for *Inside Texas*, wrote, "His 30-minute monologue of tall-tales, one-liners, and zingers had people dripping tears of laughter." [18]

That night the 1978 team and Abe and Betty Jo gathered at Scholz's Beer Garden, an ancient Austin tavern, to trade stories and relive the Longhorns' four-game sweep of Temple, Nebraska, Rutgers, and North Carolina State in the 1978 NIT.

Former players Tyrone Branyan, Jim Krivacs, Johnny Moore, Ron Baxter, John Danks, Ovie Dotson, and Gary Goodner huddled to remember the great season. Bill Little, now the assistant athletic director at UT, had a gleam in his eye as he recalled the trip to New York City. Little said, "Man, you shoulda been there." [19]

Pearle evaluated Abe's speech to his old team and supporters, "These were not the bitter ramblings of a defeated man, but the

Groundbreaking ceremonies were held in 1998 for the new Henry J. Freede Wellness and Activities Center on the OCU campus. Left to right, OCU supporter J.R. Homsey; Kent Stanley, OCU women's basketball coach; OCU men's basketball coach Win Case; and Abe. The sports arena inside the new facility will be known as the "Abe Lemons Arena". Courtesy Oklahoma City University.

sage observations of one who lived the highs and lows of coaching at a high stakes program like Texas. And the crowds ate up every word, because Lemons wrapped his brass knuckled shot to the chin within the velvet glove of humor. So by the end, you just wanted to catch your breath, hug the guy, and say to him, thanks for being here." [20]

After Abe spoke to his former players at Scholz's, John Danks took Abe by the arm and helped his exhausted coach to a chair, where a long line formed of those who wanted to touch Abe and wish him well.

One cannot be around Abe Lemons very long without realizing how his hundreds of former players worship him. Some men, now

Abe and his coach at OCU, Doyle Parrack, joined former OCU basketball stars at a 1999 reunion in Shawnee. Left to right, Arnold Short, Parrack, Hub Reed, Abe, Gary Hill, Lyndon Lee, and Bud Koper. Courtesy Oklahoma City University.

graying at the temples, and looking as if they never could have been skinny enough to get into basketball trunks, drop by when they travel near Abe's home in Oklahoma City. Players still call for advice on major questions of life or just call to tell Abe and Betty Jo how much they have meant to them.

In February, 1999, two dozen of Abe's former players met him for lunch at a barbecue restaurant in Shawnee, Oklahoma. Retired sportswriter Frank Boggs walked among the tall former stars and commented, "I don't know what kind of boys Abe recruited to OCU, but I know what kind of men they were when they left." [21]

At the reunion was Leon Griffin, whose career ended 40 years before, and four All-Americans, Gary Hill, Bud Koper, Hub Reed, and Arnold Short. Ben Ratzlaff, who was recruited in his hometown of Bessie, Oklahoma, by Abe on the day in 1954 that the OCU gym burned down, said, "I want to thank coach Lemons for getting me out of the cotton field." [22]

Toward the end of the reunion, the players gathered around their aging coach and told stories about their years at OCU and how Abe had made a difference in their lives. On cue, Abe had a funny story or quip to respond to the serious adoration being heaped upon his stooped shoulders by the kids he had helped make into men. Hub Reed said the best way he could express his feelings for his former coach was to quote from the first chapter of the Apostle Paul's letter to the Phillippians, "I thank my God upon every remembrance of you." [23]

Almost a decade after his retirement as an active coach, Abe was still often quoted by sportswriters. *The Daily Oklahoman* sports pages were sprinkled from time to time with Abe's famous quotes. Every few months *Dallas Morning News* columnist Blackie Sherrod mentions Abe. The ultimate compliment was paid Abe in January, 1999, when *USA Today* quoted Abe's comment, "Doctors bury their mistakes, ours are still on scholarship," as the best coach's comment of the century.

On February 3, 1999, two dozen of Abe's former players gathered for a reunion in Shawnee. Front row, left to right, Gary Hill, Mark Heusman, Dennis Jeter, Mike Kelley, Cecil Magana, Abe, Doyle Parrack, Fred Dunbar, Bill Juby, Lyndon Lee, Pat Petree. Back row, left to right, Manuel Heusman, Larry Faulkner, Jack Williams, Leon Griffin, Ben Ratzlaff, Roger Holloway, Bill Johnston, Gary White, Larry Bradshaw, Jerry Wallace, Arnold Short, Hub Reed, Dale Tracy. Courtesy Oklahoma City University.

Abe's correspondence files are full of letters from young men he has taught basketball and how to live in the world. Johnny Moore, whose number was retired by the NBA San Antonio Spurs in 1998, wrote, "My love and respect surpass the typical adoration felt from a coach/player relationship. My feelings are so strong that 'coach' just doesn't seem to suffice. Webster merely states a coach as a trainer of athletes. Many times I feel rather awkward because you are so much more than that. 'Coach' in itself doesn't even scratch the surface of what you have deposited in my life. You represent a friend, an advocate, and a mentor...My most earnest desire is that you are well pleased with me." [24]

Michael Tosee, a native of Apache, Oklahoma, became an FBI agent in New York City and history teacher at Haskell Indian Nations University in Kansas after playing for Abe. Tosee wrote, "You have made a difference in so many people's lives. My life changed for the better because of you and the experiences made me a stronger person, more confident about who and what I am." [25]

Jesus Guerra, Jr., who played for Abe at Pan American, wrote Abe after Guerra was inducted into the Texas Association of Basketball Coaches Hall of Fame, "I sincerely thank you for believing in me and giving me a chance to prove that I could play major college basketball...You instilled in us a mental toughness that prepared us for games and has also been invaluable to me as a person, husband, dad, and son...Thank you for providing guidance, discipline, faith, and care to me and my family." [26]

Larry Jones speaks for many of Abe's former players by assuring anyone who will listen that Abe wanted his players to do well in life. Jones says, "He felt like he could instill in you, via basketball principles, what it took for Fred Moses to become a banker or me a minister or someone else a teacher. He is more apt to talk to somebody about me than he is to me because when I'm with him, he talks about Harry Vines who coaches a wheelchair basketball team...There's a mutual understanding. Abe is proud of us, even when he doesn't say the magic words. We just know." [27]

Assistant OCU basketball coach Kenny Clark, a man who knows Abe as well as anyone outside his immediate family, said,

CLOCKWISE FROM TOP LEFT: Kip Reese, II, Dana Lemons Reese, and son Kip, III "Trey"; Jan Lemons Latimer; granddaughter Kristi Tague; Abe and Betty Jo's great grandchildren, left to right, Aerol, Logan, Lacy, and Amber; granddaughter Shauna Hedden; and grandson Ryan Tinsley.

"The proof of how genuine Abe is can be seen in the fact that he is at his funniest without trying to be funny. He is a brilliant coach without trying to be brilliant. He cares for people just because he believes that's the way you're supposed to be." [28]

The saga of Abe Lemons is not just a collection of funny stories and box scores of more than 1,000 college basketball games he coached. It is also a story of the lives of the young men he touched along the way, young men who have gone on to become lawyers, doctors, corporate executives, teachers, basketball coaches, and good husbands and fathers. Abe Lemons made the world around him a better place to live.

NOTES

Chapter 1

1. *History of Cotton County, Family and Area Stories,* Walters, Oklahoma (Cotton County Historical Society, 1979), p. 329.

2. *The Daily Oklahoman* (Oklahoma City, Oklahoma), November 30, 1969.

3. *The Sporting News* (St. Louis, Missouri), January 9, 1965.

4. *Sports Illustrated,* Vol. 37 No. 1 (January 4, 1965), p. 33.

5. *Oklahoma City Times* (Oklahoma City, Oklahoma), December 26, 1972.

6. Interview, Abe Lemons, May 20, 1998, Archives, Oklahoma Heritage Association, Oklahoma City, Oklahoma. Hereinafter referred to as Abe Lemons interview.

7. Ibid.

8. Ibid.

9. *The Daily Oklahoman,* April 27, 1988.

10. *Ibid.*

Chapter 2

1. Interview, Betty Jo Lemons, June 8, 1998, Archives, Oklahoma Heritage Association, Oklahoma City, Oklahoma. Hereinafter referred to as Betty Jo Lemons interview.

2. Ibid.

3. John Scott Douglas and Albert Salz, *He's In The Merchant Marine Now* (New York: Robert McBride and Company, 1943), p. 11.

4. Interview, Howell Ogletree, June 8, 1998, Archives, Oklahoma Heritage Association, Oklahoma City, Oklahoma.

5. Douglas and Salz, *He's In The Merchant Marine Now,* p. 9.

6. Interview, Doyle Parrack, January 19, 1999, Archives, Oklahoma Heritage Association, Oklahoma City, Oklahoma. Hereinafter referred to as Doyle Parrack interview.

7. *Keshena,* Oklahoma City University yearbook, 1948, hereinafter referred to as *Keshena.*

Chapter 3

1. Paul W. Milhouse, *Oklahoma City University: A Miracle at 23rd and Blackwelder* (Oklahoma City: Western Heritage Books, Inc., 1984), p. 18-57.

2. *Ibid.,* p. 45.

3. Betty Jo Lemons interview.

4. Interview, Carol Hansen, February 23, 1999, Archives, Oklahoma Heritage Association, Oklahoma City, Oklahoma.

Hereinafter referred to as Carol Hansen interview.

5. *The Campus* (Oklahoma City, Oklahoma), November 7, 1947.

6. 1949 *Keshena,* p. 167.

7. Abe Lemons interview.

8. Milhouse, *Oklahoma City University,* p. 105.

9. Carol Hansen interview.

10. *The Campus,* December 3, 1948.

11. *Ibid.,* November 12, 1948.

12. Interview, Bruce Hodge, January 15, 1999, Archives, Oklahoma Heritage Association, Oklahoma City, Oklahoma.

13. Interview, Jack Key, January 20, 1999, Archives, Oklahoma Heritage Association, Oklahoma City, Oklahoma.

14. Ibid.

15. Ibid.

16. *The Campus,* December 3, 1948.

17. *Ibid.,* November 12, 1948.

18. 1949 *Keshena,* p. 97.

19. *The Campus,* February 4, 1949.

20. *Ibid.*

21. Abe Lemons interview.

22. *The Campus,* December 2, 1949.

23. Frank K. Boggs and Pendleton Woods, *Myriad of Sports* (Oklahoma City: All Sports Association, 1971), p. 49.

24. *The Campus,* January 12, 1950.

25. Doyle Parrack interview.

Chapter 4

1. Abe Lemons interview.

2. John D. McCallum, *College Basketball USA* (New York: Stein and Day, 1978) p. 81.

3. *Ibid.,* p. 98.

4. Interview, Arnold Short, February 5, 1999, Archives, Oklahoma Heritage Association, Oklahoma City, Oklahoma. Hereinafter referred to as Arnold Short interview.

5. *The Campus,* September 30, 1950.

6. Carol Hansen interview.

7. Arnold Short interview.

8. McCallum, *College Basketball USA,* p. 97.

9. 1953 *Keshena,* p. 97.

10. *The Campus,* November 13, 1953.

Chapter 5

1. *The Campus,* October 30, 1953.

2. Interview, Edwin Powell Nall, December 15, 1998, Archives,

Oklahoma Heritage Association, Oklahoma City, Oklahoma. Hereinafter referred to as Ed Nall interview.

3. Ibid.

4. Ibid.

5. Ibid.

6. *The Wichita Beacon* (Wichita, Kansas), February 1, 1957.

7. *The Daily Oklahoman*, December 15, 1954.

8. Carol Hansen interview.

9. 1955 *Keshena*, p. 127.

10. *The Daily Oklahoman*, May 17, 1955.

11. *Ibid.*

Chapter 6
1. 1956 *Keshena*, p. 66.

2. Abe Lemons interview.

3. 1956 Keshena, p. 67-68.

4. *The Campus*, October 31, 1955.

5. *Ibid.*

6. *Oklahoma City Times*, December 17, 1966.

7. *The Campus*, October 31, 1955.

8. *Ibid.*

9. Interview, Roger Holloway, Archives, Oklahoma Heritage Association, Oklahoma City, Oklahoma, February 1, 1999.

10. *The Daily Oklahoman*, January 21, 1956.

11. *Ibid.*

12. *Ibid.*

13. *Ibid.*

14. *The Campus*, January 28, 1956.

15. *Ibid.*

16. *The Daily Oklahoman*, February 15, 1956.

17. *Ibid.*, January 16, 1956.

18. *Oklahoma City Times*, March 15, 1956.

19. Abe Lemons interview.

20. *The Campus*, March 9, 1956.

21. *Ibid.*, March 23, 1956.

22. *Ibid.*

23. *The Campus*, March 2, 1956.

24. *The Daily Oklahoman*, March 2, 1956.

25. *Ibid.*

Chapter 7
1. Abe Lemons interview.

2. Ibid.

3. *The Daily Oklahoman*, September 2, 1956.

4. Carol Hansen interview.

5. *The Campus*, November 2, 1956.

6. *Ibid.*

7. *Ibid.*

8. *The Daily Oklahoman*, January 10, 1957.

9. *The Campus*, January 11, 1957.

10. *Ibid.*

11. *The Daily Oklahoman*, January 31, 1957.

12. *Ibid.*

13. *Oklahoma City Times*, February 26, 1957.

14. *The Daily Oklahoman*, January 23, 1957.

15. *Dallas Morning News* (Dallas, Texas), March 17, 1957.

16. *Ibid.*

17. Robert Heard, *You Scored One More Point Than a Dead Man* (Austin, Texas: Lemons-Heard Company, 1978), p. 29-30. The book, a delightful collection of the more humorous of Abe's sayings down through the years, is hereinafter referred to as *Scored*.

18. *Ibid.*, p. 91.

19. *Ibid.*

20. *Ibid.*, p. 99.

Chapter 8
1. Heard, *Scored*, p. 73.

2. *The Campus*, March 14, 1958.

3. *Oklahoma City Times*, January 13, 1958.

4. *Ibid.*

5. 1958 *Keshena*, p. 125-128.

6. *The Daily Oklahoman*, November 30, 1969.

7. *Ibid.*

8. *The Daily Oklahoman*, May 26, 1958.

9. Abe Lemons interview.

10. Interview, Larry Jones, February 1, 1999, Archives,

Oklahoma Heritage Association, Oklahoma City, Oklahoma. Hereinafter referred to as Larry Jones interview.

11. Ibid.

12. *The Daily Oklahoman*, June 5, 1958.

13. *Ibid.*

14. *Ibid.*

15. *Ibid*, June 15, 1981.

16. *The Campus*, October 17, 1968.

17. Interview, Harry Vines, March 1, 1999, Archives, Oklahoma Heritage Association, Oklahoma City, Oklahoma.

18. Interview, Bud Sahmaunt, January 25, 1999, Archives, Oklahoma Heritage Association, Oklahoma City, Oklahoma. Hereinafter referred to as Bud Sahmaunt interview.

19. Ibid.

20. Ibid.

21. Abe Lemons interview.

22. Ibid.

23. *The Campus*, January 9, 1959.

24. *Ibid.*, February 20, 1959.

25. Bud Sahmaunt interview.

26. Carol Hansen interview

27. *The Campus*, April 17, 1959.

Chapter 9
1. Heard, *Scored*, p. 179.

2. *The Sporting News,* January 9, 1965.

3. *Oklahoma City Times,* February 16, 1967.

4. *Sports Illustrated,* January 4, 1965.

5. *Ibid.,*

6. *The Campus,* November 23, 1959.

7. Heard, *Scored,* p. 85.

8. *Ibid.,* p. 88.

9. *Ibid.,* p. 85.

10. *Sports Illustrated,* January 4, 1965.

11. *The Campus,* February 24, 1960.

12. *Ibid.,* February 19, 1960.

13. Larry Jones interview.

14. Ibid.

15. Ibid.

16. Heard, *Scored,* p. 56.

17. Interview with Gary Hill, February 5, 1999, Archives, Oklahoma Heritage Association, Oklahoma City, Oklahoma. Hereinafter referred to as Gary Hill interview.

18. Ibid.

19. Ibid.

20. 1961 *Keshena,* p. 120.

21. Interview with Manuel Heusman, January 21, 1999, Archives, Oklahoma Heritage Association, Oklahoma City, Oklahoma. Hereinafter referred to as Manuel Heusman interview.

22. *The Campus,* October 20, 1961.

23. 1962 *Keshena,* p. 106.

24. *The Campus,* January 5, 1962.

25. Manuel Heusman interview.

26. *The Campus,* February 2, 1962.

27. *Ibid.,* September 14, 1962.

Chapter 10

1. Abe Lemons interview.

2. Ibid.

3. Heard, *Scored,* p. 32.

4. *Ibid.,* p. 33.

5. *Arkansas Gazette* (Little Rock, Arkansas), August 10, 1967.

6. *Oklahoma City Times,* January 27, 1971.

7. Heard, *Scored,* p. 37.

8. *Ibid.,* p. 38.

9. *Sports Illustrated,* January 17, 1977.

10. *Dallas Times Herald* (Dallas, Texas), March 9, 1975.

11. 1963 *Keshena,* p. 128.

12. *The Campus,* November 3, 1962.

13. Carol Hansen nterview.

14. *The Daily Oklahoman,* January 22, 1963.

15. *Ibid.*

16. Abe Lemons interview.

17. *The Campus,* September 21, 1962.

18. Interview with Charles H.T. Hunter, January 7, 1999,

Archives, Oklahoma Heritage Association, Oklahoma City, Oklahoma. Hereinafter referred to as Charles H.T. Hunter interview.

19. *Dallas Times Herald,* December, 1963.

20. Interview with Gary Gray, January 27, 1999, Archives, Oklahoma Heritage Association, Oklahoma City, Oklahoma. Hereinafter referred to as Gary Gray interview.

21. Ibid.

22. *The Campus,* January 5, 1964.

23. *Ibid.*

24. Charles H.T. Hunter interview.

25. Heard, *Scored,* p. 57.

26. *The Campus,* December 17, 1964.

27. *The Daily Oklahoman,* February 4, 1965.

28. *Sports Illustrated,* January 4, 1965.

29. Heard, *Scored,* p. 51.

30. Charles H.T. Hunter interview.

31. Abe Lemons interview.

32. Charles H.T. Hunter interview.

33. Gary Gray interview.

34. *Tulsa Tribune* (Tulsa, Oklahoma), February 15, 1966.

35. *The Campus,* March 17, 1966.

36. *Ibid.*

37. Abe Lemons interview and undated Boggs column from *The Daily Oklahoman.*

38. Charles H.T. Hunter interview.

Chapter 11

1. *Sports Illustrated,* January 4, 1967.

2. Heard, *Scored,* p. 112.

3. *Oklahoma City Times,* January 5, 1965.

4. Heard, *Scored,* p. 113.

5. *Oklahoma City Times,* January 15, 1964.

6. *The Campus,* October 14, 1966.

7. Gary Gray interview.

8. Heard, *Scored,* p. 136.

9. Gary Gray interview.

10. 1967 *Keshena,* p. 120-122.

11. Gary Gray interview.

12. *The Campus,* March 15, 1967.

13. *The Daily Oklahoman,* September 1, 1967.

14. *Ibid.,* January 25, 1968.

15. Interview, Rich Travis, February 1, 1999, Archives, Oklahoma Heritage Association, Oklahoma City, Oklahoma. Hereinafter referred to as Rich Travis interview.

16. Interview, Patrick McGuigan, February 2,

1999, Archives,
Oklahoma Heritage
Association, Oklahoma
City, Oklahoma.

17. *The Campus,*
January 26, 1968.

18. Rich Travis interview.

19. Abe Lemons interview.

20. *The Campus,*
March 19, 1968.

21. *Ibid.*

22. Abe Lemons interview.

23. Memo from black
players to Lemons,
May 9, 1968, Archives,
Oklahoma Heritage
Association, Oklahoma
City, Oklahoma.

24. *The Daily
Oklahoman,* May 12,
1968.

25. Abe Lemons interview.

26. Telegram from E.
Melvin Porter to Dr.
John Olson and Abe
Lemons, May 12,
1968, Archives,
Oklahoma Heritage
Association, Oklahoma
City, Oklahoma.

27. *The Daily
Oklahoman,* February
13, 1968.

Chapter 12
1. *Oklahoma City
Times,* August 5, 1963.

2. *Texas Parade* magazine, January 7, 1964.

3. *Sports Illustrated,*
January 9, 1965.

4. Heard, *Scored,* p. 18.

5. *Ibid.,* p. 19.

6. Interview, Norm
Russell, December 28,
1998, Archives,
Oklahoma Heritage

Association, Oklahoma
City, Oklahoma.
Hereinafter referred to
as Norm Russell interview.

7. *Christian Science
Monitor* (Boston,
Massachusetts),
February 27, 1973.

8. *Sports Illustrated,*
January 9,. 1965.

9. Heard, *Scored,*
p. 114.

10. 1969 *Keshena,*
p. 47-53.

11. *The Campus,*
February 6, 1969.

12. Carol Hansen
interview.

13. *Dallas Morning
News,* January 27,
1972.

14. Heard, *Scored,*
p. 118.

15. *Dallas Morning
News,* January 9, 1977.

16. 1970 *Keshena,*
p. 105-110.

17. *Dallas Morning
News,* January 15,
1971.

18. Norm Russell
interview.

19. Carol Hansen
interview.

20. Norm Russell
interview.

21. Ibid.

22. Ibid.

23. Ibid.

24. *Oklahoma City
Times,* February 10,
1971.

25. *Ibid.*

26, *Ibid.*

27. Norm Russell
interview and Carol
Hansen interview.

28. Heard, *Scored,*
p. 145.

Chapter 13
1. Heard, *Scored,* p. 42.

2. *Ibid.,* p. 43.

3. *Ibid.,* p. 46.

4. *Seattle Post-
Intelligencer* (Seattle,
Washington), February
8, 1971.

5. *Tacoma News
Tribune* (Tacoma,
Washington), February
10, 1971.

6. *Arkansas Gazette,*
August 10, 1967.

7. *Oklahoma City
Times,* January 17,
1970.

8. *Sports Folio of the
Southwest* (Austin,
Texas), April, 1968.

9. *The Daily
Oklahoman,* December
19, 1967.

10. *Ibid.,* January 15,
1976.

11. Norm Russell
interview.

12. Ibid.

13. Ibid.

14. *The Campus,*
December 3, 1971.

15. Norm Russell
interview.

16. Ibid.

17. Heard, *Scored,* p.
147.

18. *Ibid.*

19. *Ibid.*

20. Norm Russell
interview.

21. Ibid.

22. *The Campus,*
January 26, 1973.

23. *Ibid.,* March 9,
1973.

24. *Ibid.,* March 16,
1973.

25. Abe Lemons interview.

26. *Austin American-
Statesman* (Austin,
Texas), December 20,
1977.

27. *Oklahoma City
Times,* undated.

Chapter 14
1. Abe Lemons interview.

2. *Tulsa Daily World*
(Tulsa, Oklahoma),
1973.

3. Heard, *Scored*
p. 155.

4. *Tulsa Daily World,*
1973.

5. Interview, James
"Jim" McKone,
January 28, 1999,
Archives, Oklahoma
Heritage Association,
Oklahoma City,
Oklahoma.
Hereinafter referred to
as Jim McKone interview.

6. Ibid.

7. Ibid.

8. *Tulsa Daily World,*
June 4, 1974.

9. Jim McKone interview.

10. *Dallas Morning
News,* 1974.

11. Heard, *Scored,*
p. 81.

12. *Ibid.,* p. 67.

13. Interview, Ed
Janka, January 19,
1999, Archives,
Oklahoma Heritage
Association, Oklahoma
City, Oklahoma.
Hereinafter referred to
as Ed Janka interview.

14. *Sports Illustrated,* February 17, 1975.

15. *The South Texas Reporter* (McAllen, Texas), May 14, 1998.

16. Jim McKone interview.

17. *Dallas Morning News,* February 4, 1975.

18. Jim McKone interview.

19. Abe Lemons interview.

20. Ibid.

21. Ibid.

22. NCAA Division I statistics, March 1, 1975, Archives, Oklahoma Heritage Association, Oklahoma City, Oklahoma.

23. Ibid.

24. *Oklahoma City Times,* February 17, 1975.

25. *Dallas Times Herald,* March 9, 1975.

26. *Dallas Morning News,* May 27, 1975.

27. *Oklahoma City Times,* July 25, 1974.

28. Interview, William E. "Bill" Foster, January 26, 1999, Archives, Oklahoma Heritage Association, Oklahoma City, Oklahoma. Hereinafter referred to as Bill Foster interview.

29. Ibid.

30. Heard, *Scored,* p. 53.

31. *Austin American-Statesman,* June 3, 1978.

32. Interview, Jesus Guerra, February 1, 1999, Archives, Oklahoma Heritage Association, Oklahoma City, Oklahoma.

33. *Dallas Times Herald,* March 17, 1976.

34. *Austin American-Statesman,* June 3, 1978.

35. *Dallas Times Herald,* January 19, 1976.

Chapter 15

1. Abe Lemons interview.

2. *Dallas Morning News,* January 9, 1977.

3. *Ibid.*

4. *Ibid.,* March 18, 1976.

5. *Ibid.*

6. *Ibid.*

7. Abe Lemons interview.

8. *Houston Chronicle* (Houston, Texas), May 16, 1976.

9. *Dallas Times Herald,* March 10, 1976.

10. Abe Lemons interview.

11. *Dallas Morning News,* March 18, 1976.

12. *Austin Sun* (Austin, Texas), July 13, 1976.

13. Heard, *Scored,* p. 224.

14. Interview, Ron Baxter, February 16, 1999, Archives, Oklahoma Heritage Association, Oklahoma City, Oklahoma. Hereinafter referred to as Ron Baxter interview.

15. Heard, *Scored,* p. 220.

16. *Houston Chronicle,* February 27, 1978.

17. Ron Baxter interview.

18. *Dallas Morning News,* January 7, 1977.

19. Interview, Barry Dowd, January 20, 1999, Archives, Oklahoma Heritage Association, Oklahoma City, Oklahoma. Hereinafter referred to as Barry Dowd interview.

20. Ibid.

21. Heard, *Scored,* p. 218.

22. Ron Baxter interview.

23. Ibid.

24. Barry Dowd interview.

25. Heard, *Scored,* p. 223.

26. Barry Dowd interview.

27. Ibid.

28. *Dallas Times Herald,* October 26, 1976.

29. *Daily Texan* (Austin, Texas), August 6, 1976.

30. Barry Dowd interview.

31. Interview, Johnny Moore, February 1, 1999, Archives, Oklahoma Heritage Association, Oklahoma City, Oklahoma. Hereinafter referred to as Johnny Moore interview.

32. Ibid.

33. Interview, Jim Krivacs, February 2, 1999, Archives, Oklahoma Heritage Association, Oklahoma City, Oklahoma. Hereinafter referred to as Jim Krivacs interview.

34. Ibid.

35. *Austin Citizen* (Austin, Texas), January 7, 1977.

36. *Ibid.,* January 5, 1977.

37. *Houston Chronicle,* January 5, 1977.

38. *Austin Citizen,* January 5, 1977.

39. *Houston Chronicle,* January 5, 1977.

40. *Ibid.*

41. *Ibid.*

42. *Texas Monthly,* January, 1977.

43. Abe Lemons interview.

44. *Austin American-Statesman,* January 11, 1977.

45. *Houston Chronicle,* January 11, 1977.

46. *Houston Post,* January 11, 1977.

47. *Houston Chronicle,* January 11, 1977.

48. *Dallas Morning News,* January 12, 1977.

49. *Daily Texan,* January 14, 1977.

50. *Austin American Statesman,* January 23, 1977.

51. *Austin Citizen,* February 7, 1977.

52. *Houston Chronicle,* February 27, 1978.

53. *Ibid.*

54. *Austin American Statesman*, February 13, 1977.

55. Barry Dowd interview.

56. *Houston Post* (Houston, Texas), January 25, 1977.

57. *Daily Texan*, February 21, 1977.

58. Heard, *Scored*, p. 255.

59. *Houston Post*, February 19, 1977.

60. *Daily Texan*, February 25, 1977.

61. *Austin Citizen*, March 4, 1977.

Chapter 16

1. *Daily Texan*, February 28, 1977.

2. *Ibid.*, March 1, 1977.

3. *Austin Citizen*, October 27, 1977.

4. *Houston Chronicle*, May 16, 1976.

5. Heard, *Scored*, p. 170.

6. *Houston Chronicle*, May 16, 1976.

7. *Dallas Morning News*, January 9, 1977.

8. Ed Janka interview.

9. Interview, Ronda Lands, February 15, 1999, Archives, Oklahoma Heritage Association, Oklahoma City, Oklahoma.

10. *Houston Post*, October 21, 1977.

11. *San Antonio Express-News* (San Antonio, Texas), February 22, 1996.

12. Abe Lemons interview.

13. *Austin American Statesman*, November 30, 1977.

14. 1998 University of Texas Basketball Media Guide, p. 252.

15. *Austin Citizen*, December 6, 1977.

16. Jim Krivacs interview.

17. *Austin American Statesman*, December 27, 1977.

18. *San Antonio Express-News*, February 22, 1996.

19. *Dallas Morning News*, January 24, 1978.

20. *Ibid.*

21. *Houston Post*, January 18, 1978.

22. *Austin American Statesman*, January 31, 1978.

23. *Dallas Times Herald*, February 2, 1978.

24. *Austin American Statesman*, February 8, 1978.

25. Heard, *Scored*, p. 283.

26. *Ibid.*

27. Abe Lemons interview; Heard, *Scored*, p. 285.

28. *Houston Post*, March 6, 1978.

29. Heard, *Scored*, p. 291.

30. *Houston Chronicle*, March 15, 1978.

31. *Austin American Statesman*, March 21, 1978.

32. *New York Post* (New York, New York), March 22, 1978.

33. *Austin American Statesman*, March 22, 1978.

34. *New York Post*, March 22, 1978.

35. *The Daily Oklahoman*, October 14, 1983.

36. *Austin American-Statesman*, February 27, 1998.

37. *Ibid.*

38. *Ibid.*

39. *Ibid.*

40. *Ibid.*

41. *Los Angeles Times* (Los Angeles, California), April 2, 1978.

Chapter 17

1. *The Daily Oklahoman*, January 11, 1998.

2. *Ibid.*

3. *Ibid.*, February 5, 1982.

4. *Oklahoma City Times*, January 4, 1981.

5. *The Daily Oklahoman*, January 11, 1998.

6. Abe Lemons interview.

7. Ibid.

8. Ibid.

9. Johnny Moore interview.

10. Abe Lemons interview.

11. Interview, Mike Wacker, February 10, 1999, Archives, Oklahoma Heritage Association, Oklahoma City, Oklahoma. Hereinafter referred to as Mike Wacker interview.

12. Interview, Ray Harper, February 20, 1999, Archives, Oklahoma Heritage Association, Oklahoma City, Oklahoma.

13. *Austin American Statesman*, November 11, 1980.

14. *Daily Texan*, December 5, 1980.

15. *Ibid.*

16. *Austin American-Statesman*, December 1, 1980.

17. *Ibid.*, December 15, 1980.

18. Nike television program, 1981, Archives, Oklahoma Heritage Association, Oklahoma City, Oklahoma.

19. *Fort Worth Star-Telegram* (Fort Worth, Texas), January 12, 1981.

20. *Austin American-Statesman*, January 13, 1981.

21. *Ibid.*, March 12, 1981.

Chapter 18

1. 1981 University of Texas Basketball Media Guide, p. 10, Archives, Oklahoma Heritage Association, Oklahoma City, Oklahoma.

2. *Austin City Magazine*, November, 1981.

3. *Ibid.*

4. *Dallas Morning News*, January 9, 1982.

5. *Ibid.*

6. *Austin City Magazine,* November, 1981.

7. *Austin American-Statesman,* January 15, 1982.

8. *Dallas Morning News,* January 8, 1982.

9. *Austin American-Statesman,* January 28, 1982.

10. *Ibid.,* February 7, 1982.

11. *Ibid.,* February 14, 1982.

12. *Ibid.*

13. *Ibid.*

14. *Dallas Morning News,* February 21, 1982.

15. *The Daily Oklahoman,* March 11, 1982.

16. *Ibid.*

17. Mike Wacker interview.

18. *The Daily Oklahoman,* March 11, 1982.

19. Abe Lemons interview.

Chapter 19
1. *Houston Post,* February 20, 1983.

2. Arnold Short interview.

3. *The Daily Oklahoman,* January 14, 1983.

4. *The Denver Post* (Denver, Colorado), August 21, 1983.

5. *Ibid.*

6. Doyle Parrack interview.

7. Abe Lemons interview.

8. Interview, Birdie Duniphin, January 19, 1999, Archives, Oklahoma Heritage Association, Oklahoma City, Oklahoma.

9. *Austin American-Statesman,* February 19, 1984. Heritage Archives.

10. Interview, Dan Davis, January 19, 1999, Archives, Oklahoma Heritage Association, Oklahoma City, Oklahoma. Hereinafter referred to as Dan Davis interview.

11. Bud Sahmaunt interview.

12. *The Campus,* January 27, 1984.

13. *Ibid.,* February 3, 1999.

14. *Fort Worth Star-Telegram,* March 18, 1990.

15. Abe Lemons interview.

16. *The Campus,* February 17, 1984.

Chapter 20
1. *The Campus,* October 12, 1984.

2. *The Daily Oklahoman,* March 7, 1985.

3. *The Campus,* February 14, 1986.

4. *Ibid.,* March 21, 1986.

5. *The Daily Oklahoman,* June 4, 1986.

6. *Ibid.*

7. *Ibid.*

Chapter 21
1. *The Campus,* February 23, 1990.

2. *Ibid.*

3. Abe Lemons interview.

4. *The Daily Oklahoman,* February 18, 1990.

5. *Ibid.*

6. *Ibid.*

7. *Ibid.*

8. *Ibid.*

9. *Ibid.*

10. Bud Sahmaunt interview.

11. Up Close with Roy Firestone, ESPN, April 16, 1992, Archives, Oklahoma Heritage Association, Oklahoma City, Oklahoma.

12. *Inside Texas* (Austin, Texas), November 7, 1994.

13. *Ibid.*

14. *Ibid.*

15. *The Daily Oklahoman,* January 19, 1997.

16. Letter from Norm Stewart to Abe Lemons, June 11, 1997, Archives, Oklahoma Heritage Association, Oklahoma City, Oklahoma.

17. Abe Lemons interview.

18. *Inside Texas,* March 9, 1998.

19. *Ibid.*

20. *Ibid.*

21. *The Daily Oklahoman,* February 8, 1999.

22. *Ibid.*

23. *Ibid.*

24. Letter from Johnny Moore to Abe Lemons, September, 1998, Archives, Oklahoma Heritage Association, Oklahoma City, Oklahoma.

25. Letter from Michael Tosee to Abe Lemons, December 10, 1998, Archives, Oklahoma Heritage Association, Oklahoma City, Oklahoma.

26. Letter from Jesus Guerra, Jr., to Abe Lemons, June 9, 1998, Archives, Oklahoma Heritage Association, Oklahoma City, Oklahoma.

27. Larry Jones interview.

28. Letter from Kenny Clark to authors, March 26, 1999, Archives, Oklahoma Heritage Association, Oklahoma City, Oklahoma.

BIBLIOGRAPHY

PRINTED MATERIAL

Newspapers

Arkansas Gazette,
Little Rock, Arkansas

Austin American-Statesman,
Austin, Texas

Austin Citizen, Austin, Texas

Austin Sun, Austin, Texas

The Campus,
Oklahoma City, Oklahoma

Christian Science Monitor,
Boston, Massachusetts

The Daily Oklahoman,
Oklahoma City, Oklahoma

Daily Texan, Austin, Texas

Dallas Times Herald,
Dallas, Texas

Denver Post, Denver, Colorado

Dallas Morning News,
Dallas, Texas

Fort Worth Star Telegram,
Fort Worth, Texas

Houston Post, Houston, Texas

Houston Chronicle,
Houston, Texas

Inside Texas, Austin, Texas

Los Angeles Times,
Los Angeles, California

New York Post,
New York, New York

New York Times,
New York, New York

Oklahoma City Times,
Oklahoma City, Oklahoma

San Antonio Express News,
San Antonio, Texas

Seattle Post-Intelligencer, Seattle,
Washington

The Sporting News,
St. Louis, Missouri

Tacoma News Tribune,
Tacoma, Washington

Tulsa Daily World,
Tulsa, Oklahoma

Tulsa Tribune,
Tulsa, Oklahoma

Wichita Beacon,
Wichita, Kansas

Magazines and Yearbooks

Austin City Magazine,
Austin, Texas

Dell Sport Magazine,
New York, New York

Keshena, yearbook annually
printed by Oklahoma City
University, Oklahoma City,
Oklahoma

Look Magazine,
New York, New York

New York Times Magazine,
New York, New York

Sports Folio of the Southwest,
Austin, Texas

Sports Illustrated,
New York, New York

Texas Monthly Magazine,
Dallas, Texas

Texas Parade Magazine,
Dallas, Texas

Books

Boggs, Frank K. and Pendleton
Woods. *Myriad of Sports.*
Oklahoma City: All Sports
Association, 1971.

Douglas, John Scott and Albert
Salz. *He's In the Merchant
Marine Now.* New York: Robert
McBride and Company, 1943.

Heard, Robert. *You Scored One
More Point Than a Dead Man.*
Austin, Texas: Lemons-Heard
Company, 1978.

*History of Cotton County,
Oklahoma.* Walters, Oklahoma:
Cotton County Historical
Society, 1979.

McCallum, John D. *College
Basketball USA.* New York: Stein
and Day, 1978.

Milhouse, Paul W. *Oklahoma
City University: A Miracle at
23rd and Blackwelder.*
Oklahoma City: Western
Heritage Books, Inc., 1984.

COLLECTIONS

Photographic archives,
Oklahoma Publishing
Company, Oklahoma City,
Oklahoma

Archives, Oklahoma City
University Athletic Department,
Oklahoma City, Oklahoma

Archives, Oklahoma Heritage
Association, Oklahoma City,
Oklahoma: correspondence,
telegrams, and sports
memorabilia

Interviews, Oklahoma Heritage
Association, Oklahoma City,
Oklahoma. Interviews with:

Ron Baxter.
February 16, 1999.

Frank Boggs.
September 5, 1998.

Dan Davis.
January 19, 1999.

Barry Dowd.
January 20, 1999.

Birdie Duniphin.
January 19, 1999.

William Foster.
January 26, 1999.

Gary Gray.
January 27, 1999.

Jesus Guerra.
February 1, 1999.

Carol Hansen.
February 23, 1999.

Ray Harper.
February 20, 1999.

Gary Hill.
February 5, 1999.

Manuel Heusman.
January 21, 1999.

Bruce Hodge.
January 15, 1999.

Roger Holloway.
February 1, 1999.

Charles H.T. Hunter.
January 7, 1999.

Ed Janka.
January 19, 1999.

Bill Johnston.
March 23, 1999.

Larry Jones.
February 1, 1999.

Jack Key.
January 20, 1999.

Bud Koper.
February 4, 1999.

Jim Krivacs.
February 2, 1999.

Ronda Lands.
February 15, 1999.

Lyndon Lee.
March 15, 1999.

Abe Lemons.
May 20, 1998.

Betty Jo Lemons.
June 8, 1998.

Bill Little.
February 10, 1999.

James McKone.
February 2, 1999.

Patrick McGuigan.
February 2, 1999.

Johnny Moore.
February 1, 1999.

Edwin Powell Nall.
December 15, 1998.

Howell Ogletree.
June 8, 1998.

Doyle Parrack.
January 19, 1999.

Hub Reed.
February 4, 1999.

Norm Russell.
December 28, 1998.

Bud Saumaunt.
January 25, 1999.

Arnold Short.
February 5, 1999.

Frank Thurber.
March 22, 1999.

Richard Travis.
February 1, 1999.

Harry Vines.
March 1, 1999.

Mike Wacker.
February 10, 1999.

INDEX